THE DEMOGRAPHICS OF IMMIGRATION

THE DEMOGRAPHICS OF IMMIGRATION

A Socio-Demographic Profile of the Foreign-Born Population in New York State

Nadia H. Youssef

1992
Center for Migration Studies
New York

The Center for Migration Studies is an educational, nonprofit institute founded in New York in 1964 to encourage and facilitate the study of sociological, demographic, historical, legislative and pastoral aspects of human migration movements and ethnic group relations. The opinions expressed in this work are those of the author.

The Demographics of Immigration
A Socio-Demographic Profile of the
Foreign-Born Population in New York State

First Edition
Copyright ©1992 by
The Center for Migration Studies of New York, Inc.
All Rights reserved. No part of this book may be reproduced
without written permission from the publisher.

Center for Migration Studies
209 Flagg Place
Staten Island, New York 10304-1199

Library of Congress Cataloging-in-Publication Data

Youssef, Nadia Haggag.
  The demographics of immigration: a socio-demographic profile of
the foreign-born population in New York State/by Nadia H. Youssef.
    p. cm.
Includes bibliographical references.
ISBN 0–934733-60-0 (HC) : $19.50. — ISBN 0-934733-61-9 (SC) : $14.50
1. Immigrants — New York (State). 2. Minorities — New York
(State) — Population. I. Title.
JV7045.Y68   1991
304.8'747 — dc20   91-28754
                                                           CIP

Printed in the United States of America

To Edwin,
for his continued enthusiasm and encouragement
throughout the years.

CONTENTS

List of Tables / xi
Acknowledgments / xvii

1. CONTEXTUAL BACKGROUND / 1

Contextual Background to New York's Immigrants / 3
    Volume / *3*
    Diversity / *5*

The Availability and Adequacy of Data on the Foreign-Born
Immigrant Population / 6
    The Federal Data Collection System / *6*
    The State Level Data Collection System / *9*

Overview of the Study / 10
Notes / 12

2. COMPONENTS OF THE INTERNATIONAL MIGRATORY FLOW
INTO NEW YORK STATE: 1965–1989 / 13

The Foreign-Born Resident Population / 14
    Volume and Distribution / *14*
    The New York Profile / *16*
    Residential Choices / *17*

The Legal Immigrant/Permanent Resident Population / 21
    Documenting the Legal Immigrant Population / *22*
    Volume / *23*
    Class of Admission / *25*
    Residential Preferences of Recent Legal Immigrants: 1980–1989 / *28*

The Refugee Population / 29
    Refugee Admissions Nationwide / *31*
    The Presence of Refugees in New York State / *33*

The Undocumented Resident / 39
    Estimating the Numbers of Undocumented Residents / *40*
    The Undocumented Resident in New York / *41*
    Social Characteristics of the Undocumented Resident / *42*

Implementing the 1986 Immigration Reform and Control Act / 44
    The IRCA Experience in New York State / 47
    Social Characteristics of Applicants Seeking Status Adjustment:
        Nationwide Trends / 47
    New York's Applicants / 48

Notes / 49

3. NATIONALITY, ETHNICITY AND RACE IN THE
   DEMOGRAPHY OF IMMIGRATION / 51

The Changing Character of Legal Immigration: Nationwide Trends / 52

Shifts in the Regional/National Origin of New York's
Foreign-Born Community / 57
    Major Immigrant Supplier Countries to New York / 60
    Principal Immigrant Communities / 62
    Recent Compositional Trends: 1980–1989 / 66
    Residential Choices of the Foreign Born in New York City / 68

Accompanying Changes in Racial and Ethnic Diversity / 70

Summary / 73

Notes / 74

4. SOCIODEMOGRAPHIC CHARACTERISTICS OF NEW YORK'S
   FOREIGN-BORN RESIDENTS / 75

Demographic Characteristics / 76
    The Age Composition / 76
    Sex Ratio, Marital Patterns and Fertility / 78
    Household Composition and Structure / 85

The Changing Educational Profile / 88
    The Educational Profile of New York / 88
    Comparative Differences in Educational Attainment among Regional
        and National-Origin Groups / 91

Notes / 94

5. ECONOMIC CHARACTERISTICS OF NEW YORK'S
   FOREIGN-BORN RESIDENTS / 95

Foreign-Born Workers in the Labor Market / 96
    Labor Market Conditions in New York / 97
    Employment and Unemployment Trends in 1980 / 98

The Population At Work / 98
The Unemployed / 102
The Timing of Arrival / 102
Questioning the Quality of Immigrant Labor / 105
The Marginalization of Immigrant Workers in the Labor Market / 111

Income Attainment among New York's Foreign-Born Residents / 114
Total Income / 114
Income from Labor / 117

Poverty among New York's Foreign-Born Residents / 124
Age and Gender / 125
National Origin / 127
Race and Ethnicity / 127

Notes / 129

6. THE CONTRIBUTION OF FOREIGN-BORN WORKERS TO THE
ECONOMY OF NEW YORK / 131

Industrial and Occupational Distribution: An Overview / 133
The Industries / 135
Occupations / 136

Subsectors in the Occupations with High Immigrant
Labor Concentration / 138

Stratifying Immigrant Supplier Regions by Human Capital
Characteristics Exported / 139
Volume of Immigrant Labor Contributed / 139
Skill-Level of Resources Exported / 140

Factors of Gender, Race and Ethnicity in Employment Distribution / 143
Gender Differences / 143
Race and Ethnicity in Relation to Occupational Location / 145

Additional Human Capital Resources Available to New York
During the 1980s / 150
Occupational Background of the Post-1980 Immigrants / 150
Immigrants Admitted Under the Worker Provision / 152

Notes / 154

7. CONCLUSION: CONSEQUENCES OF FUTURE IMMIGRATION
FOR NEW YORK / 156

Consequences of Immigration / 157
  Sustaining Population Growth / 157
  Complementing Labor Market Needs / 158
    Nationwide Educational and Occupational Demands / 158
    New York's Demand for Specialized Manpower / 159
    The Immigrant Potential / 159
    *Considerations in the Implementation of a Labor-Market Conscious
      Immigration Policy* / 161

Data Gaps and Research Directions / 162
  Data Adequacy / 162
  Research Directions / 163
    Assessing impact / 163
    The Importance of a State-Specific Focus in Immigration Research / 164

Notes / 166

Appendix A / 167

References / 169

Index / 179

LIST OF TABLES

2.1 Foreign-Born Persons as Percent of the Total Population in the United States, New York State and New York City, 1900–1980   15

2.2 Distribution of the Foreign-Born Population in Selected States, 1970 and 1980   17

2.3 Total and Foreign-Born Population Residing in Five Metropolitan Areas, 1980   18

2.4 Total and Foreign-Born Population Residing in Seven Central Cities, 1980   19

2.5 Population Changes in the Total and Foreign-Born Population in the United States and Selected Cities, 1970–1980   19

2.6 New York City Population by Nativity, 1900–1980   20

2.7 Legal Immigrants Admitted as Permanent Residents to the United States and the Number Declaring New York State as Intended Residence, 1965–1989   24

2.8 Immigrants Admitted into the United States by Major Category of Admission, 1988 and 1989   26

2.9 Distribution of New York State-Bound Foreign-Born Persons Admitted as Permanent Residents to the United States by Class of Admission, 1978–1986   27

2.10 Refugee Approvals and Admissions by Geographical Area of Chargeability, 1981–1989   30

2.11 Refugee Admissions into the United States, 1975–1980   31

2.12 Refugee Arrivals into the United States by Selected Nationality, 1982–1989   32

2.13 Refugees Granted Lawful Permanent Resident Status in 1988 by Calendar Year of Entry, Region and Selected Country of Birth   34

2.14 Number of Individuals Granted Asylum by INS District Directors by Selected Nationality, 1984–1989   36

2.15 Refugee Arrivals by Selected Area of Citizenship and
      State, 1980–1986   37

2.16 Refugee Arrivals in New York State Classified by
      Country of Origin, 1983–1989   38

2.17 Refugee Arrivals to New York State in Relation to Nationwide
      Refugee Admissions, 1985–1987   38

2.18 Aliens and Estimated Undocumented Aliens Counted in the
      1980 Census by Period of Entry in the 15 States with the
      Largest Numbers of Aliens   43

2.19 Age and Sex Composition of Undocumented Aliens Counted
      in the 1980 Census for Selected States of Residence   45

2.20 1980 Census Estimated Count of Undocumented Aliens
      in Relation to Provisional Applications Filed for
      Status Adjustment Under the 1986 IRCA Provisions, by
      Selected States, January, 1989   46

3.1   Percent Distribution of Legal Immigrants Admitted by Region
      of Origin and Period of Entry, 1955–1989   54

3.2   Changing Composition of the Foreign-Born Population
      According to Period of Immigration, 1980   55

3.3   Changes in the National Origin of Immigrants Admitted
      from the 1989 Top Fifteen Countries of Birth   55

3.4   The Composition of the Foreign-Born Population Residing
      in New York State in 1980 Classified by Period of Arrival to
      the United States and Region of Birthplace   58

3.5   Percent Distribution of the Foreign-Born Population Residing
      in the United States, California and New York State in 1980
      by Region of Birthplace   59

3.6   California and New York State Share in Regional Origin
      Groups in Relation to Nationwide Totals in Each Group, 1980   59

3.7   Rank Order of Top 10 Largest Supplier Countries to New
      York City by Period of Immigration to 1980   62

3.8   Comparative Differences in the Numerical Importance of
      Nationality Groups among Foreign-Born Residents in
      New York City, 1960–1980   64

3.9 Top 8 Countries Dominating the Post-1980 Legal Immigrant
    Flow into New York State   67

3.10 Ten Leading Immigrant Supplier Countries to New York State in
     Relation to Their Importance to California and the
     United States, 1989   67

3.11 Distribution of the Foreign-Born Population of New York City by
     Birthplace and Borough of Residence, 1980   69

3.12 Self-Reported Racial and Ethnic Categories of U.S.-Born
     and Foreign-Born Residents of New York City by
     Period of Immigration, 1980   72

3.13 Self-Reported Racial and Ethnic Categories of U.S.-Born
     and Foreign-Born Residents of New York State by Region of
     Birthplace, 1980 (Population 16+)   72

4.1 Age Distribution of the U.S.-Born and Foreign-Born Residents of
    New York State and the United States, 1980   77

4.2 Marital Status of the U.S.-Born and Foreign-Born Residents by
    Period of Entry to the United States, 1980   81

4.3 Characteristics of Family-Based Households by Nativity of
    Householder and Period of Arrival to the United States,
    New York and the United States, 1980   84

4.4 Children Ever Born of Recent Immigrant Women by Nationality
    and Age Group, New York, 1980   85

4.5 Educational Attainment of U.S.-Born and Foreign-Born
    Residents Ages 25+ by Period of Arrival to the United States,
    New York, 1980   90

4.6 Comparative Differences in Educational Attainment between
    U.S.-Born and Foreign-Born Residents of the United States
    and New York State, 1980   91

4.7 Distribution of U.S.-Born and Foreign-Born Residents Ages 25+
    by Educational Level Completed and Region of Birthplace,
    New York, 1980   92

4.8 Educational Levels Completed by the Post-1970 Foreign-Born
    Residents of New York State by Selected Regions/Countries
    of Birth, New York, 1980   93

5.1 Economically Active and Inactive Men Ages 16 + in
    New York State by Nativity, Ethnicity and Region
    of Birthplace, 1980   99

5.2 Economically Active and Inactive Women Ages 16 + in
    New York State by Nativity, Ethnicity and Region of
    Birthplace, 1980   100

5.3 Labor Force Status of Recently Arrived Immigrants Residing in
    New York State by Sex, 1980   101

5.4 1980 Labor Force Status of Foreign-Born Residents Ages 16 + by
    Period of Immigration to the United States and Birthplace   103

5.5 Distribution of Foreign-Born Residents Ages 16 + by Labor Force
    Status and Educational Attainment According to Year of Arrival
    in the United States, New York, 1980   107

5.6 Percentage of Foreign- and U.S.-Born Workers with
    College Degrees and Graduate Education in Selected
    Occupational Subcategories, New York, 1980   108

5.7 Percentage of Foreign- and U.S.-Born Workers Ages 16 + at
    Different Educational Levels in Selected Areas of Precision
    Production and Repair and Semiskilled Labor Categories,
    New York, 1980   109

5.8 Self-Reported Proficiency in English Among New York's
    Foreign-Born Residents Ages 16 + by Labor Force Status, 1980   110

5.9 Race/Ethnic-Specific Labor Force Rates of Foreign- and
    U.S.-Born Residents of New York State by Sex, 1980   112

5.10 Median Income of Foreign- and U.S.-Born Persons Ages 16 +
     from "All Sources" for Those Who Are Income Recipients,
     New York, 1980   115

5.11 Median Income of Foreign- and U.S.-Born Men and Women
     Ages 16 + from "All Sources" for Those Who Are Income
     Recipients, New York, 1980   116

5.12 Median Wages and Salary Income per Person Ages 16 + by
     Nativity and Region of Birthplace, New York, 1980   119

5.13 Median Wage and Salary Income Per Person Ages 16 +
     Receiving Wages and Salary by Nativity, Selected Regions
     of Birthplace, Race and Ethnicity, New York, 1980   119

5.14 Median Wage/Salary Income Per Person Ages 16 + in the
       Work Force by Nativity, Educational Attainment and Sex,
       New York, 1980   121

5.15 Median Wage/Salary Income per Person Ages 16 + in the
       Work Force by Broad Occupational Category, Nativity, and
       Foreign- and U.S.-Born Income Differentials, New York, 1980   123

5.16 Median Wage/Salary Income per Men and Women Ages 16 + in
       the Work Force by Broad Occupational Category, Nativity
       Foreign- and U.S-Born Income Differentials, New York, 1980   123

5.17 Fraction of Individuals Living Below Poverty Line and Those
       with Incomes 200% and More Above the Poverty Threshold by
       Sex and Period of Arrival to the United States, New York, 1980   126

5.18 Poverty Differences in the Foreign-Born Population by Age
       and Sex, New York, 1980   126

5.19 Poverty Rate Differences among National Origin Groups,
       New York, 1980   128

5.20 Race and Ethnic-Specific Poverty Rates of Foreign- and
       U.S.-Born Persons by Selected Regions of Birthplace,
       New York, 1980   128

6.1 Percent Distribution of Foreign- and U.S.-Born Workers
      Ages 16 + by Industry Sector, New York, 1980   134

6.2 Percent Distribution of the Work Force Ages 16 + by Broad
      Occupational Category and Nativity of Workers, New York, 1980   134

6.3 Distribution of the Foreign-Born Resident Population Ages 16 +
      and of Foreign-Born Workers in the Occupations by Region
      of Birthplace, New York, 1980   140

6.4 Internal Distribution of Foreign-Born Workers from Different
      Regions into Occupational Groupings Ranked According to
      Skill Level, New York, 1980   141

6.5 Sex Distribution of U.S.-Born and Foreign-Born Workers Ages
      16 + into Broad Occupational Categories and Proportion in All
      Occupational Categories Who Are Women, New York, 1980   144

6.6 Occupational Distribution of Foreign-Born Male Workers
      from Selected Regions of Birthplace by Race/Ethnicity,
      New York, 1980   147

6.7 Occupational Distribution of Foreign-Born Asian Male Workers
      by Ethnicity, New York, 1980   148

6.8 Occupational Distribution of Foreign-Born Women Workers
      from Selected Regions of Birthplace by Race/Ethnicity,
      New York, 1980   149

6.9 Occupational Distribution of Foreign-Born Asian Women
      Workers by Ethnicity, New York, 1980   150

6.10 Occupational Composition of Immigrants Admitted as Legal
      Permanent Residents with Intended Settlement in New York
      State, 1980–1986   151

6.11 Number of Persons Legally Admitted to the United States
      Under the Work Provision with Intended Residential Settlement
      in New York State, 1980–1986   153

ACKNOWLEDGMENTS

This study began in the fall of 1988 and became a sustained and focused research project of the Center for Immigrant and Population Studies until the summer of 1990. From its inception, the project has continuously received vital support and encouragement from Dr. Edmond Volpe, President of the College of Staten Island and Dr. Barry Bressler, Vice President for Academic Affairs. The interest and initial guidance of the then Director of the Center, Dr. Roy Bryce LaPorte, are deeply appreciated and this research has certainly benefited from his helpful and insightful comments. Acknowledgment is also extended to the Wagner Institute of Urban Public Policy at the City University of New York for a grant made to the Center which provided computational support.

I am especially thankful to Dr. Demetrios Papademetriou of the U.S. Department of Labor and Dr. Charles Keely of Georgetown University for the time they spent from the outset discussing this project and, subsequently, for their thorough review and invaluable comments on the first draft of this study. The several meetings held with Dr. Robert Warren of the Immigration and Naturalization Service to discuss documentation sources to account for the various subcategories of the forcign-born population were very valuable. Very special thanks goes to Dolores Hayes who contributed long hours of work to this project and takes full credit for the programming and processing of the computer runs which constitute the basis for much of the analysis presented here. Upula Liyanarachi, who accurately typed and retyped all the tables included here, and Tina Quilty, who kindly accepted the task of typing the first rough draft have contributed generously to this work. Many thanks are also extended to Eileen Reiter for her editorial talent. Carmela Richards deserves special mention for her patience and efficiency. She was the ultimate link between the many drafts and the conclusive draft of the book, carrying the full responsibility for finalizing the presentation of the product in its present form.

1

CONTEXTUAL BACKGROUND

Since the late 1970s the United States has been the recipient of a large influx of immigrants. Because these recent settlers come predominantly from Third World countries and are distinctive ethnically and racially from the migratory flows of the late 1880s and early decades of the 1900s, the presence of an immigrant population in the country has become decidedly more visible.

Concern over the immigrant presence has heightened recently, the issue having become the subject of considerable scrutiny, conjecture and debate (Jensen, 1989). In the overall mix of expressed public sentiments, three distinct positions may be singled out. One demands a more restrictive and exclusionary immigration policy. This stems from the dramatic rise in the volume of legal entries originating from the lesser developed countries, the seeming inability of the government to control the inflow of undocumented aliens, and the overall feeling that immigration policy has been allowed to function without regard to its economic consequences (Briggs, 1985). The second position is grounded in humanitarian concerns and calls for an overall increase of immigration quotas and the lifting of restrictions imposed on political refugees and asylees (DiMarzio and Papademetriou, 1988; Gibney, 1989). The third stance has argued for a labor market conscious immigration policy that would increase admission ceilings selectively for holders of special job qualifications to compensate for the nationwide demographic deficit in the working age population and deepening manpower shortages in critical professional specialties and technical areas (Vernez and McCarthy, 1990).

Two major legislative responses to these public sentiments have been enacted. The Immigration Reform and Control Act (IRCA) was legislated in 1986 for the dual purpose of offering amnesty and legalization provisions to selected groups from among the undocumented and demagnetizing the labor market to discourage the further inflow of illegal aliens by way of imposing sanctions against

U.S.-based employers who hire undocumented persons for labor (Morrison, 1990).

The second legislative response is contained in Senate Bill 358 – the Immigration Act of 1990 – which was passed by the 101st Congress on October 27 of that year. As the first major revision of immigration policy since 1965, this Act represents a definite move toward the adoption of a labor market approach in linking immigrant admission criteria to the enhancement of the country's capacity to effectively compete in the international marketplace. The Bill raises the yearly total of immigration from a 530,000 average to 700,000 through 1994 and thereafter to 675,000, and calls for greater diversity in the nationality make-up of future migratory streams in favor of those groups least represented in past flows. Its most notable feature, however, is that it nearly triples the "skilled professional" quota that had been set aside under the 1965 Act, increasing occupational slots from 54,000 to 140,000 for priority workers (and their close family members) with specialties in scientific, medical and technology fields. The numbers of immigrants to be admitted on the basis of family reunification and permanent resident status under the new provisions total 465,000 through 1994 and 480,000 in 1995 and thereafter.

The 1990 Act responds, in part, to the humanitarian concerns voiced by advocacy groups in granting a "special temporary protected status" to Salvadoran nationals already in the United States through June 30, 1992, and giving new explicit authority to the Attorney General to extend their stay beyond that date. The holder of this position is vested with additional legal power to offer protected status to aliens from other countries where there have been "physical" and/or "environmental disasters."

This study examines the particular international migration streams into New York State between 1965 and 1989 and analyzes the social, economic and demographic characteristics of foreign-born persons/immigrants who settled in this state at some point in time and were New York residents in 1980.[1] The year 1965 is taken as benchmark because the enactment of the Immigration and Nationality Act that took effect in that year radically transformed the immigration experience of the United States.

The principal reasons for drawing this data together are to 1) highlight major shifts in the trends and character of New York-bound immigration brought about by the 1965 Immigration Act which encouraged a large scale entry of Third World persons to the United States; 2) present elements of a socioeconomic and demographic profile of foreign-born New Yorkers – examining such variables as their immigrant status, national and ethnic diversity, demographic, social and economic characteristics, and the occupational and industrial structure of their work force; and 3) compare and contrast distinguishing characteristics among foreign-born New Yorkers by way of developing a typology of immigrant supplier countries organized into geographical regions of birthplace.

Immigrants are not a homogenous population. They differ from native-born persons and from one another, and the statistical profile presented in this study reveals that there is no such thing as a typical immigrant. It is hoped that the insights and observations presented — drawn as they are from a comparative profile of all reported foreign-born persons residing in New York State, classified by birthplace and disaggregated by socioeconomic variables — will punctuate the importance of differentiating one immigrant from another; break down some of the stereotypical impressions about immigrants held by the public and sustained by the media; point to the contributions and not only the problems that foreign-born persons bring to the state; and single out for policy consideration at the state level those groups in the foreign-born population that appear to be experiencing greatest difficulties in being assimilated into the mainstream.

For many years most immigration literature focused attention on the portrayal of the foreign-born/immigrant population in the United States as a whole. A regional and state level perspective in immigration studies began to surface in the late 1970s, heavily dominated by research on the disparate immigrant experience of Mexicans in California, Central American political asylees in the southern border states and, more recently, the state level impact of the 1986 Immigration Reform and Control Act. Research on the latter centered around the impact of legalization provisions, application of employer sanctions and resultant discrimination practices against foreigners in the labor market. Comprehensive immigration research on international migratory flows that is specific to New York other than that of the social history nature is recent. Important work along those lines appeared in the 1980s in the writings of Richard Alba and M. Batutis (1984), Richard Alba and Katherine Trent (1988), Roger Waldinger (1984, 1986, 1988), Dimitri Papademetriou and Nicholas DiMarzio (1986), Dimitri Papademetriou and Thomas Muller (1987), Elizabeth Bogen (1987), in the edited volumes by Nancy Foner (1987), Constance R. Sutton and Elsa Chaney (1987) and in Louis Winnick (1990), to mention only some (*see,* also, Shokeid, 1988; Weisser, 1989; Cominolli, 1990).

Contextual Background to New York's Immigrants

Volume

The prominence of New York, New York City in particular, in the nation's immigration history has been well documented. Although patterns of immigration into the state in the past few decades mirror national trends, the composition of the New York immigrant population reveals a high degree of selectivity compared to the characteristics of the overall foreign-born population in the country. New York City has always had a larger percentage of foreign-born persons than the national population, but the factor of difference is on the order of three or four times in each census year when compared to nationwide trends (Kraly, 1987). During each of the first three decades of the century, mass immigration accounted for between one third and one half of the state's population growth. As a result of restrictions imposed by three successive legislations in the 1920s (1921, 1924, 1928) — each fine-tuning the National Origins legislation — the Depression of the 1930s and the immediate effects of World War II, immigration fell sharply after 1930 and did not resurge until the late 1950s, reflecting in part the influx of Cuban and Hungarian refugees. It was not the McCarran-Walter Act of 1952, which still upheld the National Origin Quota System, but the immigration policy reforms enacted in 1965 as amendments to the 1952 Act that renewed the importance of international migration both in the United States and in New York.

As of this writing, the 1990 census count of the foreign-born population had not been released. In 1980, the census identified 2.4 million persons of foreign birth residing in New York State, or 14 percent of its 17 million residents. About one half that number — 1.2 million — had arrived in the United States after 1965 and settled in New York sometime between then and 1980. Of the foreign-born population enumerated in New York in 1980, 29 percent had arrived before 1950, 21.6 percent between 1950 and 1964, 14.6 percent between 1965 and 1969, and 34.8 percent between 1970 and 1980. From 1975 to 1980 alone, over 500,000 persons of foreign birth established legal residence in the state.

During the decade of the 1980s, the number of legally admitted persons granted permanent resident status settling in New York State averaged yearly 80,000 to 90,000 during 1982–1983, and 107,000 during 1984–1986. In 1987 they totaled 114,194, dropping to 109,300 in 1988, then increasing to 134,766 in 1989. These figures are inclusive of new entries and of refugees, asylees and previous nonimmigrants processed for status adjustment; they do not include newly-arrived refugees nor, of course, the undocumented. The number of persons admitted to the United States in permanent resident status between 1982 and 1989 who selected to establish residence in New York State totaled 858,300, representing 16.5 percent of the 5.2 million admitted as legal immigrants nationwide during that period. Tentative figures for legal immigrant admissions in 1990 place the number establishing residence in New York at 189,589, comprising 12.1 percent of the 1.5 million entries nationwide. No one can say with confidence how many illegal aliens are presently residing in the state and how many more are coming.

Diversity

The effect of the 1965 Immigration and Nationality Act on the population composition of New York has been significant. Through this Act, the United States announced that it would look impartially on the world in providing a more equitable worldwide distribution of visas. The outcome was not only a dramatic increase over the past decades in the volume of foreign-born persons settling in New York, but radical shifts in the origin points of the immigrant supplier countries. Throughout the nineteenth and early twentieth centuries, mass immigration into New York originated overwhelmingly in Europe – the Irish and Germans during the 1840s, other northern Europeans until the 1880s – then gave way to southern and Eastern Europeans in the 1890s and early years of the twentieth century. By contrast, the majority of the 1970 and 1980 cohorts of immigrants living in New York come from the Caribbean countries, Asia and Latin America. Until 1950, New York City was still predominantly populated by persons of European descent, though it had black, Caribbean, Puerto Rican and Chinese neighborhoods. An influx of Caribbeans and Chinese had come to the city beginning with World War II and such moves were accelerated from the 1960s onward, setting in motion a chain of dramatic changes in the ethnic and racial composition of New York City.

Records documenting legal immigrant admissions from 1965 through 1989 show the gradual, though persistent, consolidation of a set of source countries which have consistently been supplying and replenishing the bulk of New York's foreign-born community. In the late 1970s and the decade of the 1980s, these supplier countries were identifiable by rank and order as follows: the Dominican Republic, Jamaica, Guyana, Haiti and China, followed at a considerable distance by India and Korea. Some of these countries already have in the past and most probably will continue to supply the state with large numbers of undocumented foreigners as well. The particular nationality composition of these flows is expected to continue in years to come, despite the 1990 mandate calling for greater diversification in the nationality mix, and carries significant implications for accelerating the pace of change of New York's ethnic make-up.

The diversity that has characterized the inflow of foreign-born persons into the state has given the population of New York City, in particular, the advantage of drawing upon a multitude of different cultures while undergoing its own transformation as a result of the new lifestyles introduced through the spectrum of immigrant life. Immigration to the State of New York has essentially meant establishing residence in the city. In 1930, one third of all New York City residents had been born outside the United States; between 1930 and 1960 one in every six foreign-born persons in the United States lived in New York City. The magnetism of the city has persisted throughout the 1980s. New York City has been particularly appealing to foreigners because new immigrants do not stand out as much as they would in some other urban centers. The city has a tradition of having hosted many nationalities and social groups, and many newcomers gravitate to New York in large numbers because of historical patterns of immigrant settlement (Foner, 1987). Whereas the share of foreign-born residents in the U.S. population in 1980 was 6.2 percent, in New York City the corresponding share was close to 25 percent. Current (1990) data show the city's population to be 30 percent foreign-born, with the percentage increasing as we approach the year 2000. Roughly 85 percent of all legally admitted immigrants with set destination to New York State selected residence in the New York City area, continuously adding new dimensions and vitality to the international character of this metropolis. A continuing concentration similar to this has not been observed in other major cities in the United States.

The Availability and Adequacy of Data on the Foreign-Born Immigrant Population

The Federal Data Collection System

The current availability of immigration data sources and their adequacy for national policy analysis and sociodemographic research have been documented and evaluated by Kraly (1979), Briggs, Jr. (1984), Levine *et al.* (1985), Kraly and Gnanasekaran (1987) and the U.S. General Accounting Office (GAO) (1988) among others. While there is general agreement that current data generation, collection and classification procedures permit analysis of changing trends in volume and composition, the available data are not adequate for more sophisticated studies attempting to trace the impact and consequences of immigration, particularly at local (state) levels (GAO, 1988).

The elementary question of how many foreign-born persons reside within New York State at a given time cannot be adequately addressed in traditional demographic analysis, complicating the task of developing their sociodemographic profile since this foremost requires a definition of the universe to be studied. Yet defining and counting are not in themselves as simple as might appear. The complexity surrounding the issue is best illustrated by the response one would have to give to the question: How many persons of foreign birth reside in New York State today? An informed reply would be, to the 2.4 million recorded in the 1980 census, add persons in the following categories: post-1980 legal immigrants and nonimmigrants (data available); legal refugees resettled and residing in New York since 1980 (data only partly available); political refugees, asylees, undocumented aliens and persons in other marginal status groups residing in New York but missed in the 1980 census (data on asylees only available); above categories of persons who settled in New York since 1980 (data not available); certified alien (temporary) workers arriving in New York after 1980 who do not fall into any of the above categories (data available on alien labor certification but not accessible to researchers); undocumented aliens in New York legalizing their status through provisions of the 1986 Immigration Reform and Control Act (data available); undocumented aliens in New York not applying for legalization (data not available); and family members of all the above categories of persons not accounted for before and after 1980 (data not available). From this sum total should be deducted the number of foreign-born persons who since 1980 1) emigrated out of New York State, 2) were deported and 3) have died (based on an educated estimate of losses incurred through mortality).

The question is, therefore, more complex than a mere differentiation between "legal" and "undocumented" entrants. In fact, the legalization provisions of the 1986 Immigration Reform and Control Act have further complicated the status issue by creating a marginal situation for persons previously designated as "illegals" who now find themselves in a "transitional" category bordering between nonlegal and lawful status. They are referred to as legal temporary residents on their way to becoming permanent residents.

The perennial difficulty in researching the foreign-born immigrant population in the United States, even when the objective is to document volume only, is the absence of an integrated body of data generated at either the federal or state level reporting system that accounts for the sum total of all persons of foreign birth, at the same time that it differentiates this population according to their specific immigrant status category. The population census has the mandate to enumerate all U.S. foreign-born residents, but does not designate the immigrant status category or subcategory to which persons of foreign birth belong. In addition, by missing large groups of inner city poor, minorities, transients and agricultural workers, in general, the census tends to undercount some marginally situated foreign-born residents as well.

Statistics on particular foreign-born groups such as recently arrived refugees, asylees, undocumented, those in transitional status, etc., are gathered primarily as byproducts of the administrative output of several federal agencies other than the Census Bureau and are subject to the internal priorities of these agencies (Briggs, 1984). Basically, then, the researcher must deal with a variety of data sets, different data collection and codification systems, and the changing priority agendas of the various administrative entities who have the responsibility to account for those distinct segments that make up the larger universe of the foreign born. The sum total of these different segments does not, unfortunately, yield the universe in its entirety.

Within the boundaries of the segmented data system just described, there nevertheless has been considerable progress made over the last few years in expanding the data base of the foreign-born/immigrant population to be more comprehensive. For example: there is greater awareness among the personnel of agencies responsible for data generation and collection of the problems involved in conceptualizing the multidimensional facets of immigration and differentiating immigrant status categories.

Also, the response in the agencies' reporting systems has been favorable to the growing diversity of nationalities and racial groupings comprising the post-1965 migratory streams, as evidenced in the expanded listing given in the census to birthplace, nationality, race and ethnicity. The 1970 Census listed six regions of origin (three of which are European) and a large listing of individual European countries of origin (listing only three countries of origin in Asia and two in Central/South America). The classification by race included only white, black and other. However, the 1980 Census lists five regions of birthplace, 26 individual countries and a thirteenfold classification for race and ethnicity. The 1980 public use microdata file (developed from a 5% sample of the census population) lists eight regions, nineteen subregions and 246 individual countries to designate birthplace. The design of the 1980 census tables facilitates immigration research by providing socioeconomic information for recent cohorts of arrivals who came to the United States during 1970 and 1980 and classifying these by birthplace.

As a reflection of the importance of immigration-related research, the Census Bureau's Center for International Research and Population Division prepared, for the first time in 1984, an extensive compilation in microfiche format of the socioeconomic characteristics of the U.S. foreign-born population. This information was essentially extracted from the 1980 census volumes and is presented at the nationwide level. State level data is reproduced only for residential patterns of foreign-born persons in metropolitan areas. This compilation was made for a variety of users, including the U.N. Statistical Office and the International Union for the Scientific Study of Population.

The limited state level information provided by the federally published *Statistical Yearbook of Immigration and Naturalization* has been supplemented with magnetic tapes providing information on birthplace and on selected sociodemographic characteristics of all persons granted permanent resident status between 1978 and 1988 by state of intended residence. This new data source makes it possible to single out individual states for indepth analysis, pursue interstate comparisons of legal immigration patterns, and obtain sociodemographic information on legally admitted immigrants that is not made available in the *Statistical Yearbook*.

However, it is one task to identify available data sources for immigration research; it is another to obtain access to such sources. The original intent in this study was to construe a "dynamic" sociodemographic profile from information that is not restricted to conventional demographic sources. A selective search was made of national surveys (identifying states); federal, state and city reports, surveys and statistics; application forms; certifications, etc., that might include the birthplace variable. The idea was to gain some insight into attitudinal and behavioral traits among the foreign born that cannot be captured by either the census or the immigration statistics data collection system. The effort was not successful.

The data sources that ultimately yielded the bulk of information on foreign-born New Yorkers utilized in this study were of the "conventional" demographic type generated by the federal data system in published format or on public use tapes. The public use microdata file developed from a 5 percent sample of the 1980 population census showed to be the most comprehensive of all the data sources reviewed for a study of this nature. The *Immigration and Naturalization Service Statistical Yearbooks* — though limited in coverage to persons legally admitted into the United States — made it possible to update information on the majority of immigrants, refugees and asylees residing in New York up to 1989. The same agency also made available 1989 data on the sociodemographic characteristics of those "undocumented" aliens residing in the state who had applied for legalization. The Bureau for Refugee Programs at the State Department and the Office of Refugee Resettlement at the Department of Health and Human Services maintain yearly records of the number of refugees located in resettlement programs in the different states throughout the country. These records were drawn upon to identify the number of refugees resettled in New York at various time periods. Unfortunately, no information is available regarding the secondary migration patterns of refugees to trace their moves during the period that follows the resettlement program through to the timing of their status adjustment to become legal immigrants.

Large-scale national sample surveys which included the variable of birthplace and residence by state could not be drawn upon for additional information because of the selectively small or unrepresentative base of foreign-born persons included in the sample. The sampling size of most national surveys is adequate when applied nationwide; state level subsamples are generally too small to allow for valid generalizations and, of course, the foreign-born population sampled is even smaller.

The State Level Data Collection System

Data generated by the New York State and New York City agencies on their foreign-born/immigrant residents are scarce and in certain cases not made accessible to researchers. Attempts made through the state and city public service agencies to gain access to nonconventional demographic sources such as alien verification system records, entitlement program records, social security application forms, alien labor certification records, public assistance records and survey reports were mostly unsuccessful.

New York State disseminates some immigrant-related information through its Department of Social Services in Albany. The New York Inter-Agency Task Force on Immigrant Affairs, which is housed within this department, made available the reports they had prepared on the impact of the 1986 Immigration Reform and Control Act, the legalization process, the workings of the State Legalization Impact Assistance Grant program (SLIAG), and discriminatory hiring practices resulting from the employer sanction provisions contained in IRCA. The actual generation of data included in some of the New York State reports may, however, have been the responsibility of the federal data collection system.

Though the New York Department of City Planning does not generate its own data, the demographic unit in this agency has been prolific in disaggregating city-relevant immigration data from the 1970 and 1980 censuses, publishing and disseminating these data sets in thematic form, compiling Directories of Immigrant Services and mapping patterns of immigrant residential concentration across the different boroughs of the city.

Overview of the Study

The central interest in this study is to construe a comprehensive profile that captures the demographic, social and economic characteristics of New York's foreign-born/immigrant residents taking into account comparative differences and similarities among the different regional and nationality groupings. Such an objective exacts the coverage of a diversity of issues.

Following this introductory background discussion, Chapter 2 pursues the complexity involved in defining the universe of the study and accounting statistically for the different categories and subcategories comprising the foreign-born population within a framework that takes into consideration the legal basis of their admission into the country.

Chapter 3 deals with the changing composition of the foreign-born population in New York by way of documenting the overall shift in the origin of immigrants coming to the United States after 1965. Particular attention is given to highlight differences in the nationality, ethnic and racial origin of New York's "new" immigrants and the implications this has had for the ethnic and racial make-up of New York City. The configuration of the nationality mix of New York's post-1965 foreign-born arrivals is compared to other states, and those nationality groups which have become major immigrant suppliers to New York over the past 23 years are detailed.

Chapters 4, 5 and 6 examine various aspects of the socioeconomic and demographic profile of the foreign-born/immigrant resident population of New York in 1980: age composition, family structure and fertility characteristics; educational attainment; economic circumstances and labor force behavior; and the productive role of immigrant workers in the occupational and industrial structure of the state.

In singling out the demographic and educational characteristics of the foreign born in New York in Chapter 4, some comparisons are drawn between the native-born population of the state and the foreign-born averages nationwide. The main interest in this comparative presentation is to explore whether or not there is a distinctiveness to the foreign-born community residing in New York in 1980 relative to U.S.-born New Yorkers and to persons of foreign birth residing in all parts of the country.

The thrust of Chapter 5 is to examine selected economic characteristics of New York's foreign-born residents; namely, their incorporation into the labor market, income attainment and exposure to poverty. These are examined with a dual purpose: from the perspective of New York as host state, to inquire into whether or not the presence of an immigrant population represents an economic liability to the state; from the perspective of the immigrant community itself, to examine some of the economic consequences of foreign birth, in combination with gender and race, as stratifying variables that condition the economic circumstances that confront immigrants.

The focus of attention, Chapter 6 centers around two issues: to identify the location of foreign-born workers in the broad industrial and occupational structure of the state and to locate the specific subcategories of occupations with the highest concentration of foreign-born workers. Examining these issues yields a typology of immigrant supplier countries based on the characteristics of the human capital resources each geographical region of origin "exports" to New York.

The findings presented in this study are based on the analysis of population and labor force data available from the sources identified earlier. The data have been collapsed and/or disaggregated further to construct detailed tables that effectively illustrate some of the specific immigrant patternings, highlight the central issues raised, and serve as reference points for future immigration research on New York.

Though much of the analysis is based on the 1980 Census, the findings may be utilized as background information for future studies interested in exploring the effects of immigration on New York State. Hopefully, this study will serve as a stimulus to encourage more comparative systematic research in the field of international migration, particularly that which is directed at analyzing and contrasting the socioeconomic characteristics of immigrants in different parts of the United States and at assessing their impact upon regions, states and localities of high immigrant concentration.

NOTES

[1] Though the terms "immigrant" and "foreign-born" are used interchangeably in this study, there is a crucial difference between the two designations. The foreign born is a collective which theoretically should include all persons of foreign birth, regardless of their legal status and intention to stay in the country. Place of birth defines the universe of the foreign born. "Immigrant" is a legal status referring to one who has entered the country as "permanent resident" or awaits that status. The term "illegal immigrant" is also problematic since it is contradictory—as long as a person is illegal, he or she is not an immigrant. The Census use of the term "period of immigration" in relation to the arrival of the foreign-born population is confusing unless referring to the specific entry into the United States of persons who received permanent resident status. For all other status categories, the appropriate term would be "period of arrival."

2

COMPONENTS OF THE INTERNATIONAL MIGRATORY FLOW INTO NEW YORK STATE: 1965–1989

This chapter presents an overview of the reported presence of persons born outside the United States who entered this country and settled residentially in New York at different times during the 1965–1989 period. The discussion centers on identifying the various components that make up the foreign-born population in the state. Comparable data for the United States as a whole are introduced to situate the migratory experience of New York within the context of processes occurring nationwide.

The key to accounting and understanding the dynamics of international migration in any part of the United States lies in the legal basis on which noncitizens are admitted into the country. Conceived in its entirety, the foreign-born population of New York, as in other parts of the country, consists of several categories and subcategories — some defined sociologically, others more often in terms of legal distinctions, some more nebulous or transitory than others. They are a complex array of citizens and residents, legal immigrants and nonimmigrants, and various kinds of refugees, illegal immigrants, deportees and prospective immigrants (Bryce-LaPorte, 1985:14) who need to be differentiated. How these various components of the foreign-born population are statistically accounted for and how the contour of their migratory flows into New York have been shaped by changes in the 1965 Immigration Act, the political events of the 1970s and 1980s in Indochina and Central America and the 1986 Immigration Reform and Control Act will serve as contextual background to the discussion.

Examined are four major categories into which the foreign-born population is classified pursuant to immigration law, policy and practice, and the different data sources which account statistically for their presence are identified. These components are the all-inclusive category of the foreign-born resident population which includes naturalized citizens, and three specific categories — the permanent resident/legal immigrant, the refugee and the asylee, and the undocumented alien. A fifth status category has been recently created by the 1986 Immigration Reform and Control Act. This is the "non-permanent" resident alien who resides in the United States "lawfully." The five categories are not mutually exclusive at all times; they are often interchangeable, overlapping and interrelated.

The Foreign-Born Resident Population

Volume and Distribution

Of the many terms used to designate non-native Americans, that of "foreign born" is the most inclusive and comprehensive of all. Though used coterminously with immigrant, it is important to note that not all foreign-born persons are immigrants in the legal sense of the term. As a segment of the U.S. population, the foreign born are identified and enumerated in the United States Census of Population which is constitutionally mandated to account for all native and foreign-born inhabitants in the country regardless of the legal status of the noncitizen resident.[1]

As of this writing, the 1990 Census count of the foreign-born population had not been released. Earlier census data reported that in 1960, 1970 and 1980, New York State maintained a stable number of foreign-born persons in excess of two million at each of the enumerations. These residents accounted for 13.6, 11.5 and 13.6 percent of New York's population at those three decennial periods. Their demographic presence was and continues to be dramatically visible in New York City, where typically 85 percent of foreign-born arrivals to New York State congregate and settle. In 1980, foreign-born New Yorkers represented close to 25 percent of all city residents and 21 percent of the population of the larger metropolitan area of New York; in 1990 their proportion in the New York City population has been estimated at 30 percent (Inter-Agency Task Force on Immigration Affairs, 1990). These numbers, while significant, are by no means outstanding in the context of the historical role of New York as a gateway for immigrants well before the turn of the century. During the first three decades of the twentieth century, the foreign born accounted for 25 to 30 percent of the New York State population, and levels of immigration were high enough to account directly for no less than one-third and as much as one half of the state's population growth (Alba and Trent, 1988), even though this immigration was offset by emigration estimated to be one-third as high.

It must be remembered that during the latter part of the nineteenth century and throughout the early decades of the twentieth century there was a massive influx of persons from abroad into the United States, the peak of which was reached in 1910 when 14 percent of the nation's population was foreign born. It was both the magnitude of their presence and the transformations taking place in the national origin composition of the foreign-born population that fueled a rise in nativist sentiments and eventually led, in the 1920s, to the passage of three restrictionist legislations (1921, 1924 and 1928), each fine-tuning the National Origin Quotas System (Bean and de la Garza, 1988). Because of these restrictions, coupled with the effects of the Depression in the 1930s and later the impact of World War II, the presence of the foreign born declined continually after 1930 in absolute numbers and in relation to the total population, reaching its lowest ebb by 1970. During the 1970s, however, there was a remarkable increase in the international movement of migrants into the country. According to the 1980 census count, between 1970 and 1980 the number of foreign-born persons had increased from 9 million to 14 million.

These trends were clearly reflected in the demography of New York. The data presented in Table 2.1 provide an historical perspective of the importance of immigration both nationwide and in New York from 1900 to 1980. Changes in the influx of immigrants into the country are indexed by the relative percentage the foreign-born component represented in the population of the United States, New York State and New York City.

Following the 1965 Amendments to the Immigration Act, immigration once again assumed a major role in both the aggregate population and labor force

TABLE 2.1

FOREIGN-BORN PERSONS AS PERCENT OF THE TOTAL POPULATION IN THE UNITED STATES, NEW YORK STATE AND NEW YORK CITY, 1900–1980

| | Foreign-Born Population | | | | | |
| | United States | | New York State | | New York City | |
Year	Number	% of Total Population	Number	% of Total Population	Number	% of Total Population
1900	10,444,717	13.7	1,900,425	26.1	1,270,100	37.0
1910	13,630,073	14.8	2,729,272	29.9	1,944,400	40.8
1920	14,020,203	13.2	2,786,112	26.8	2,028,200	36.1
1930	14,283,405	11.6	3,193,942	25.3	2,358,700	34.0
1940	11,656,641	8.8	2,853,530	21.1	2,138,700	28.7
1950	10,431,093	6.9	2,500,429	16.8	1,860,900	23.6
1960	9,738,143	5.4	2,289,314	13.6	1,558,700	20.0
1970	9,619,302	4.7	2,109,776	11.5	1,437,100	18.2
1980	14,079,906	6.2	2,388,938	13.6	1,670,200	23.6

Sources: U.S. Bureau of the Census, *Census of Population: 1980.* Vol.1. Chapter C. General and Social Characteristics, Part 1. United States Summary. (Washington, DC: U.S. Government Printing Office, 1983). Table 77; U.S. Bureau of the Census, *Census of Population: 1950.* Vol. 2. New York. (Washington, DC: U.S. Government Printing Office, 1952). Table 68.

growth. The reported numbers in the 1980 count marked the first increase in the foreign-born segment of the U.S. population since 1930. In 1920, foreign-born residents numbered 14 million nationwide and accounted for 13.2 percent of the total population; by 1970, their numbers had declined to 9.6 million, representing a 4.7 percent share in the population. By 1980, however, this segment had increased their numbers by about 4.5 million, or 1.5 percentage points, over the 1970 figure and accounted for 6.2 percent of the national population. This rapid growth is traced to both legal and undocumented entries.

In preparation for the 1980 census count, the Census Bureau addressed for the first time in its history the subject matter of the undocumented resident. At the conclusion of the 1980 census coverage, demographers at the bureau estimated that 2.1 million undocumented persons had been included in the 1980 nationwide count. This differentiation by legal status introduced a new term into census parlance: "the legally resident foreign-born population" – reported in 1980 to total 12.1 million persons – to be distinguished from the overall "foreign-born population" – which totaled at the time 14.1 million.[2]

The New York Profile

The census identified 2,388,980 persons of foreign birth residing in New York State in 1980, 56 percent of whom were nationalized citizens. These 2.4 million comprised both early and recent arrivals to this country: 29 percent had immigrated before 1950; 13 percent between 1950 and 1960; 23.4 percent between 1960 and 1970; and 34.8 percent between 1970 and 1980. A total of 1,180,000, or 49 percent of their total number in 1980, had arrived in the United States after the 1965 Immigration Act and settled in this state some time between then and 1980; they represented 16 percent of all the post-1965 arrivals to the United States.

Certainly New York was not the exclusive destination of those heading for the United States. The 2.4 million foreign-born New Yorkers reported in 1980 represented 17 percent of all foreign-born residents nationwide in that year. Other preferred destinations have been California, Texas, Florida, New Jersey and Illinois; together with New York, these five states absorbed over 70 percent of all foreign-born persons in 1980. California and New York together hosted 45 percent of the total number.

Table 2.2 provides data on the distribution of foreign-born residents in the six principal host states in 1970 and 1980. When changes in the proportion of the population who are foreign born in these states are compared over the ten-year period, the increase registered in New York State – from 11.5 percent to 13.6 percent – was relatively modest in relation to California and Texas. In California, the proportion of the foreign born rose from 8.8 percent to 15.1 percent, while in

TABLE 2.2
DISTRIBUTION OF THE FOREIGN-BORN POPULATION IN
SELECTED STATES, 1970 AND 1980

| | Foreign-Born Population | | | |
| | 1970 | | 1980 | |
Country/State	Number	% Total Population	Number	% Total Population
United States	9,619,302	4.7	14,079,906	6.2
New York	2,109,776	11.5	2,388,980	13.6
California	1,757,990	8.8	3,580,033	15.1
Texas	309,772	2.7	856,213	6.0
Florida	540,284	7.9	1,058,372	10.8
New Jersey	634,818	8.8	757,822	10.2
Illinois	628,890	5.6	823,696	7.2

Sources: U.S. Bureau of the Census, *Census of Population: 1980.* Vol. 1. Detailed Population Characteristics. Part 1. Chapter C. Part 6. California. Section 1. Table 61, Illinois. Section 1. Table 61, Part 11. Florida. Section 1. Table 61, Part 32. New Jersey. Section 1. Table 61, Part 34. New York. Section 1. Table 61, Part 45. Texas. Section 1. Table 61; Chapter D. United States Summary. (Washington DC: U.S. Government Printing Office,1983). Table 61.

Texas their representation in the state more than doubled—from 2.7 to 6.0 percent. Gains made in other host states were not as significant.

Certainly, there have been distinct changes in the destination points selected by foreigners coming to the United States over the past 25 years. The geographic and cultural origins of the newcomers figure prominently in these changing trends, but so does the population distribution that occurred nationwide over the 1970 to 1980 period (Kraly, 1987). Kraly has documented the swing of the pendulum to the west and southwest regions, drawing parallels between the geographical moves of native workers and their families to southern and western areas of the state and changing patterns in immigrants' residential choices. In both cases, these were responses to the relative economic decline and absolute loss of population experienced during the 1970s in the urban areas of the northeast and north central regions.

Residential Choices

Foreign-born persons overwhelmingly choose to live in highly urbanized areas. These residential choices are well documented and highlight the heavy concentration levels of the foreign born in metropolitan areas and central cities.

Table 2.3 illustrates comparative differences in the clustering of the foreign-born and the total population in five major metropolitan areas across the country. In 1980, the sum total of all foreign born residing in the New York, Los Angeles,

Chicago, San Francisco and Miami metropolitan areas in relation to the total foreign-born population nationwide was 38.7 percent; the corresponding percentage in the total population was only 12.6. The threefold differential holds true for all metropolitan areas except Chicago. It is, in particular, immigrant cohorts arriving after 1965 who have contributed so significantly to expanding the metropolitan area population base. By 1980, post-1965 arrivals had added 1.1 million persons to each of the New York and Los Angeles metropolitan areas, 400,000 persons to Chicago and roughly 300,000 to San Francisco and Miami. This cohort also accounted for over half of the foreign-born residents of the larger New York metropolitan area. But New York was not alone in this. The metropolitan areas of Chicago, San Francisco and Miami showed the same pattern, with the experience of Los Angeles being the most dramatic: seven in every ten foreign-born residents in 1980 had arrived in the United States after 1965.

TABLE 2.3

TOTAL AND FOREIGN-BORN POPULATION RESIDING IN
FIVE METROPOLITAN AREAS, 1980

Metropolitan Areas	Total Population	% U.S. Total	Foreign-Born Population	% U.S. Foreign-Born
United States	226,545,805	100.0	14,079,906	100.0
Total Five SMSAs	28,577,884	12.6	5,443,930	38.7
New York	9,120,346	4.0	1,946,800	13.8
Los Angeles	7,477,503	3.3	1,664,793	11.8
Chicago	7,103,624	3.1	744,930	5.3
San Francisco	3,250,630	1.4	509,352	3.6
Miami	1,625,781	0.7	578,055	4.1

Source: E. Bogen, *Immigration in New York.* (New York: Praeger, 1987). Table 5.4.

Residential choices are basically guided by individual and family preferences to live in a particular city or town, not a metropolitan area. The data in Table 2.4 documents the presence of the foreign born in the central cities of the United States relative to the total population and highlights the particular position of New York City in relation to cities in other host states. When the proportion who are foreign born is compared among central cities, New York shows a slightly lower percentage (23.6%) than Los Angeles and San Francisco (27.5%). None, however, surpass Miami, a city where over one half of the residents were born outside the country.

In Table 2.5, information has been compiled to compare the relative growth of the foreign-born population to that of the total population over the 1970 to 1980 period in five major cities. The size of the two populations obviously varies

TABLE 2.4

TOTAL AND FOREIGN-BORN POPULATION RESIDING IN SEVEN CENTRAL CITIES, 1980

Cities	Total Population	Foreign-Born Population	Foreign-Born as Percent of Total
New York	7,071,639	1,670,199	23.6
Los Angeles	2,966,850	804,818	27.1
Chicago	3,005,078	435,232	14.5
San Francisco	678,974	192,204	28.3
Miami	346,865	186,280	53.7
Houston	1,595,138	155,577	9.8
San Diego	875,538	130,906	15.0

Source: U.S. Bureau of the Census 1983, *Census of Population: 1980.* Vol. I. Chapter C. General Social and Economic Characteristics. Part 1. United States Summary, (Washington, DC: U.S. Government Printing Office, 1983).

TABLE 2.5

POPULATION CHANGES IN THE TOTAL AND FOREIGN-BORN POPULATION IN THE UNITED STATES AND SELECTED CITIES, 1970–1980

Location	Total 1970 Population	Foreign Born 1970 Population	Total 1980 Population	Foreign Born 1980 Population	% Change of Total	% Change of Foreign Born
United States	203,210,158	9,619,302	226,545,805	14,079,906	+11.5	+46.4
New York City	7,894,798	1,437,058	7,071,639	1,670,199	-10.4	+16.2
Los Angeles	2,815,998	410,870	2,966,850	804,818	+5.4	+95.9
Chicago	3,362,947	373,919	3,005,078	435,232	-10.6	+16.4
San Francisco	715,673	154,507	678,974	192,204	-5.1	+24.4
Miami	335,062	140,207	346,865	186,280	+3.5	+32.9

Source: E. Bogen, *Immigration in New York.* (New York: Praeger, 1987). Table 5.3.

and comparisons in growth patterns are in relative proportion to the respective population size. The overriding pattern is, however, clear. The population size in the foreign-born segment showed positive growth over the ten-year period in each of the cities listed, whereas the national population experienced a loss in numbers in three cities: New York, Chicago and, (only slightly) San Francisco. If the growth patterns of the foreign born in New York City are compared with other cities, New York (16% increase) loses to San Francisco and Miami (a 24% and 33% increase respectively), not to mention Los Angeles where an increase of 96 percent was registered — about six times as high as the growth rate for New York.

Despite this slack, New York City's flair remains unsurpassed. Its historical prominence as an "immigrant city" is best illustrated in Table 2.6, which presents a profile of the concentration of foreign-born persons in New York City indicating the proportion in the nationwide total of U.S. foreign-born residents that this city has been absorbing. Even during the economic recession of the late 1970s and early 1980s, when the state experienced a considerable outflow of American-born New Yorkers, the city remained the preferred residential choice of foreign-born people settling in New York State. Of the 1.2 million people who arrived in the United States after 1965 and were residing in New York State by 1980, 80 percent were New York City residents. According to the 1980 census, 75 percent of the state's foreign-born residents were living in the New York City proper, with another 15 percent in the surrounding counties of the greater metropolitan area of New York: Westchester, Rockland, Nassau and Suffolk. Since 1900, more than 10 percent of the foreign-born population in the United States resided in New York City, but the clustering became more visible since 1970 when foreign-born city residents totaled 1.4 million and represented 18.2 percent of the city's total population. Ten years later, nearly a quarter of a million additional foreign-born persons were added to the city count, bringing their total number to 1.7 million, over half of whom had arrived after 1965. This was at a time when New York City experienced an exodus of 800,000 American-born New Yorkers.

The respective losses and gains in population experienced by the city during the 1970s were not distributed equally among the different counties, the Bronx having witnessed the largest decline — almost 300,000 persons. However, as each of the boroughs, with the exception of Richmond (Staten Island), were losing in

TABLE 2.6

NEW YORK CITY POPULATION BY NATIVITY, 1900–1980 (NUMBERS IN THOUSANDS)

Year	Total	Foreign Born	% Foreign Born	% of U.S. Foreign Born in New York City
1900	3437.2	1270.1	37.0	12.2
1910	4766.9	1944.4	40.8	14.3
1920	5620.0	2028.2	36.1	14.5
1930	6930.4	2358.7	34.0	16.5
1940	7455.0	2138.7	28.7	18.3
1950	7892.0	1860.9	23.6	17.8
1960	7783.3	1558.7	20.0	16.0
1970	7894.9	1437.1	18.2	14.9
1980	7071.6	1670.2	23.6	11.9

Source: Rosenwaike, 1972, Table 69; U.S. Bureau of the Census, 1972, Table 138; U.S. Bureau of the Census, 1981, Tables 77, 78, 79; U.S. Bureau of the Census, 1983a, Table 172; cited in Kraly, 1987.

population that decade, the foreign-born population was increasing. Brooklyn and Queens, in particular, were favorite residential choices and in these two localities the number of foreign-born residents increased by 16 and 29 percent respectively. As a ratio of the American-born population, persons of foreign birth were distributed along the following proportions in 1980: 1:4 in Queens, Manhattan and Brooklyn; close to 1:5 in the Bronx and 1:15 in Staten Island.

The Legal Immigrant/Permanent Resident Population

An up-to-date profile of a significant portion of New York's foreign-born population may be drawn from the annual statistical records collected and published by the Immigration and Naturalization Service (INS) in the form of their *Statistical Yearbook*. These records identify the number of persons in the foreign-born population who have been legally admitted to the status of permanent resident, and to this category the term "immigrant" is the most appropriate. The permanent resident/legal immigrant component takes into account two categories of the foreign-born population: all persons entering legally into the United States with permanent resident visas obtained at U.S. consular offices abroad and all persons already residing in the United States as nonimmigrants who have adjusted their status to become legal permanent residents. The latter group includes persons who had earlier entered the country for a temporary period, such as students, temporary workers, resident refugees, asylees and undocumented persons, and who have applied and been approved for legalization of their status. The statistics on legal immigrants exclude from the count newly admitted refugees, asylees and other resident aliens who have not fulfilled their residence requirements to qualify for legal immigrant status, and all nonlegal residents who include, but are not limited to, the category labeled "illegals."

When the term "admission" to legal immigrant status is thus clarified, it corrects the common perception that annual figures published on the number of legal admissions signify newcomers that are an addition to the volume of foreign-born persons already living in the country. For example, of the number of legal immigrants admitted nationwide between 1980 and 1988, around 60 percent were "new arrivals" to the country. The remaining 40 percent involved adjustment from nonimmigrant to immigrant status. The ratio was reversed in 1989 when the fraction who were "new arrivals" dropped to 37 percent. Close to two thirds of all legal immigrant admissions during the 1988–1989 fiscal year were cases of status adjustment activated in large part by the legalization program. The particular group among those legally admitted to the United States during 1980 and

1988 who declared intention to reside in New York State, however, included a higher proportion (75%) of "new arrivals" than the nationwide profile. This would suggest that entries to New York during that eight year period were more heavily weighted toward new immigrants seeking family reunification or occupational opportunities than adjustment from nonimmigrant to immigrant status.

Documenting the Legal Immigrant Population

Generally, documenting the number of foreign-born persons admitted to permanent resident status is important since this particular component has the greatest impact on the country: technically speaking, only they are "immigrants" in the legal sense and can become U.S. citizens. Additionally, and in the context of this research in particular, the INS data base identifies the particular destination point of the newly admitted immigrant by state, (and until recently by urban and rural locality), making it possible to delineate the demographic profile of legal flows establishing residence across different regions of the country and to examine some aspects of their social and economic impact upon individual states. Also, since INS records are collected and published annually, they provide the most recent information on the changing volume and nationality composition of legal migratory flows into each state from one year to the next. This permits the updating of legal immigration trends during intercensus periods. In this particular study, INS data sources allowed for the inclusion of information up to 1989.

However, the INS data base also has some serious limitations. In geographical settings where the presence of nonlegal residents is particularly high, the data fall short of identifying/estimating the total number of foreign-born persons in the given population. More importantly, the annual legal immigration totals lend themselves to incorrect interpretation or inappropriate usage as a proxy for stock, fed by additional migratory flows. One reason for this is that appropriate adjustments for legal emigration have not been made. In addition, the time lag between refugee/asylee entry and the recording of refugee adjustment to legal immigrant status continues to be a constant and nagging problem. Refugee admissions are not recorded as formal immigration until these individuals "adjust" to immigrant status – a process that usually starts one or two years after arrival in the United States (Warren, 1976).

Until recently, state level information available in the published INS data sets was too scanty to encourage comparative research on local/regional immigration issues. Geographic distribution patterns by national origin, however, have been available by state for some time, based on information provided by immigrants regarding their destination points. Although such indications are conveyed as expressions of an immigrant's "intent" to reside in a particular state, they are taken as proxy for the actual distribution of immigrants across the country. By and large, statements of "intent" have coincided with the de facto residential location of the foreign-born population as reported in the decennial census. Residential location of legal immigrants is significant because it has shown in many cases to be a predictor of the residential concentration of undocumented aliens as well, given that the latter are known to join and live with or close to family members who have legal status in the country.

Allowing for some of the limitations of the INS reporting system, the following account may be rendered of the volume of persons admitted as legal immigrants into the United States since 1965 and of those amongst them who expressed intent to reside in New York State.

Volume

Historically, the reported immigration to the United States increased from 1,563,470 during the 1931 to 1950 period to 5,837,156 from 1951 to 1970, reaching 10,294,893 between 1971 and 1989. The implementation of the 1965 Immigration Act was not finalized until 1968, and in that year alone legal admissions climbed to 450,000, marking an increase over the 320,000 average recorded in the three previous years. Throughout the 1970s the annual legal admission figure averaged 422,000. A peak in the number of legal entries was reached in 1986, and from then on yearly admissions exceeded the 600,000 figure – doubling the number of legal admissions reported in 1965 (Table 2.7). Despite what may appear at first as a steady progression in admission levels beginning in 1968, the indications are that immigration into the United States was in fact a binding constraint until 1977. As shown in Table 2.7, the number of legal admissions in 1968, the year marking the end of the transition phase following the enactment of the 1965 Act, totaled 454.4 thousand, a figure that was not matched for another decade – to be precise, in 1977, when admissions totaled 462.3 thousand. In the years between, the numbers admitted annually were much lower.

In 1989, legal admissions exceeded the one million figure, the highest yearly total reported since 1915, marking a 69.5 percent increase over the 1988 entries. This increment was in large part due to status adjustments under the 1986 IRCA legalization provisions. Entries under this program accounted for 44 percent of all legal admissions in 1989. It is expected that the volume of legal immigration will level off in the next few years as the bulk of legalization applications have now been filed and processed.

Side by side with the national figures in Table 2.7, corresponding entries of legal immigrants into New York State are shown. With 1965 (the last year under the McCarran-Walter Act) selected as the index year, the data indicate clearly that in proportionate terms New York was receiving fewer immigrants than those coming into the United States as a whole during the 1965 to 1989 period. The

TABLE 2.7

LEGAL IMMIGRANTS ADMITTED AS PERMANENT RESIDENTS TO THE
UNITED STATES AND THE NUMBER DECLARING NEW YORK STATE
AS INTENDED RESIDENCE, 1965–1989

Arrival Year	Total Admissions to the U.S. (000s)	Changes with 1965 as Index Year	Number Declaring New York as Intended Residence (000s)	Changes with 1965 as Index Year
1965	296.7	100	69.0	100
1966	323.0	108	77.3	112
1967	362.0	122	86.3	125
1968	454.4	153	97.8	142
1969	358.6	121	94.4	137
1970	373.3	126	97.8	142
1971	370.5	125	92.5	134
1972	384.7	130	93.8	136
1973	400.0	135	93.6	136
1974	394.8	133	88.1	128
1975	386.2	130	86.5	125
1976	398.6	134	86.0	125
1977	462.3	156	88.8	129
1978	601.4	203	100.5	146
1979	460.3	155	94.4	137
1980	530.6	179	n.a.[a]	—
1981	596.6	201	n.a.[a]	—
1982	594.1	200	85.0	123
1983	559.7	189	93.1	135
1984	543.9	183	107.0	155
1985	570.0	192	104.7	152
1986	601.7	203	110.2	160
1987	601.5	203	114.2	165
1988	643.0	217	109.3	158
1989	1,091.0	368	134.8	195

Sources: U.S. Immigration and Naturalization Service, (INS), *Annual Report Statistical Yearbook 1965–1987*. (Washington DC: U.S. Government Printing Office, unpublished); INS, *1988 Statistical Yearbook of the Immigration and Naturalization Service*. (Washington DC: U.S. Government Printing Office, 1989). Table 17; INS, *1989 Statistical Yearbook of the Immigration and Naturalization Service*. (Washington DC: U.S. Government Printing Office, 1990). Table 16.

Note: [a] Tape documentation on *Immigrants Admitted into the U.S. as Legal Permanent Residents, FY 1978–1986*, reports the following number of legal immigrants declaring New York State as intended residence: 1980 – 80,148; 1981 – 80,590.

increase in legal admissions in the two populations in relation to a basic index figure equivalent to 100 in each case in 1989 totaled 368 nationwide, but only 195 in New York State. In the 1980s, the peak admission year for New York was 1989, when 134,766 legal entries were reported. Entries were at their lowest from 1979 to 1983, corresponding to the period of New York's economic recession and to a more general economic decline in the northeast and north central regions. From 1984 onward, however, legal entries increased in excess of 100,000 yearly, reaching a peak in 1989. The 1988–1989 increase in New York's entries – from 109,300 to 134,766 – is impressive but in no way commensurable with the corresponding increase in admissions nationwide. These increased over the 1988–1989 period by 69 percent for the country as a whole, but by only 23 percent in New York State. The differential reflects in part the relatively few applications filed for status legalization in New York following the IRCA provisions of 1986, thereby depressing the numbers who would have eventually become permanent residents by 1989.

Class of Admission

Upward trends in the nationwide volume of legal admissions are not due to increased quotas, but to an expanded legal entry of foreigners into the country who are not subject to numerical limitation. The number of immigrants admitted nationwide who are subject to worldwide limitation has been relatively constant since 1978 – around the limit of 270,000 with no more than 20,000 coming from any independent country and no more than 500 from a dependency. The visa allocation for this group is determined by a preference system of six categories, each with its own numerical limitation (see, Appendix) which includes relatives and occupational preferences. Categories of immigrants who are exempt from the worldwide limitation include immediate relatives of U.S. citizens; refugees and asylees who adjust their status; special immigrants; and, since 1986, aliens who have unlawfully resided in the country since January 1972 and seasonal agricultural workers. The national immigration statistics show that throughout most of the 1980s, a 55 percent average of all yearly admissions pertained to categories exempt from numerical limitations: this proportion increased from 59 percent in 1988 to 74 percent in 1989. As shown in Table 2.8, two major categories account for this expansion in exemptions: aliens adjusting for status legalization who totaled 478,814 in 1989 and Amerasians who were added as an immigrant category in 1988. Only 319 children born in Vietnam, their families and guardians entered under the latter provision in 1988 as compared to 8,589 in 1989. The INS estimated that an additional 15,000 may have entered in 1990.

The situation was somewhat different for the 1978–1986 cohort of immigrants who selected New York State as destination point. In the majority of cases, these

TABLE 2.8

IMMIGRANTS ADMITTED INTO THE UNITED STATES BY
MAJOR CATEGORY OF ADMISSION, 1988 AND 1989

Category of Admission	1989	1988	Change Number	%
Grand Total	1,090,924	643,025	447,899	69.7
Total, IRCA Legalization[a]	478,814	NA	478,814	NA
Total, Except IRCA Legalization	612,110	643,025	-30,915	-4.8
Subject to Worldwide Limitation	280,275	264,148	16,127	6.1
Relative Preferences	217,092	200,772	16,320	8.1
First	13,259	12,107	1,152	9.5
Second	112,771	102,777	9,994	9.7
Fourth	26,975	21,940	5,035	22.9
Fifth	64,087	63,948	139	0.2
Occupational Preferences	52,755	53,607	-852	-1.6
Third	26,798	26,680	118	0.4
Sixth	25,957	26,927	-970	-3.6
Nonpreference	7,068	6,029	1,039	17.2
Other	3,360	3,740	-380	-10.2
Exempt from Worldwide Limitation	331,835	378,877	-47,042	-12.4
Immediate Relatives of U.S. Citizens	217,514	219,340	-1,826	-0.8
Spouses	125,744	130,977	-5,233	-4.0
Parents	50,494	47,500	2,994	6.3
Children	41,276	40,863	413	1.0
Orphans	7,948	9,120	-1,172	-12.9
Other Children	33,328	31,743	1,585	5.0
Refugee and Asylee Adjustments	84,288	81,719	2,569	3.1
Amerasians	8,589	319	8,270	25.92
Special Immigrants	4,986	5,120	-134	-2.6
1972 Registry	10,570	39,999	-29,429	-73.6
Cuban/Haitian Entrant	2,816	29,002	-26,186	-90.3
Other	3,072	3,378	-306	-9.1

Source:　U.S. Immigration and Naturalization Service, *1989 Statistical Yearbook of the Immigration and Naturalization Service.* (Washington, DC: U.S. Government Printing Office, 1990). Table E.

Note: [a] IRCA legalization is also exempt from limitations.

TABLE 2.9

DISTRIBUTION OF NEW YORK STATE-BOUND FOREIGN-BORN PERSONS ADMITTED AS
PERMANENT RESIDENTS TO THE UNITED STATES BY CLASS OF ADMISSION, 1978–1986

Class of Admission	1978	1979	1980	1981	1982	1983	1984	1985	1986
Worldwide Limited Subtotal	73.5	75.0	71.0	76.3	74.1	73.2	66.2	66.3	66.4
1st Preference	0.8	1.0	1.0	1.1	1.2	1.2	1.1	1.2	1.4
2nd Preference	21.7	38.1	32.6	39.1	39.7	41.7	35.0	37.9	36.5
3rd Preference	1.3	1.3	1.6	1.3	2.9	2.8	2.6	2.5	3.0
4th Preference	1.9	3.5	3.3	3.6	5.1	5.7	3.7	3.7	4.3
5th Preference	18.6	22.0	22.2	25.1	17.5	14.6	17.3	14.9	15.1
6th Preference	2.1	4.1	7.1	6.1	7.7	7.2	6.5	6.1	6.1
7th Preference[a]	4.5	4.5	3.2	–	–	–	–	–	–
Nonpreference	22.6	0.5	–	–	–	–	–	–	–
Other	–	–	–	–	–	–	–	–	0.1
Exempt from Limitation Subtotal	26.5	25.0	29.0	23.7	25.9	26.8	33.8	33.7	33.6
Recap Cuban NUMS	3.2	4.1	5.1	3.0	0.3	–	–	–	–
Immediate Relatives	18.1	18.6	20.7	17.7	21.5	23.1	23.9	26.7	26.7
Special Immigrants	0.3	0.3	0.5	0.7	0.9	0.5	0.3	0.4	0.4
Adj/Not Sect. 245	4.4	1.5	2.2	1.6	1.2	0.7	1.7	1.1	1.4
Other Adjustments	0.5	0.5	0.5	0.6	0.5	0.6	0.5	0.5	0.5
Refugee Act	–	–	–	0.1	1.5	1.9	7.4	5.2	4.6

Source: U.S. Immigration and Naturalization Service, *Immigrants Admitted into the United States as Legal Permanent Residents. FY 1978–86.* Tape Documentation. (Washington DC: Statistical Analysis Branch, 1987).

Notes: [a] Abolished in 1980 with the Refugee Act.

were admitted under categories and provisions subject to numerical limitation, namely, the second preference category (spouses and unmarried sons and daughters of permanent resident aliens) and fifth preference (adult brothers and sisters of U.S. citizens and their spouses and children). From 1983 on, immigrants admitted under the fifth preference category continued to increase in New York as did others entering as "immediate relations" of U.S. citizens, a category that is exempt from worldwide limitation (Table 2.9).

Few persons among the 1978–1986 cohort of immigrants settling in New York State were admitted under the third preference category of "professionals of exceptional ability." They represented on the average 1.3 percent of the yearly admissions during 1978 and 1981 and slightly under 3 percent during 1982 and 1986. Admissions were higher for those entering under the sixth preference category designated for "workers in skilled and unskilled occupations." They averaged just under 7 percent of all admissions, twice the percentage of those applying to enter as "professionals." The relative scarcity of immigrants entering under the worker provision category does not necessarily imply a lack of qualified resources coming into the state. Applications under third and sixth preference categories require labor certification which can entail a lengthy process. If qualified persons are eligible to file under the family reunion provisions they are more likely to do so to expedite entry into the United States.

Residential Preferences of Recent Legal Immigrants: 1980–1989

It was mentioned previously that residential choices indicated by legal immigrants upon entry to the United States for the most part coincided with the actual geographical distribution of the foreign-born population as reported in the 1980 census. The top six states of intended residence for immigrants since 1971 are California, New York, Texas, Illinois, Florida and New Jersey. They accounted for 80 percent of the immigrants' intended place of residence in 1989. Until 1976, New York had been the single most favored destination point selected by legal immigrants, and until that time the state's share in the total number of legal immigrant admissions approximated 25 percent. Since then it has decreased to 17 percent in 1988 and 12 percent in 1989. Over the past 14 years, California has been the lead receiving site, hosting close to 30 percent of all persons admitted as legal immigrants from 1985 to 1988 and as many as 42 percent in 1989. Legal immigrants were heavily concentrated in California in 1989 (58%), while New York held a strong lead as the preferential choice of undocumented immigrants. Among these, the state received 16 percent of the nationwide total in 1989. Whether or not New York can regain the momentum it held in the 1980s following its economic recession is not known.

Nationality and cultural origin figure prominently in the modified geographical distribution of immigrants in the country. The rising importance of California as first host state and the relative decline of New York has come about because of the combined effect of four major factors: 1) the overall economic decline experienced in the northeastern and north central regions; 2) the nationality profile of new immigrants and refugees who show particular preference for the western region: approximately one third of the foreign-born population living in western states in 1980 was born in Mexico and another one-fourth was Asian; 3) the decline in immigration among Europeans who have shown a distinct preference to reside in New York; and 4) the high concentration of undocumented residents in California who applied for legalization and regularized their status to become permanent residents, thereby boosting the California numbers further.[3]

The magnetism of New York City as the "city of immigrants" still persists and is best documented with INS information detailing the particular urban and rural localities within the selected states that immigrants have indicated as residence site. Almost all legal immigrants coming to New York chose to live in New York City, a percentage not matched by any other city in California, Texas and Florida, and immigrants intending to reside in the other three states selected a more balanced and diversified set of localities for residence site, including not only a variety of central cities, but smaller urban localities as well.[4]

The Refugee Population

The heavy flow of Southeast Asian refugees into the country after 1975 prompted Congress to enact the 1980 Refugee Act, which opened a special category for refugee admission separate from the jurisdiction of immigration policy and established a policy to extend federal funding for resettlement assistance to all groups of refugees equally (Simcox, 1988). A process for Presidential and Congressional consultations was developed to set an annual ceiling for the number of refugees to be admitted for each area of chargeability. Table 2.10 provides detailed information of refugee approvals and actual arrivals between 1981 and 1989 by geographic area of chargeability.

Upon arrival to the United States, "legal" refugees enter into the statistics of the nonimmigrant population for that year. Being exempt from the worldwide annual limitation of 270,000 immigrants, they become eligible to adjust to lawful permanent resident status after one year. The current data collection system allows for a yearly accounting of 1) the number of refugee entries (INS); 2) the numbers placed in resettlement programs across the country (Department of Health and Human Services and Department of State; and 3) the number and residential locations of refugees who adjust their status to become permanent residents (INS). There is no estimate of the number of persons wishing to be accepted as political refugees but who are not recognized as such by the United States government.

Consistent with the 1967 United Nations Protocol on Refugees,[5] the 1980 Act also introduced for the first time a statutory basis for granting asylum to persons already in the country or at a U.S. port of entry who fear persecution if forced to return to the homeland. Persons already in the United States who desire to apply for asylum are not identifiable as a distinct group within the larger foreign-born population, for they can be part of any one of the nonimmigrant visa holders or undocumented aliens. As a distinct group of asylees, they are recognized statistically only after they apply for asylum, when being granted asylee status and when they adjust status from asylee to permanent resident, which requires a one-year residence in the United States.

No legal limits are set as to the number of individuals granted asylum within a year, since this category is exempt from the worldwide limitation of 270,000 authorized immigrant entries. However, no more than 5,000 persons granted asylee status may "adjust" to become lawful permanent residents within a given year.

TABLE 2.10

REFUGEE APPROVALS AND ADMISSIONS BY GEOGRAPHIC AREA OF CHARGEABILITY, 1981–1989

Geographic Area of Chargeability	1981	1982	1983	1984	1985	1986	1987	1988	1989[a]
Authorized Admissions	217,000	140,000	90,000	72,000	70,000	67,000	70,000	87,500	104,500
Africa	3,000	3,500	3,000	2,750	3,000	3,000	2,000	3,000	2,000
East Asia	165,600	96,000	64,000	52,000	50,000	45,500	40,500	38,000	38,000
Eastern Europe & Soviet Union	39,900	31,000	15,000	11,000	10,000	9,500	12,300	30,000	50,000
Latin America & Caribbean	4,000	3,000	2,000	1,000	1,000	3,000	1,000	3,500	3,500
Near East	4,500	6,500	6,000	5,250	6,000	6,000	10,200	9,000	7,000
Unallocated Reserve	X	X	X	X	X	X	4,000	4,000	4,000
Approvals	155,291	61,527	73,645	77,932	59,436	52,081	61,529	80,282	95,505
Africa	3,784	4,198	2,642	2,743	1,943	1,329	1,974	1,304	1,825
East Asia	124,719	37,481	51,476	58,697	39,628	35,193	37,082	41,450	35,196
Eastern Europe & Soviet Union	18,845	13,778	13,382	10,917	9,999	9,515	12,290	26,645	48,620
Latin America & Caribbean	1,210	580	710	156	1,868	99	99	2,452	2,848
Near East	6,733	5,490	5,435	5,419	5,998	5,997	10,084	8,431	7,016
Admissions[b]	NA	93,252	57,064	67,750	62,477	58,329	66,803	80,382	101,072
Africa	NA	3,259	2,382	2,704	1,952	1,279	2,068	1,708	1,998
East Asia	NA	69,712	35,861	49,154	44,972	41,673	40,046	35,160	36,989
Eastern Europe & Soviet Union	NA	13,438	12,986	10,497	9,720	9,270	12,450	28,906	48,416
Latin America & Caribbean	NA	453	724	152	159	48	902	4,319	5,033
Near East	NA	6,350	5,110	5,242	5,674	6,059	10,619	9,486	7,699
Unknown	NA	40	1	1	--	--	718	803	937

Source: Immigration and Naturalization Service, *1988 Statistical Yearbook of the Immigration and Naturalization Service.* (Washington DC: U.S. Government Printing Office, 1989). Table 25. *1989 Statistical Yearbook of the Immigration and Naturalization Service.* (Washington DC: U.S. Government Printing Office, 1990). Table 26.

Notes: Beginning in 1987, refugee admission data were compiled through the Nonimmigrant information system. Since the system collects all entries of persons with nonimmigrant status, initial arrivals of refugees may be overstated. In 1988, approximately 700 reserve slots were used to admit Cuban refugees.

[a] The authorized admission level for 1989 was set at 118,500, including 12,000 admissions for Amerasians (P.L. 100-202) under the East Asia ceiling of 80,000 Since Amerasians enter the United States on immigrant visas, they are not included as refugee arrivals in the INS data. As a result, the authorized admission levels for 1989 have been reduced accordingly. In Fiscal Year 1989, 8,589 Amerasians entered the United States.

[b] Admissions may by higher than approvals because of the arrivals of persons approved in previous years.

NA = Not available. X = Not applicable .

Refugee Admissions Nationwide

Prior to the 1980 Refugee Act, the United States had recognized refugees for entry into the country since 1946. International events taking place in Southeast Asia, most particularly during the mid and late 1970s, acted as catalysts to the formulation of a separate refugee policy in 1980. From 1975 to 1980, prior to the Act, 548,296 refugees had been admitted; among these, 417,894, or 76 percent, came from the Southeast Asia region (Table 2.11). Though admission trends in the early 1980s were still dominated by Southeast Asians, approvals extended in the latter part of the decade gave visibility to refugees from other parts of the world.

TABLE 2.11

REFUGEE ADMISSIONS INTO THE UNITED STATES, 1975–1980

Fiscal Year	Africa	East Asia	Eastern Europe	Soviet Union	Latin America	Near East/ South Asia	Total
1975	—	135,000	1,947	6,211	3,000	—	146,158
1976	—	15,000	1,756	7,450	3,000	—	27,206
1977	—	7,000	1,755	8,191	3,000	—	19,946
1978	—	20,574	2,245	10,688	3,000	—	36,507
1979	—	76,521	3,393	24,449	7,000	—	111,363
1980	955	163,799	5,025	28,444	6,662	2,231	207,116
Total 1975–80	955	417,894	16,121	85,433	25,662	2,231	548,296
Percent	0.17	76.2	2.9	15.6	4.7	0.4	100.0

Sources: D. Simcox, *U.S. Immigration in the 1980's.* (Boulder: Westview Press, 1988). p. 53.

Between 1981 and 1989, 918,000 admissions for refugees were authorized and 717,228 applications were approved. The number of refugees actually admitted into the United States between 1982 and 1989 totaled 587,129 (*see,* Table 2.10). A comprehensive documentation of refugee arrivals by selected nationality groups for that period is provided in the data compiled in Table 2.12. The expansion of refugee source countries beyond the orbit of Vietnam (1982–1989), Cambodia (1982–1985), Laos (1986–1989), Poland and Romania (1982–1989) to include the Soviet Union (1987–1989), Ethiopia (1982–1988), Cuba (1988–1989) and Iran (1985–1989) is evident. This expansion was in no way the result of policy dictates in immigration and refugee policy per se; rather, it reflected changes in demand and in the country's perception of its responsibilities vis-à-vis certain nations (Papademetriou, 1990).

Refugee arrivals reached a peak in 1982 with the entry of 93,252 persons within a single year. After this, a steady decline set in until 1987, with increases noted in

TABLE 2.12

REFUGEE ARRIVALS INTO THE UNITED STATES BY
SELECTED NATIONALITY, 1982–1989

Nationality	1982	1983	1984	1985	1986	1987	1988	1989
All Nationalities	93,252	57,064	67,750	62,477	58,329	66,803	80,382	101,072
Afghanistan	4,282	2,475	2,231	2,094	2,478	3,241	2,380	1,991
Albania	15	61	45	43	78	49	74	44
Bulgaria	117	158	137	122	148	110	147	110
Cambodia	19,832	11,161	17,785	16,647	9,133	1,772	2,802	2,110
China[a]	21	155	210	82	39	416	162	210
Cuba	453	723	81	158	43	314	3,006	3,742
Czechoslovakia	697	1,191	773	959	1,447	373	247	257
El Salvador	—	—	67	—	—	74	60	74
Ethiopia	3,050	2,275	2,347	1,773	1,248	1,858	1,539	1,750
Hungary	534	651	519	545	635	690	810	1,071
Iran	16	1,017	2,812	3,292	3,246	7,075	6,920	5,466
Iraq	1,986	1,577	152	244	311	186	37	115
Laos	9,215	2,631	7,423	4,724	11,130	15,508	14,561	12,779
Nicaragua	—	—	—	—	—	486	1,155	1,053
Poland	6,312	5,520	3,794	2,806	3,617	3,734	3,670	3,792
Romania	2,907	3,758	4,281	4,488	2,573	3,203	2,953	3,359
South Africa	6	13	10	22	8	69	35	22
Soviet Union	2,747	1,363	803	643	744	3,652	20,533	39,076
Vietnam	40,604	21,463	23,372	22,831	20,821	22,320	17,626	21,865
Yugoslavia	6	9	15	25	2	578	400	619
Other	452	863	893	979	628	1,095	1,265	1,567

Sources: Immigration and Naturalization Service, *1988 Statistical Yearbook of the Immigration and Naturalization Service.* (Washington, DC: U.S. Government Printing Office, 1989). Table 26. INS, *1989 Statistical Yearbook of the Immigration and Naturalization Service.* (Washington, DC: U.S. Government Printing Office, 1990). Table 27.

Notes: Data for Fiscal Years 1980–81 are not available. Beginning in 1987, refugee admission data were compiled through the Nonimmigrant Information System. Since the system collects all entries of persons with nonimmigrant status, initial arrivals of refugees may be overstated.

[a] Data for Mainland China and Taiwan are included in China.

1988 and again in 1989. Refugee arrivals increased by 25 percent between 1988 and 1989 from 80,382 to 101,072 for five areas of chargeability: Africa; East Asia; Eastern Europe and the Soviet Union; Latin America and the Caribbean; the Near East, with the Soviet Union, Vietnam and Laos leading the arrival list. The three countries combined accounted for almost three fourths of all refugee arrivals. By 1988, 93,398 refugees who arrived in the United States between 1981 and 1987 were granted lawful permanent resident status, and these came in overwhelming numbers from Asia and the Caribbean. The two regions represented 55 percent and 32 percent, respectively, of the 93,398 cases of status adjustment that were effected for refugees arriving from 1981 to 1987, with Haiti heading the list of individual countries (Table 2.13).

Between 1980 and 1989, the immigration authorities had received 395,795 requests for asylum: 43 percent of these were presented for adjudication, and of these an average of 30 percent were approved. The approval rate was highest (over 50%) in 1980 and 1987 and lowest in 1989 (18%). Asylum applications received in 1989 were 67 percent higher than the number filed the previous year — increasing numerically from 60,736 to 101,679, with nationals from El Salvador and Nicaragua heading the list. The number of applicants granted asylum in 1988 increased by over 40 percent from 1987 — from 5,093 to 7,340 — but by only 25 percent from 1988 to 1989 when 9,229 requests were approved. In these three years, Nicaraguans were the leading nationality granted asylum, followed at some distance by Iranians. A select nationality breakdown of persons granted asylum between 1984 and 1989 is presented in Table 2.14.

The Presence of Refugees in New York State

State level information concerning refugees and asylees — their numbers, social characteristics, resettlement experience, secondary migration patterns, etc. — is scanty. State-specific data are published yearly on the numbers of resident refugees granted lawful permanent resident status, applications filed for asylum and persons granted asylee status, and asylees granted permanent resident status. If these are taken as an approximate measure of the overall volume of refugees/asylees residing in the various states and compared accordingly, then New York State lags far behind other states as host site to these groups. For example, applications requesting asylum filed in New York represented only 7.7 percent of the nationwide figure. In the total population of refugees and asylees granted permanent resident status in 1989, only 7.4 percent were residing in New York. The state accounted for 7.2 percent of the 79,143 refugees and for 11.6 percent of the 5,145 asylees who adjusted their status nationwide. The corresponding proportions in California were 43.5 and 33.2 percent. Foreign-born New Yorkers showed greater visibility in the group of individuals who were naturalized be-

TABLE 2.13

REFUGEES GRANTED LAWFUL PERMANENT RESIDENT STATUS IN 1988
BY CALENDAR YEAR OF ENTRY, REGION AND SELECTED COUNTRY OF BIRTH

Region and Country of Birth	Total	1987	1986	1985	1984	1983	1982	1981	Before 1981	Uknown/ Not Reported
All Countries	105,276	15,029	29,273	10,164	4,859	1,804	30,093	969	11,878	1,207
Europe	10,558	3,283	4,870	915	359	227	170	102	325	307
Bulgaria	121	40	60	12	–	1	–	1	3	4
Czechoslovakia	1,131	361	565	98	21	25	5	10	12	34
Germany, West	85	27	47	5	3	1	–	1	–	1
Hungary	693	159	353	69	43	28	7	2	17	15
Poland	3,738	1,070	1,850	336	148	99	89	13	32	101
Romania	2,882	841	1,485	282	102	40	16	22	29	65
Soviet Union	1,581	707	391	86	34	24	33	52	173	81
Spain	84	4	7	10	2	1	14	1	45	–
Other Europe	243	74	112	17	6	8	6	–	14	6
Asia	52,638	10,898	23,361	8,842	4,307	1,455	862	777	1,289	847
Afganistan	2,434	869	1,157	190	78	17	20	7	8	88
Cambodia	9,254	492	1,611	3,706	1,934	697	229	252	182	151
China, Mainland	564	199	273	46	14	3	2	3	10	14
Hong Kong	147	4	113	12	9	–	1	3	2	3
Indonesia	80	10	36	15	8	1	7	2	–	1
Iran	3,883	1,563	1,870	286	54	21	5	3	12	69
Iraq	231	81	93	12	8	14	6	9	8	–
Laos	10,348	1,552	6,469	681	574	124	170	168	492	118

TABLE 2.13
(Continued)

Malaysia	68	15	33	9	2	1	3	–	3	2
Philippines	404	42	157	105	47	17	12	11	9	4
Thailand	3,587	308	1,279	1,162	482	124	59	40	71	62
Vietnam	21,398	5,667	10,172	2,602	1,093	434	343	278	479	330
Other Asia	240	96	98	16	4	2	5	1	13	5
Africa	1,773	738	775	100	72	20	21	9	14	24
Ethiopia	1,522	639	672	88	53	18	17	9	7	19
Sudan	80	33	41	3	1	2	–	–	–	–
Other Africa	171	66	62	9	18	–	4	–	7	5
Oceania	1	1	–	–	–	–	–	–	–	–
North America	40,047	95	239	274	102	92	29,024	75	10,119	27
Caribbean	39,812	85	220	249	84	73	29,006	63	10,005	27
Cuba	13,556	85	213	243	84	72	2,806	57	9,969	27
Haiti	25,476	–	–	–	–	–	25,442	6	28	–
Other Caribbean	780	–	7	6	–	1	758	–	8	–
Central American	191	10	16	17	14	17	12	11	94	–
Other North America	44	–	3	8	4	2	6	1	20	–
South America	257	13	28	33	19	10	15	6	131	2
Born on board ship	1	–	–	–	–	–	1	–	–	–
Unknown or not reported	1	1	–	–	–	–	–	–	–	–

Source: Immigration and Naturalization Service, *1988 Statistical Yearbook of the Immigration and Naturalization Service*. (Washington, DC: U.S. Government Printing Office, 1989). Table 27.

tween 1985 and 1989, representing 15 percent of the total number as compared to 30 percent in California. The 1989 statistics illustrate the point.

Data on the geographic distribution of refugees by state establish the fact that during the 1970s and early 1980s New York did not act as a major host to the initial resettlement programs organized for arrivals. When it did, it received mostly refugees coming from Eastern Europe and the Soviet Union. The state fared poorly, particularly in relation to Southeast Asian refugees, when compared to other parts of the country. During the early 1980s when New York resettled 3.6 percent of all Southeast Asian refugees, California was hosting ten times as many (30%) and Texas twice as many (7%). Though the state still captured 17 percent of East European and Soviet refugees, in the mid-1980s a larger fraction from among this group – 20 percent – were resettled in California (Table 2.15).

As shown earlier, from the mid to the late 1980s a more diversified refugee population outside the Southeast Asian orbit was being admitted into the country. New York State began to reflect this diversification. Of the 479,237 refugees who arrived into the country during 1983 and 1989, 52,481, or 10.9 percent of the total,

TABLE 2.14

NUMBER OF INDIVIDUALS GRANTED ASYLUM BY INS DISTRICT
DIRECTORS BY SELECTED NATIONALITY, 1984–1989

Nationality	1984	1985	1986	1987	1988	1989
All Nationalities	11,627	6,514	4,284	5,093	7,340	9,229
Afghanistan	268	92	91	24	50	23
China, Mainland	16	74	22	27	90	150
Cuba	18	65	17	73	36	107
Czechoslovakia	51	47	39	13	17	48
El Salvador	503	129	90	39	149	443
Ethiopia	361	210	217	205	570	517
Ghana	18	8	13	4	34	–
Guatemala	6	11	7	7	42	102
Hungary	82	65	26	14	40	33
Iran	7,442	4,087	1,568	1,346	1,107	723
Lebanon	19	27	4	48	73	76
Libya	17	88	55	115	79	39
Nicaragua	1,153	557	1,284	2,213	3,725	5,092
Pakistan	8	15	5	7	51	23
Poland	953	549	456	558	488	329
Romania	192	113	152	137	398	650
Somalia	35	22	16	14	79	128
Soviet Union	70	35	44	33	47	127
Syria	36	41	57	67	36	28
Other	379	279	121	149	229	591[a]

Source: Immigration and Naturalization Service, *1988 Statistical Yearbook of the Immigration and Naturalization Service.* (Washington, DC: U.S. Government Printing Office, 1989) Table 31.

Note: [a] The category "Other" in 1989 included 318 Panamanian nationals.

were resettled in programs located in New York. The state absorbed 33.5 percent of all Soviet refugees, 18 percent each of the Afghani, Polish and Romanians, 14 percent of the Hungarians and 12 percent of the Iranians, yet still only a minute fraction of Southeast Asians — under 5 percent (Table 2.16).

By the close of the 1980s, New York had assumed a more active role in relation to refugee arrivals. The numbers of refugees absorbed in initial resettlement programs increased both in absolute terms and as a portion of the national total. Whereas in 1985 only 5,000 refugees were resettled in New York State upon arrival, by 1988 the figure had risen to 7,582. In 1989, the state received 20,033 refugees or 18.7 percent of the nationwide arrivals in that year (Department of Health and Human Services, Office of Refugee Resettlement, 1990). As of this date, the Office of Refugee Resettlement has not released statistics for 1990. Early estimates indicate that New York was absorbing in that year a total of 25,500 refugees in their initial settlement phase (Inter-Agency Task Force on Immigration Affairs, 1990) (Table 2.17).

The expanding role of the state in relation to refugees is in large part due to increasing flows coming from the Soviet Union, their numbers having risen from 950 in 1987 to 4,099 in 1988 and to 15,898 in 1989 (U.S. Department of Health and Human Services, Office of Refugee Resettlement, 1991; Inter-Agency Task Force on Immigration Affairs, 1990). As a proportion of the nationwide total of Soviet arrivals, New York has resettled 28 percent in 1987 and 40.3 percent in 1989. These high levels are expected to be sustained since, according to immigration authorities, as many as 50,000 more Soviet refugees may have arrived in 1990 (Immigration and Naturalization Services, 1990). New York's share in the settlement of the 12,440 refugee arrivals to the United States in 1989 from Latin

TABLE 2.15

REFUGEE ARRIVALS BY SELECTED AREA OF CITIZENSHIP AND STATE, 1980–1986

State	South East Asia[a]			Eastern Europe Soviet Union[b]	Other[c]
	1980	1985	1986	1986	1986
U.S.	166,727	49,853	45,391	9,077	7,204
California	48,540	16,107	15,168	1,811	3,066
Florida	2,926	1,104	883	217	121
Illinois	7,012	1,776	1,548	847	239
New York	5,938	2,185	1,946	1,602	729
Texas	12,251	4,219	3,493	376	477

Source: U.S. Department of Commerce, *Statistical Abstract of the United States.* (Washington, DC: U.S. Government Printing Office, 1988). Table 12.

Notes: [a] Vietnam, Laos and Cambodia.

[b] Czechoslovakia, Hungary, Poland and Romania.

[c] Afghanistan, Iran, Iraq and Ethiopia.

TABLE 2.16
REFUGEE ARRIVALS TO NEW YORK STATE CLASSIFIED BY
COUNTRY OF ORIGIN, 1983–89

Country of Origin	Nationwide	New York State	% New York Arrivals of Total
Total	479,237	52,481	10.9
Afghanistan	1,659	3,039	18.3
Ethiopia	13,044	810	6.2
Iran	28,198	3,427	12.0
Cambodia	69,400	3,121	4.4
Laos	71,252	1,071	1.5
Vietnam	166,737	7,897	4.7
Czechoslovakia	7,043	747	10.6
Hungary	4,851	693	14.2
Poland	26,289	4,950	18.8
Romania	24,252	4,421	18.2
U.S.S.R.	66,512	22,305	33.5

Source: U.S. Department of Health and Human Services, Office of Refugee Resettlement (unpublished data), 1990.

TABLE 2.17
REFUGEE ARRIVALS TO NEW YORK STATE IN RELATION TO
NATIONWIDE REFUGEE ADMISSIONS, 1985–1987

Refugee Admissions	1985[a]	1986[a]	1987[a]	1988[b]	1989[c]	(Est.) 1990[b]
U.S. Admissions	67,680	61,957	64,643	77,356	106,902	125,000
New York State Arrivals	4,992	4,316	5,461	7,582	20,033	25,500
% New York Arrivals of total Admissions	7.3	6.9	8.6	9.8	18.7	20.4

Sources: [a] U.S. Department of State, Bureau of Refugee Programs (unpublished data).

[b] U.S. Department of Health and Human Services. Office of Refugee Resettlement, cited in Inter Agency Task Force on Immigration Affairs, *Immigration in New York State: Impact and Issues.* (Albany: New York State, 1990).

[c] U.S. Department of Health and Human Services, Office of Refugee Resettlement, Report to the Congress. (Washington DC: U.S. Government Printing Office, 1990).

Note: Figures on refugee admissions to the United States cited by the Department of State and the Department of Health and Human Services do not correspond exactly to the data published by the Immigration and Naturalization Service.

America, Ethiopia and the Near East was 9.4 percent. The state also received 3.5 percent of the 45,787 Southeast Asian refugees and Amerasians arriving in that year (U.S. Department of Health and Human Services, Office of Refugee Resettlement, 1990)

The Undocumented Resident

The term "undocumented resident" refers to persons living in the United States who do not possess the prerequisite documents to legalize their stay in the country. This population includes both illegal entrants and legal entrants who have overstayed their visas.

Until 1980, the size of the undocumented population, the volume of illegal entries or overstays and rough estimates of their yearly net or gross increase in numbers were a matter of speculation and conjecture. A myriad of national estimates as to the size of this population were publicized in the 1970s ranging anywhere between two to twelve million—none based on large-scale empirical data subjected to careful demographic analyses.[6] Since the early 1980s, analytical estimates based on demographic research have become available that provide a more solid reference point for examining the size of the undocumented population. The application of careful estimation techniques have all pointed to levels that are at the lower end of the wild speculations made earlier. Reviewing the methodologies and outcomes of the numerous studies undertaken on the subject, Bean and de la Garza (1988) write:

> Suffice it to note that one of the earliest of these reviews conducted by Siegel, Passell and Robinson at the U.S. Census Bureau concluded that in 1980 the number of undocumented aliens probably fell within the 3 to 6 million range; recent research conducted by Kenneth Hill for the National Academy of Sciences and by Passell suggest that the figure may even be lower. Because of its potential significance for apportionment outcomes, of greater importance is Warren and Passell's estimate that the number of undocumented aliens included in the 1980 census was 2,057,000. (p. 49)

The only data against which the validity of the earlier indirect assumptions can be contested are the legalization application statistics compiled by the Immigration Service to monitor and document the process of implementing the 1986 IRCA provisions. The statistical monitoring has provide information on selected sociodemographic characteristics for those undocumented aliens who applied for status legalization and whose applications were not denied. This includes place of residence in the United States, age, sex, marital status, birthplace and occupation. Whether the successful group of applicants provides a proxy sample of the larger universe of the undocumented population cannot be ascertained.

Estimating the Numbers of Undocumented Residents

Theoretically, the decennial census includes in its coverage undocumented residents as part of the larger foreign-born population, without identifying them as such. The only agency that has collected data directly on the undocumented population is the Immigration and Naturalization Service through yearly statistics compiled on the number of apprehensions of illegal aliens and on numbers of those deported. Apprehensions have increased from a low of 110,000 in 1965, to 756,819 in 1975, to over one million yearly from 1977 to 1988, excepting the 1980–1982 interim when apprehensions declined to 900,000 per year. Between 1985 and 1986 alone, however, the number of apprehensions increased from 1.3 to 1.7 million.[7] These figures have often been used by the Immigration Service as a proxy indicator of the relative increase and/or decline of illegal migratory flows into the country and publicized for political purposes accordingly, a procedure which is highly questionable.[8]

In 1980, a serious attempt was made by the census to distinguish "legal" from "illegal" residents. The estimate derived at from the census coverage of the foreign-born population in each state and in the District of Columbia was that 2,057,000 individuals had been reached who were residing in the country without legal documents. This number represented 15 percent of the reported 14.1 million foreign-born persons in the United States in 1980.[9] Based on this figure, Passel and Woodrow (1984) estimated the nationwide size of the undocumented population in 1980 to range between 2.5 to 3.5 million persons.

How many undocumented persons were missed in the 1980 census coverage is not known. Davis *et al.* (1983) have maintained that the number missing must be less than the number counted because of concerted efforts made by the Census Bureau both in the design and field stages to maximize outreach to all layers of the foreign-born Hispanic community—the largest of the undocumented group.

Subsequent analysis of immigration trends between 1980 and 1983 led the Census Bureau to arrive at a nationwide estimate of the annual growth of the population of illegal entrants and of those legal entrants overstaying their visas. The figure arrived at for both groups ranged between 100,000 and 300,000 yearly. In the absence of a precise consensus figure, the yearly increase has been placed at 200,000 for the decade of the 1980s for purposes of intercensus national estimates, and this number is widely used by public officials, journalists and most researchers. Based on this estimation, the nationwide size of the undocumented population in 1986 was estimated to have ranged between 3.1 to 5.3 million persons and projected to reach anywhere between 4 to 6 million by 1990. Neither of these estimates allow for status adjustment, mortality or emigration. In light of the IRCA provisions, the figures projected for 1990 would now have to be corrected to reflect the removal of those persons who benefited from the legalization program and thereby graduated out of the category of the "illegal" alien segment.

Among the 2.1 million undocumented residents estimated to have been reached by the 1980 census, by far the largest number – 1,023,700 persons or 49.8 percent of the estimated total – were residing in California. The number of those reached in New York ranked second in numerical importance, but was much smaller in size – only 234,000 individuals, comprising 11.5 percent of the estimated total reached. Texas, Illinois and Florida followed behind New York with an estimated undocumented population of 186,000, 135,000 and 80,000 respectively.

Can one treat the 2.1 million undocumented persons reached by the census as representative of illegal immigration in the country as a whole? Keely (1989) maintains that the 2 million figure is in no way intended to represent any particular proportion of their true number; it represents at least one half of the total so that the undercount is less than 50 percent. Passel and Woodrow's upper limit of 3.5 million implies a 40 percent undercount if this were the correct number. Woodrow, Passel and Warren (1987) have stated that the internal consistency of the estimates and the comparisons made with other independent data sources strongly support treating the figures derived both at the national and state levels as a lower bound of the undocumented alien population.

The Undocumented Resident in New York

The U.S. Census Bureau estimated in the early 1980s that around 22,000 or 11 percent of the approximately 200,000 undocumented persons who enter into the United States each year come to New York State. Prior to the IRCA legalization program, the number of persons living in New York City without proper documents and those in nonlegal status were estimated to range between 500,000 to 750,000 based on census estimates and certain demographic assumptions (Papademetriou and Muller, 1987; City of New York, Department of City Planning, 1985). In their 1987 report, the New York State Inter-Agency Task Force on Immigration Affairs cites a higher estimate for the undocumented in the state – ranging from 850,000 to 1.5 million persons; this being considered by the Task Force as an additional component to the 2.5 million (legal) immigrants residing in New York in 1987.

Undocumented aliens reside predominantly in the New York City area. Of the 234,000 undocumented persons reached by the 1980 census in the state, 212,000, or 90 percent, lived in the larger New York metropolitan area and 14,000, or 6 percent, in the New York/Suffolk area, mirroring the residential location of the legal immigrant. How many among them were actually missed in the New York City census coverage in 1980 cannot be established; at the time, city officials claimed that 550,000 undocumented aliens had been left out of the official count. In 1987, New York's Task Force estimated that only 75 percent of the undocumented lived in the larger New York metropolitan area, including New York City, Long Island and Westchester and Rockland counties.

The estimated number of undocumented persons reached in 1980 relative to the total size of the reported foreign-born population was much lower in New York than in other states in the country. Table 2.18 illustrates this with data for fifteen states. Two cohorts of undocumented residents are identified in that data set—those estimated to have entered the country between 1960 and 1980, and those who arrived more recently, between 1975 and 1980. Among the 1960 to 1980 cohorts in New York, the proportion of "illegals" to all foreign born was 22 percent. In California, Illinois and Maryland, the corresponding percentages were 40.2, 30.6 and 33.0 percent respectively. Among the more recent cohort of arrivals, the proportion of "illegals" to all foreign born was 12.5 percent in New York as compared to 44 percent in California, 35 percent in Texas and an average of 30 percent in each of Illinois, Arizona, Maryland and Virginia. Assuming consistency in the techniques applied to the population in every state in estimating the numbers of undocumented reached, the above figures show that other areas have been absorbing almost three to four times as many undocumented persons as New York.

Social Characteristics of the Undocumented Resident

Census information points to selected social and demographic characteristics of the 2.1 million undocumented persons reached in the 1980 coverage: 54.9 percent were born in Mexico, 7.1 percent in the Caribbean and 8.6 percent in South and Central America; close to one-half their number had entered the United States during 1975 and 1980, while three-fourths came between 1970 and 1980; 53 percent were men; among both the men and women, 49 percent were between the ages of 15 and 29 years; 32 percent lived in the greater Los Angeles-Long Beach metropolitan area, 10.3 percent in the larger New York metropolitan area and 6 percent in Chicago. Other major cities of residence included: Orange County, California; Washington, DC; San Francisco, California; Houston, Texas and Miami, Florida. The percentages residing in each of these areas ranged from 2.4 percent to 3.8 percent.

TABLE 2.18

ALIENS AND ESTIMATED UNDOCUMENTED ALIENS COUNTED IN THE 1980 CENSUS BY PERIOD OF ENTRY IN THE 15 STATES WITH THE LARGEST NUMBERS OF ALIENS (POPULATION IN THOUSANDS, FIGURES ROUNDED INDEPENDENTLY)

State of Residence	All Periods of Entry[a]			Entered During 1975–80		
	Total Aliens	Undocumented Aliens	% Undocumented	Total Aliens	Undocumented Aliens	% Undocumented
United States	7,440	2,057	27.6	3,326	941	28.3
California	2,543	1,024	40.2	1,157	507	43.8
New York	1,066	234	22.0	431	54	12.5
Texas	691	186	26.9	296	106	35.9
Florida	507	80	15.8	168	39	23.2
Illinois	442	135	30.6	200	61	30.4
New Jersey	318	37	11.6	119	2	1.3
Massachusetts	192	17	9.0	78	5	6.5
Michigan	131	8	5.9	62	4	6.1
Pennsylvania	114	7	6.5	59	–	–
Washington	103	22	21.6	58	11	19.9
Arizona	100	25	24.8	35	11	30.9
Maryland	99	32	32.6	49	14	29.4
Virginia	97	34	35.6	56	19	33.7
Connecticut	94	4	4.2	35	–	–
Ohio	86	10	11.4	43	2	5.6

Source: J. Passel and K. Woodrow, "Geographic Distribution of Undocumented Immigrants: Estimates of Undocumented Aliens Counted in the 1980 Census by State," *International Migration Review*, 18(3)1984:642–671.

Note: [a] Covers 1960–1980 period of entry for all countries except Mexico.

The undocumented residents reached in New York in 1980 were socially and demographically distinctive from the national profile (Table 2.19). Most particularly they were characterized by: 1) a high female ratio—86 men for every 100 women; 2) an older age structure—one-third were 35 years and older whereas in the nationwide average of the undocumented only 20 percent were in that age range; 3) long-standing residence—44 percent had arrived in the United States prior to 1970; and 4) a predominance of Caribbean-born persons from the Dominican Republic, Haiti, Jamaica, Trinidad and Tobago. Whereas nationwide the number of undocumented persons of Caribbean birth estimated to have been reached by the census totaled 147,000, the data indicate that 84,000 persons, or 57 percent of that population, were reached in New York State alone.

Implementing the 1986
Immigration Reform and Control Act

The Immigration Reform and Control Act of 1986 was the first federal legislative response to the growing number of undocumented persons in the country. The effort was basically directed at halting illegal immigration by 1) discouraging further entry and encouraging departure of illegals through prohibiting employers from hiring undocumented persons and 2) providing amnesty for certain groups among the undocumented to apply for legalization of status.

Based on the 1986 estimates of the undocumented population, it was forecast that between 2.5 and 4 million persons would be eligible for amnesty under the provisions of the 1986 Act. As of May 1990, a total of 3,038,825 applications had been filed nationwide: 1,762,143 (or 58%) under the General Legalization Act and 1,276,682 under the Special Agricultural Workers (SAW) provision. These figures are not final, for although the application period has ended the numbers may change due to late filings or pending court decisions. Applicants have shown to be highly concentrated in five leading states: California (54.7% of all applicants filing for the General Legalization provision resided in that state); Texas (17.8%); New York and Illinois (each state accounted for roughly 7%) and Florida (2.8%). California-based aliens also accounted for 53.7 percent of all the SAW applicants, followed by Texas (10.2%) and Florida (9.2%). SAW applications filed in New York accounted for only a 3.6 percent share of the total number. The data shown in Table 2.20 are based on applications filed in January 1989 and coincide closely with the latest legalization statistics reported by the INS in May 1990.

TABLE 2.19

AGE AND SEX COMPOSITION OF UNDOCMENTED ALIENS COUNTED IN THE
1980 CENSUS FOR SELECTED STATES OF RESIDENCE

State of Residence	Number of Undocumented Aliens	All Ages	Under 15 Years	15–34 Years	35 Years and Over
		% Age Group			
All States	2,057	100.0	18.1	62.2	17.8
California	1,024	100.0	19.6	62.6	17.8
New York	234	100.0	10.9	56.3	32.8
Texas	186	100.0	20.1	68.6	11.3
Illinois	135	100.0	16.0	64.7	19.3
Florida	80	100.0	15.8	56.2	28.0
New Jersey	37	100.0	14.6	55.7	29.7
Virginia	34	100.0	18.6	51.5	29.9
Maryland	32	100.0	17.5	50.0	32.5
Arizona	25	100.0	23.9	61.6	14.6
Washington	22	100.0	16.9	67.1	16.0
		% Sex Ratio			
All States	2,057	1.14	—	1.07	1.24
California	1,024	1.15	1.94	1.26	0.94
New York	234	0.86	1.16	0.87	0.76
Texas		1.23	1.09	1.37	0.78
Illinois	135	1.34	1.03	1.43	1.31
Florida	80	0.97	1.23	0.99	0.82
New Jersey	37	0.86	1.02	0.92	0.70
Virginia	34	1.09	1.15	1.19	0.90
Maryland	32	0.85	0.86	0.84	0.86
Arizona		0.99	1.01	1.10	0.61
Washington	22	1.70	1.48	1.83	1.47

Source: J. Passel and K. Woodrow, "Geographic Distribution of Undocumented Immigrants: Estimates of Undocumented Aliens Counted in the 1980 Census by State," *International Migration Review,* 18(3)1984:642–671.

Note: Populations in thousands. Sex ratio is number of males per female. All computation based on unrounded figures.

TABLE 2.20

1980 Census Estimated Count of Undocumented Aliens in Relation to Provisional Applications Filed for Status Adjustment under the 1986 IRCA Provisions, by Selected States, January 1989

State and National	1980 Census Estimated Count of Undocumented Aliens		General Legalization Applications Filed to Date		Total SAW Applications Filed to date		Legalization and SAW Applications Combined	Combined Applications as Percentage of Total Number Filed
	Number	%	Number	% Share of Total	Number	% Share of Total		
New York	234,000	11.4	120,800	6.8	46,500	3.6	167,300	5.5
California	1,024,000	49.8	967,400	54.7	691,500	53.7	1,658,900	54.3
Oregon	15,000	0.7	3,800	0.2	27,400	2.1	31,200	1.0
Illinois	135,000	6.6	118,000	6.7	31,300	2.5	149,300	4.9
Texas	186,000	9.0	314,200	17.8	131,000	10.2	445,200	14.6
Florida	80,000	3.9	48,100	2.8	120,200	9.3	168,300	5.5
Washington	22,000	1.1	8,700	0.5	26,700	2.1	35,400	1.2
Pennsylvania	7,000	0.3	2,800	0.2	5,000	0.4	7,800	0.3
Massachusetts	17,000	0.8	9,600	0.5	5,400	0.4	15,000	0.5
Other States	337,000	16.4	173,633	9.8	202,824	15.7	376,457	12.2
National	2,057,000	100.0	1,767,033	100.0	1,287,824	100.0	3,054,857	100.0

Source: U.S. Immigration and Naturalization Service, Statistical Analysis Branch, Office of Plans and Analysis, *Provisional Legalization Application Statistics: May 12, 1989.* (Washington, DC: U.S. Government Printing Office, 1989).

The IRCA Experience of New York State

The legalization process in New York presented a number of barriers to prospective applicants. In 1986, state officials had estimated the number of undocumented residents eligible to apply for status adjustment under the legalization program to approximate 440,000 (Helton, 1988), a figure which the director of the INS Statistical Analysis Branch believes to have been too high (Warren, 1989). The Inter-Agency Task Force on Immigration Affairs (1990) was more cautious in their assessment of the eligible population, which they estimated to range between 250,000 to 400,000.

The 1989 legalization statistics show 170,601 applicants for New York State; 119,156 who applied under the Legalization Act and 51,445 under the SAW provisions. Under the first category, 58 percent had entered prior to January 1, 1982 and 40 percent were overstayers. Under the second category, 96 percent of the applicants had been seasonal agricultural workers during 1985 and 1986.

As a proportion of what was earlier cited as the lower bound estimate of the number of undocumented aliens eligible to apply for legalization in New York — 250,000 — the number of applications filed in the state represent a 68 percent share. In relation to the upper bound estimate — 440,000 — the corresponding share is 38 percent. In relation to the total number of legalization applications filed, the New York share is only 5.6 percent despite the fact that in 1980 the state was estimated to house the second largest concentration of undocumented persons in the country.

According to the 1990 report of the New York State Inter-Agency Task Force on Immigration Affairs, the status of the 119,000 legalization applications processed as of November 2, 1989, was as follows: 103,752 were approved (87%); 9,653 were still pending (8%); 6,154 (5%) had been denied. Among those approved at the time, 46,187 persons (45% of the total) had requested adjustment to permanent resident status. The INS had processed 29,556 of those cases and in that pool rejected only three applications. Among the applications filed in New York under the Special Agricultural Workers provision, 19,500 had been processed by November 1989 and of these 57.5 percent were rejected. At that point in time immigration officials did not have plans to initiate deportation proceedings against aliens filing fraudulent documents.[10] Applicants who were rejected will most probably be (re)classified as part of the undocumented population (New York State Inter-Agency Task Force, 1990).

Social Characteristics of Applicants Seeking Status Adjustment: Nationwide Trends

National data show that more than 2.2 million legalization and SAW applications were filed by Mexicans. They accounted for over 70 percent of all those filing under the General Legalization provision, followed by Salvadorans (8%) and Guatemalans (3%). Each of the other nationalities included in the applications accounted for roughly one percent of all applications filed. Applicants were typically 30 years old, and 81 percent fell within the fifteen to 44 age range. The reported occupation of applicants identifies one in every four as blue-collar, one in every five in service-related jobs, ten percent as skilled craftsmen and 12 percent as students. Mexican nationals also dominated the applicant list of those filing under the SAW provisions (80%). Among these applicants, nine in every ten were within the fifteen to 44 age range, with 28 years as the median; almost all were men and slightly more than one-half were married.

New York's Applicants

New York-based applicants represented 153 countries of origin, with Spanish-speaking Caribbeans (Dominicans), Central Americans and South Americans leading the list of nationalities. French-speaking (Haitian) and English-speaking Caribbeans were also well represented in the pool of applicants, which included as well Asian nationals from Taiwan, Hong Kong, Korea, the Philippines and China. Very few persons from Europe, the Middle East, Africa, India and Pakistan applied (New York State Inter-Agency Task Force on Immigration Affairs, 1987). One third of all the applicants resided in Brooklyn, 29 percent in Queens, followed by the Bronx (12%) and Manhattan (5%). Applicants filing for General Legalization were most heavily represented by persons from Haiti, Mexico, El Salvador, the Dominican Republic, Colombia, Ecuador, China and Jamaica. Asian nationals — Pakistanis, Indians, Koreans, Bangladeshi and Chinese — dominated the list of SAW applicants. This is surprising since these nationality groups are not associated with immigrant farm labor in the United States.

Regardless of whether or not the eligibility estimates projected for New York aliens at the outset of IRCA were too high to be realized, a series of factors did operate in the state to depress the turnout rate of those technically qualified to apply: namely, fear of deportation, if rejected, of self and other family members and deep concerns about disqualification under the restrictive administration criteria applied. These anxieties were probably operating in all other states, but — according to Arthur Helton (1988) of the Lawyers Committee for Human Rights — they appear to have been more widespread in New York. One reason is that undocumented residents in New York are more vulnerable than their counterparts in border states, such as California and Texas, to have their brief entries and departures recorded, thereby risking automatic placement outside the purview of the legalization program. The fact that this particular administrative barrier was somewhat relaxed in 1987 had not been sufficiently publicized to the immigrant community in New York and many continued to fear its consequences. It is also true that undocumented persons living in New York tend more frequently than those in other states to reside in households composed of members with mixed eligibility. This, too, could have generated grave concerns about being exposed to INS scrutiny, lest other "illegals" in the family be uncovered and become subject to deportation (Helton, 1988). According to lawyers representing the Committee for Human Rights, the Immigration and Naturalization Service could have been more forthcoming in undertaking some of the specific measures recommended to them during the legalization program period in order to achieve a better turnout of aliens in New York State (Helton, 1988). The recommendations made at the time included 1) publicizing to the immigrant community at large the favorable disposition of the Immigration and Naturalization Service to allow ineligible parents, spouses and children of qualified applicants to remain in the United States until they also can secure a durable immigration status; 2) modifying the eligibility criteria to disregard absences, brief visits and reentries, etc. as factors that break the residency requirement, so long as aliens can demonstrate intent to return and remain in the United States; and 3) announcing the extension of the time period for the acceptance of applications.

The State and City of New York can also be faulted for some of the procedures and policy guidelines followed during the implementation of the amnesty program. New York State provided over $900,000 in funding to assist community organizations and service providers to maximize outreach. However, of the 107 legalization offices set up nationwide, only five were established in New York and three of these were located in New York City. These may not have been sufficient and more should have been requested. Furthermore, both the state and city could have provided more effective and widespread publicity and outreach public education programs, taking into account the particular multilingual and ethnic diversity of the city's foreign-born population.

NOTES

[1] The population census excludes in its coverage foreign nationals who are in the country on a very temporary basis such as tourists, but includes others who are only temporarily present such as students and businessmen.

[2] To estimate the size of the legal foreign-born population the Census Bureau supplemented data on legal immigrants admitted to the country (from INS records) with data on refugee arrival provided by the Department of State. The estimate corrects for a loss of population through mortality, but does not adjust for emigration. As such it represents a maximum (Woodrow, K., J. Passell and R. Warren, 1987).

[3] California also "gained" immigrants through the large scale refugee resettlement programs taking place in the state which brought in a heavy influx of Southeast Asian refugees who later were admitted to permanent resident status. It was estimated that 40% of the 800,000 Southeast Asian refugees who arrived since 1975 now reside in California, with Orange County, Los Angeles, as the preferred geographical site.

[4] The leading metropolitan areas of settlement for legal immigrants admitted in 1988 were New York City (93,106); Los Angeles-Long Beach (88,211); Miami-Hialeah (38,259); Chicago (21,183) and Washington, DC-Maryland-Virginia (18,032). California cities account for 5 of the top 10 areas of intended residence; Los Angeles-Long Beach, San Francisco, Anaheim-Santa Ana, San Diego and San Jose.

[5] The definition of refugee set forth in the Refugee Act of 1980 conforms to that of the 1967 United Nations Protocol of Refugees. A refugee, as defined by the Act, is any person who is outside his or her country of nationality and unable or unwilling to return to that country because of persecution or a well-founded fear of persecution. Claims of persecution may be based on the alien's race, religion, nationality, political opinion or membership in a particular social group.

[6] The presence of undocumented aliens in official survey data was first empirically detected in the 1979 Current Population Survey (U.S. Department of Commerce, 1982). The CPS yielded a sample estimate of 1.25 million undocumented persons in the United States who had entered the country between 1970 and 1979 and who were represented in the CPS; 734,000 or 60% of these aliens were estimated to have been born in Mexico.

[7] It must be noted that apprehension statistics reflect variations in the manner in which INS border patrol and detection procedures are enforced and the particular priority of the Agency at a given point in time.

[8] For methodological reasons, apprehension statistics cannot be taken as reliable indicators of "illegal" entries. The figures reported do not correct for multiple apprehensions, which are frequent within the same year, nor do they record permanent movements of illegal residents out of the country (Davis et al., 1983). Despite these limitations, the General Audit Office in 1982, following an exhaustive literature review of the estimated size of the undocumented population, reached the conclusion that apprehension statistics are the most comprehensive data on illegal aliens (Glazer, 1985).

[9] The 2 million or so figure is not based on individual records, but is an aggregate estimate derived by a residual technique in which selected characteristics of the foreign-born population identified in the census (age, sex, country of birth, period of entry to the United States) are compared with parallel information recorded in the 1980 estimate of the legally resident alien population derived from the 1980 INS Alien Registration System (Form I-53). This comparison yielded both a national and state level estimate of the number of undocumented persons reached by census enumerators (Passel and Woodrow, 1984).

[10] The processing of some applications has been problematic nationwide because of extensive fraud and the widespread filing of false documents. This was perceived to be particularly noticeable in applications filed under the SAW provisions and those submitted under the extension period granted to the amnesty program. Immigration officials have been accused of accepting late amnesty applications "that were patently fraudulent or determinable to be fraudulent upon minimal scrutiny and investigation." M. Howe, "Fraud Charges Rise as Aliens Seek to Enter Through Rulings," The New York Times, 16 April 1990. P. A13.

3

NATIONALITY, ETHNICITY AND RACE IN THE DEMOGRAPHY OF IMMIGRATION

The 1965 Amendment to the Immigration and Nationality Act, known as the Hart-Cellar Act, changed the profile of the foreign-born population in the United States in terms of national origin, ethnicity and race. It abandoned the National Origins Quota System favoring northwestern European immigration, swung the "Golden Door" open to Asian entry which had been severely restricted from immigration and, along with subsequent legislation in 1976 and 1978, left the door relatively more open than before to other nationalities. Caribbeans who had been subject to very small quotas for dependencies were now included in the 120,000 ceiling for the Western Hemisphere (South and North America and the Caribbean), with a national limit of 20,000 added in 1976. The strong emphasis the Amendment placed on family reunification instead of national origin and the downplaying of labor certification as a basis for admission paved the way for Asia, South America and Central America to emerge from the late 1960s as predominant immigrant supplier sources. This legislation was not alone, however, in setting into motion the transformation in composition that ultimately took place. The political events of the 1970s and 1980s in Southeast Asia, Central America, Cuba and Haiti (to a much lesser extent in Iran and Afghanistan) generated massive refugee flows into the United States and these contributed significantly to the heterogeneous mix of the foreign-born population residing in the country over the past 25 years.

This chapter focuses on shifts in the national origin, ethnic and racial composition of immigrant flows since 1965, highlights the resulting heterogeneity of today's foreign-born residents, and points out how the particular mix of immigrants in New York State differs in relation to other host states. To update migratory trends beyond those identified in the 1980 census, an extensive review has been made of information available in the files of the Immigration and

Naturalization Service (INS) covering the 1980 to 1989 period in published form and tape documentation. Because the INS records are restricted to legal admissions, it is not possible with the information available to capture in full the dynamics of the changing scenario in composition experienced in the nation and in New York State.[1]

The Changing Character of Legal Immigration:
Nationwide Trends

On paper, the 1965 legislation was simply an amendment to the 1952 Immigration and Nationality Act. In truth, it was the most far-reaching change in immigration legislation enacted since 1924. It came in the wake of four decades of overt racism manifested in restrictions imposed by the 1924 National Origins Act which assigned to each country outside the Western Hemisphere an annual quota initially based on the national origins of the United States population in 1890; modified in 1928 to correspond to the population reported in the 1910 census. This meant earmarking large quotas to northern and Western European nationals since they had contributed significantly to early immigration and settlement in the United States. Warren (1976) writes:

> Of the 43 million immigrants admitted between 1870 and 1965, about 81 percent or 35 million were from Europe. Before the establishment of the National Origins quota, millions of Europeans had immigrated to the country. By reserving 94 percent of the visas for European countries, the system assured that most post-1925 immigrants would also be from Europe. Prior to 1965, Western Hemisphere immigrants constituted only 15 percent of the total entrants and most of these were from Canada. (pp. 1–14)

The demographic implications of the 1965 Immigration Act in adopting the family reunification principle as the cornerstone of U.S. immigration policy was referred to earlier in terms of the nearly unrestricted entry this granted to close relatives of U.S. citizens and immediate relatives of resident aliens. Two other demographic consequences brought about by the Immigration Act will be examined: 1) the decline in immigration from European countries and 2) the entry of Third World nationals.

The changes enacted in the 1965 Act were accompanied by a gradual increase in the volume of immigration and by shifting patterns in its composition. Neither of these changes were fully felt until 1968 when the 1965 Immigration and

Nationality Act was actually implemented. Following World War II, southern and Eastern Europeans began to replace those from the north and west of the continent, and in the late 1960s both waves gave way to immigration from the Third World. The most striking change since then has been the dramatic growth in the legal entry of South and East Asians into the United States – from just over 17,000 in 1965 to an average of over a quarter of a million yearly since 1981. Within that same time span the demand for immigration from Europe diminished, declining from 114,329 persons in 1965 to 65,000 in 1981. Whereas Europe had been supplying 50 percent of all legal immigrants to the country between 1955 and 1964 and 30 percent between 1965 and 1974, from 1985 to 1988 the proportion of the immigrant population born in Europe dwindled to account for 10 percent of yearly legal admissions, down to 7.5 percent in 1989. In addition to Asians, the new immigration wave also accelerated entries from Mexico, the Caribbean countries and Central and South America. By 1978, Asia had overtaken all other regions to become the single largest immigrant supplier to the United States until 1989.

This expansion is in large part attributed to the inflow of refugees from Vietnam, Cambodia and Laos during the 1970s, which continued into the early 1980s. By the mid-1980s, even though the refugee flow had been somewhat contained, Asian nationalities continued to dominate the annual migratory streams. Legal admissions in 1985 and 1986 reported 45 percent of all entries into the country as coming from the Asian region, as compared to 33 percent from North America, 10 percent from Europe and 7 percent from South America. By 1988, the proportion of the immigrant population born in Asia declined to 41 percent, in favor of those born in North America which had by then increased to 39 percent of the total (Table 3.1).

In 1989, the Asian share was further reduced by status adjustment procedures legislated under the 1986 IRCA legalization provisions. The predominant nationality origin groups represented in the pool of those who qualified for status legalization were Mexicans, Salvadorans and, in lesser number, Guatemalans. In the total numbers admitted from these nationality groups in 1989, 83 percent, 76 percent and 70 percent, respectively, were status legalization immigrants. This particular situation positioned the North American region as top-most immigrant supplier in 1989, representing 55.7 percent of all the admissions. As a consequence, the share of Asian nations dwindled to 28.7 percent. With the bulk of legalization applications filed and processed, the 1990 admission profile is not expected to be as heavily represented by North American nationals.

The census points to shifts in the distribution of the foreign-born resident population by birthplace as well, but not as sharply as the annual records of legal immigrant admissions compiled by the immigration authorities. This is because census data are cumulative and the immigration profile presented therein neces-

TABLE 3.1

PERCENT DISTRIBUTION OF LEGAL IMMIGRANTS ADMITTED BY REGION OF
ORIGIN AND PERIOD OF ENTRY, 1955–1989

Region	1955–64	1965–74	1975–84	1985	1986	1987	1988	1989
All Regions (%)	100.0	100.0	100.0	100.0	100.0	100.0	100.0	100.0
Europe	50.2	29.8	13.4	11.1	10.4	10.2	10.1	7.5
North and West	28.6	11.0	5.2	5.0	5.0	5.2	5.1	—
South and East	21.6	18.1	8.1	6.0	5.4	5.0	5.0	—
Asia	7.7	22.4	43.3	46.4	44.6	42.8	41.1	28.7
Africa	0.7	1.5	2.4	3.0	2.9	2.9	2.9	2.3
Oceania	0.4	0.7	0.8	0.7	0.6	0.7	0.6	0.3
North America	36.0	39.6	33.6	31.9	34.5	36.0	38.9	55.7
Caribbean	7.1	18.0	15.1	14.6	16.9	17.1	17.5	8.1
Central America	2.5	2.6	3.7	4.6	4.7	4.9	4.8	9.2
Other No. America (Including Mexico)	26.4	19.0	14.8	12.7	12.9	14.0	16.6	38.4
South America	5.1	6.0	6.6	6.9	7.0	7.4	6.4	5.5

Sources: U.S. Immigration and Naturalization Service, *1988 Statistical Yearbook of the Immigration and Naturalization Service.* (Washington DC: U.S. Government Printing Office, 1989). Table B; U.S. Immigration and Naturalization Service, *1989 Statistical Yearbook of the Immigration and Naturalization Service.* (Washington, DC: U.S. Government Printing Office, 1990). Table 6.

sarily carried the legacy of the early European migratory waves into the country, contrary to immigration statistics which capture the changing dynamics of annual flows. Notwithstanding this limitation, comparison of the 1970 and 1980 inter-census data point to a definite decline in the proportion of European-born residents — from 54.6 percent in 1970 to 33.7 percent in 1980 — at the same time that the share of foreign-born Asians in the population increased from 8.6 percent to 18.0 percent.

Census data also provide information on the distinctive period of entry of the foreign born from the various regions of birthplace. The sharp shifts in points of origin by year of arrival into the United States is shown in Table 3.2. Close to one half of all foreign-born Asians in the country had arrived during the five years preceding the 1980 census count — in itself a statement of the demographic impact that refugee flows generated by the Vietnam War had upon the compo-sition of the foreign-born segment. A contrasting situation is the case of foreign-born residents from Europe, the Soviet Union and Canada: 65 to 70 percent among them had come to the United States before 1960.

A more contemporary profile of the modified composition of foreign-born residents is presented in Table 3.3. The data trace the changing national origin mix of the leading immigrant suppliers from 1985 to 1989. To allow for a more

TABLE 3.2

CHANGING COMPOSITION OF THE FOREIGN-BORN POPULATION
ACCORDING TO PERIOD OF IMMIGRATION, 1980

Region of Birth	Number Foreign-Born	% Immigrated to the U.S. by Period of Immigration			
		< 1960	1960–69	1970–74	1975–80
Total	14,079.9	38.2	22.3	15.8	23.7
Europe	4,743.3	65.2	19.1	7.5	8.1
Soviet Union	406.0	70.4	5.3	3.2	21.1
Asia	2,539.8	12.5	18.1	22.4	47.0
Central America[a]	2,553.1	19.4	22.5	24.5	33.7
Caribbean	1,258.4	11.9	45.5	24.1	18.6
South America	561.0	10.7	33.0	23.6	32.6
Canada	842.9	64.7	20.1	5.4	9.8

Source: U.S. Dept. of Commerce, *Statistical Abstract of the United States.* (Washington, DC: U.S. Government Printing Office, 1988). Table 45.

Notes: [a] Includes Mexico.

TABLE 3.3

CHANGES IN THE NATIONAL ORIGIN OF IMMIGRANTS ADMITTED FROM
THE 1989 TOP FIFTEEN COUNTRIES OF BIRTH

Country of Birth	Numbers Admitted			% Change	
	1989[a]	1988	1985	1985–1989[a]	1988–1989[a]
All Countries	612,110	643,025	570,609	7.2	-4.8
Mexico	66,445	95,039	61,077	8.7	-30.1
Philippines	49,749	50,697	47,498	3.7	-1.9
Vietnam	37,572	25,789	31,895	17.8	45.7
Korea	32,218	34,703	35,253	-8.6	-7.2
India	28,517	26,268	26,026	9.5	8.6
China (mainland)	27,489	28,717	24,787	10.9	-4.3
Dominican Republic	25,622	27,189	23,787	7.7	-5.8
Jamaica	21,991	20,966	18,923	16.2	4.9
Iran	17,155	15,246	16,071	6.7	12.5
El Salvador	13,585	12,045	NA	–	12.5
United Kingdom	12,892	13,228	13,408	-3.8	-2.5
Taiwan	12,470	9,670	14,895	-16.3	29.0
Laos	12,467	10,667	NA	–	16.9
Soviet Union	11,009	2,949	NA	–	273.3
Colombia	10,578	10,322	11,982	-11.7	2.5
Other	232,351	259,530	245,007	-5.2	-10.5

Source: U.S. Immigration and Naturalization Service, *1989 Statistical Yearbook of the Immigration and Naturalization Service.* (Washington DC: U.S. Government Printing Office, 1990). Table D; *1985 Statistical Yearbook of the Immigration and Naturalization Service.* (Washington, DC: U.S. Government Printing Office, 1986). Table C.

Note: [a] The 1989 admissions include nonlegalization immigrants only.

rigorous basis for comparisons, admissions effected under the IRCA legalization provisions have been excluded from the 1989 listing. In 1985, 1988 and 1989, Mexico and the Philippines surpassed all other countries as the largest non-legalization suppliers. Combined, they exported to the United States 109,055 immigrants in 1985, 145,736 in 1988 and 116,192 nonlegalization immigrants in 1989, accounting for 19 to 22 percent of all admissions in those three years. In addition to the Philippines, four other Asian nationality groups stood out as important suppliers in the mid and late 1980s: the Vietnamese, Koreans, Asian Indians[2] and (mainland) Chinese, each supplying between 25,000 and 37,000 legal immigrants yearly. Combined, these four countries represented 20 percent of all admissions in 1985 and 1989, declining to 18 percent in 1988. When Taiwan and Laos — each averaging between 9,000 and 15,000 admissions — and the Philippines are included, the sum total of Asian immigrants from the top fifteen supplier countries averaged 30 percent of the yearly admissions during the mid and late 1980s.

Shifts in the rank and order of the top-listed Asian countries did take place during that period. Second to the Philippines, Korea headed the supplier list in 1985 and 1988 but was superseded by Vietnam in 1989. India, which had out-numbered China in 1985, fell behind in 1988, regaining its earlier position by 1989. Laos, absent from the list in 1985, remained third to last in rank in 1988 and 1989. One immediate result of the large influx of Asians into the country was to effect a 45 percent increase in the proportion of population classified under categories of race other than "white" or "black." The entry of Asian refugees certainly accounts for the major force bringing about this ethnic diversity, yet nonrefugee Asians as well had increased their presence in the mid 1970s, particularly among Indians, Koreans and Filipinos.

Second in rank in the top list of immigrant suppliers during the mid to late 1980s were the Caribbeans — the Dominican Republic and Jamaica, in particular. In 1985 and 1988, Haiti, Cuban and Guyana had also been major contributors. They have not been included in Table 3.3 because they failed to appear on the 1989 top list of nonlegalization source countries. In 1985 and 1989, the leading Caribbean suppliers contributed 73,209 and 100,519 immigrants respectively, representing 14 percent of the nationwide admissions in those two years. The Cuban contribution was the second largest in 1985 (20,334 admissions)[3] while Haiti ranked as the third largest supplier to the United States in 1988 (34,000 admissions). By 1989, only the Dominican Republic and Jamaica remained on the top list, with the leading Caribbean contribution to nonlegalization immigra-tion declining to 47,600, or 8 percent of the total admissions.

In relation to the top nonlegalization suppliers in 1989, the nationality config-uration of the major source countries underwent the following changes since 1985. Cambodia disappeared as leading supplier after 1985 and Cuba and Haiti were dropped after 1988. The 1989 nonlegalization top listing introduced three new major source countries: El Salvador, Laos and the Soviet Union. In other respects, increases and losses in the relative positioning of the individual supplier countries remaining on the list between 1985 and 1989 were not dramatic. Relative declines in migratory flows were evident in the case of Taiwan (-16%), Colombia (-11.7%) and Korea (-8.6%), coupled with increments among the Vietnamese (17.8%) and Jamaicans (16.2%). Three notable changes did occur in the one-year interim between 1988 and 1989 — a 273.3 percent increase in the admission of Soviets, a 45.7 percent rise among the Vietnamese and a significant drop in the number of Mexican immigrants entering under provisions other than the IRCA legalization.

Will the legal flows into the 1990s replicate this pattern? According to the waiting lists for U.S. visas filed in the various consulates abroad in 1986 and 1987, Mexican and Filipino nationals continued to lead as top applicants while Hong Kong and Pakistan — countries not previously included in the top supplier list — have now emerged as important new immigrant sources. By and large, it can be expected that immigration patterns in the 1990s will replicate the national origin profile of the non-IRCA legalization population admitted in the late 1980s, with increasing representation of Soviets and Eastern Europeans.

With this as a background to the national scenario, the discussion now examines the particular experience of New York State.

Shifts in the Regional/National Origin of New York's Foreign-Born Community

Two distinctive traits characterize New York's immigrant population. The first is its extreme heterogeneity. Relative to the total foreign-born population of the United States, New York continues to attract diverse range of nationality groups. The second trait is that the state does not allure IRCA legalization immigrants. Though second in rank as immigrant host state, New York in 1989 was a preferred destination point for newly admitted immigrants who had applied for permanent resident status under provisions other than the legalization program.

In 1980, the last year the Alien Registration requirement was in effect, the number of foreign-born persons registered in the State of New York represented 165 countries of birth. In fact, the heterogeneity of the foreign-born population in the northeast region in 1980 was in large part due to the nationality composition of New York's immigrants; nearly half of the foreign-born population in the northeast resided in the larger New York-New Jersey metropolitan area (Kraly, 1987a). In addition to diversity, New York's immigrant groups are well represented so as to make their presence quite visible, drawing large numbers of nearly all European and Caribbean and most Asian and South American nationalities.

Overall, the census-based profile of New York's foreign-born population registered changes in national origin after 1965 that mirrored national trends. The distribution of New York's foreign-born residents in 1980 by period of immigration surfaced the same sharp shift in points of origin by year of entry to the United States as indicated earlier for the foreign born nationwide. As shown in Table 3.4, the timing of immigration is distinctive for the different nationality groups: Europeans residing in New York in 1980 had entered the United States prior to 1960, while Asians, North and Central Americans and South Americans increased their presence after 1965. Increases reported for the North and Central American region were accounted for mainly by stepped-up migration among Caribbeans, particularly in the years immediately following the 1965 Immigration Act. Certain nationalities accelerated their entry into the United States after 1975 – Vietnamese as a refugee population, Indians, Koreans and Japanese. For example, two thirds of the Japanese and over one half the Koreans living in New York in 1980 immigrated during the 1975 to 1980 period. The pace of immigration from Guyana to New York increased as well during the late 1970s (Kraly, 1987).

Was the outcome in composition resulting from the overall shift in national origin different in California, which has been the leading host state for the past 14 years? Information compiled in Tables 3.5 and 3.6 partially address this

TABLE 3.4

THE COMPOSITION OF THE FOREIGN-BORN POPULATION RESIDING IN
NEW YORK STATE IN 1980 CLASSIFIED BY PERIOD OF ARRIVAL TO THE
UNITED STATES AND REGION OF BIRTHPLACE

	Period of Arrival % Immigrated in Each Period		
Region of Birthplace	1950–64	1965–69	1970–80
Total Foreign Born	516,030 (100.0%)	348,379 (100.0%)	832,804 (100.0%)
Europe	54.0	26.0	17.0
USSR	2.0	–	4.0
Asia	7.0	12.0	23.0
North & Central America[a]	22.0	40.0	35.0
South America	5.0	11.0	13.0
Africa	1.1	1.0	2.0

Source: U.S. Bureau of the Census, *Census of Population: 1980.* Vol. 1. Chapter D. Detailed Population Characteristics. Part 34. New York. Section 1. (Washington, DC: U.S. Government Printing Office, 1983). Table 195.

Notes: [a] Includes Mexico, Canada, Greenland, Bermuda and the Caribbean.

TABLE 3.5

PERCENT DISTRIBUTION OF THE FOREIGN-BORN POPULATION
RESIDING IN THE UNITED STATES, CALIFORNIA AND NEW YORK STATE
IN 1980 BY REGION OF BIRTHPLACE

Region of Birthplace	United States	California	New York
All Foreign Born	14,079,906	3,580,003	2,388,938
	(100.0%)	(100.0%)	(100.0%)
Africa	1.4	0.9	1.3
Asia	18.1	24.0	12.1
Caribbean	8.9	1.7	19.4
Central America[a]	18.0	40.2	3.2
South America	3.9	2.7	7.6
North America[b]	6.0	4.5	3.1
Europe	33.6	17.6	42.0
Soviet Union	2.8	1.6	4.7
Oceania	0.5	0.8	0.1
All Others and Country Not Reported	6.8	6.0	6.5

Source: U.S. Bureau of the Census, *Statistical Profile of the Foreign-Born Population: 1980.* (Washington, DC: U.S. Government Printing Office, 1983). Tables 1 and 3.

Notes: [a] Includes Mexico.

[b] Includes Canada, Greenland and Bermuda.

TABLE 3.6

CALIFORNIA AND NEW YORK STATE SHARE IN REGIONAL ORIGIN GROUPS IN
RELATION TO THE NATIONWIDE TOTAL IN EACH GROUP, 1980

	% Share in U.S. Total	
Region of Birthplace	California (N = 3,580,033)	New York (N = 2,388,938)
All Regions	25.4	16.9
Africa	17.2	16.3
Asia	34.5	11.4
Caribbean	5.0	36.8
Central America[a]	56.4	2.9
South America	17.2	32.6
North America[b]	19.2	8.7
Europe	13.3	21.5
Soviet Union	14.4	27.7
Oceania	38.2	5.3
All Others and Country Not Reported	20.5	16.7

Source: U.S. Bureau of the Census. *Statistical Profile of the Foreign-Born Population: 1980.* (Washington, DC: U.S. Government Printing Office, 1983). Tables 1 and 3.

Notes: [a] Includes Mexico.

[b] Includes Canada, Bermuda and Greenland.

question. Table 3.5 shows the 1980 distribution of the foreign-born population by region of birth in the nation as a whole, in California and in New York State. Table 3.6 compares the respective share in each state of the foreign born from the various regions of birthplace in relation to the nationwide total.

The geographic origins of foreign-born persons figure prominently in the particular way in which they are distributed across the different regions of the country, and it is precisely these differences that accounted for the contrasting profile of New York and California in 1980. California's foreign born were overwhelmingly Mexican and Asian with few Europeans and smaller numbers of Caribbeans and South Americans. The foreign-born mix in New York was much more heterogeneous. The state absorbed significant numbers of Europeans of nearly all nationalities, most of the Soviet and Asian nationalities, Caribbeans, Central Americans and South Americans. Whereas in California immigrants were spread geographically over several major central cities and urban centers, in New York State it is New York City that is the only immigrant city.

The contrast between the two principal host states in terms of the nationality mix of their foreign-born resident population may best be summarized as follows: in California, immigrants born in Asia and Central America (including Mexicans) accounted for practically two thirds of the state's foreign-born population in 1980; that same proportion was matched in New York City by immigrants born in Europe, the Soviet Union and the Caribbean.

The respective share of New York and California in the nationwide total of foreign-born residents in 1980 stood as follows: California — which accounted for 10 percent of the U.S. population — was hosting nearly 25 percent of the nation's foreign-born population. That population represented 56 percent of all foreign-born Central Americans (predominantly Mexicans), 35 percent of all Asians and 38 percent of all persons born in Oceania residing in the country. New York State — which carried 8 percent of the country's population — was hosting 17 percent of all the foreign born and these accounted for 37 percent of all Caribbeans, 32 percent of all South Americans, 28 percent of the Soviets and 21 percent of all Europeans in the United States (Table 3.6).

Major Immigrant Supplier Countries to New York

The discussion has, for the most part, centered around regions of birth to document changes in the geographical origin of New York's immigrants. The following places importance on the principal supplier countries that have been instrumental in shaping the contour of New York's foreign-born community since 1965. The presentation of data for the discussion draws on census material and on the yearly influx of new immigrants into New York during the 1980s.

The population profile drawn in the 1980 census punctuates the numerical importance of the European-born community in New York State, which at the time totaled 1,022,524 residents representing nine countries and accounted for 42 percent of the 2.4 million foreign-born New Yorkers. Ten years earlier, the European-born population totaled 1,290,538 persons, accounting for 61.2 percent of New York's foreign-born residents. Italians have been, for some time, the largest nationality represented: in 1980 they totaled 240,000 persons and accounted for one fourth of the European-born community. Additionally, there were Germans (134,991), Poles (113,262), Soviets (112,725) and other smaller groups of nationalities making up this multiregional European group. Most of these residents were part of the legacy of earlier migratory waves whose representative communities have not been replenished with newcomers. In fact, except for Greeks and Yugoslavs, few European nationalities have actually increased in population size following the 1965 Immigration Act. Since 1986, the Soviet-born community has been bolstered with the entry of increasing numbers of refugees who appear to continue the historical legacy of their predecessors in establishing residence in New York State.

By 1980, the presence of a growing Third World immigrant community had made itself fully visible in New York. Caribbeans, mostly from the Dominican Republic and Jamaica, totaled 463,759 persons at that time and represented 19.4 percent of the estate's foreign-born population; Asians, the majority from China and the Philippines followed in lesser numbers by Indians and Koreans, totaled 290,456 persons or 12.2 percent of the total, while South Americans, mostly from Colombia and Ecuador, numbered 182,779 representing about 8 percent of all foreign-born New Yorkers.[4]

Shifts in the national origin of foreign-born persons coming into New York City from before 1965 to 1980 are documented in detail in Table 3.7. The importance of the information presented is that it identifies changes in the rank order of the top country suppliers over different time periods. To be noted is how European countries listed as leading immigrant suppliers prior to 1965 disappear from the list or fall in rank after 1965, best illustrated by the experience of Poland, Germany, Austria and Hungary. Concurrent with the declining importance of the European nations, the Dominicans, Jamaicans and Chinese effectively consolidated their position after 1965 to emerge as New York City's top suppliers. In the collective profile of 1980, Italy still maintained the lead position.

Two immigrant communities need special mention — the Caribbeans and the Asians. Combined they represent seven in every ten of the legally admitted immigrants who have come into New York each year since 1982. Information on the birthplace of New York-bound legal immigrants admitted into the United States between 1978 and 1986 drawn from the INS files substantiate this. Overall, the compositional profile of the state's immigrants has been astonishingly stable

TABLE 3.7

RANK ORDER OF TOP 10 LARGEST SUPPLIER COUNTRIES TO NEW YORK CITY
BY PERIOD OF IMMIGRATION TO 1980

Pre-1965	1965–1974	1975–1980	Total 1980
1. Italy	1. Dominican Rep.	1. Dominican Rep.	1. Italy
2. Poland	2. Jamaica	2. USSR	2. Dominican Rep.
3. Germany	3. China	3. China	3. China
4. USSR	4. Italy	4. Jamaica	4. Jamaica
5. Ireland	5. Haiti	5. Guyana	5. USSR
6. Cuba	6. Trinidad-Tobago	6. Haiti	6. Poland
7. Austria	7. Ecuador	7. Korea	7. Germany
8. China	8. Colombia	8. Colombia	8. Haiti
9. Dominican Rep.	9. Cuba	9. Trinidad-Tobago	9. Cuba
10. Hungary	10. Greece	10. India	10. Ireland

Source: City of New York, Department of Planning, Office of Immigrant Affairs and Population
Analysis Division New York, 1988. "Caribbean Immigrants in New York City."

during the 1980s, except for the Asian nationality groups who have increased their
share in the total annual entry into New York—from 20 percent in 1980 to 26
percent in 1986.

Principal Immigrant Communities

The New York metropolitan area witnessed a dramatic influx of English-speaking Caribbeans in the post-1965 years. Before that time, not one country in the
Caribbean basin had been placed on the top list of New York's immigrant
suppliers. By the mid-1970s, however, their presence in New York City had
become very noticeable. According to the 1980 census, 82 percent of the Jamai-
can-born and 88 percent of the Trinidadian-born residents in the New York area
were post-1965 arrivals. United States refugee policy had also permitted a large
scale admission of Cubans who were prominent in the New York area and later
of Haitians. By the late 1970s, five countries among the ten listed as leading
suppliers to New York City were Caribbean: the Dominican Republic (first in
rank), followed by Jamaica (fourth), Guyana (fifth), Haiti (sixth) and Trinidad-
Tobago (ninth).

Though labor migration from the Caribbean basin to the United States has
been longstanding, an intensification in the movement to emigrate in the direction
of New York, in particular, took place at the end of the 1960s. It drew from among
the West Indies more because of Britain's refusal to further accept immigrants
from black Commonwealth nations (City of New York, Department of City
Planning, 1985). Among Dominicans, the stimulus was provided by more liber-

alized internal policies allowing citizens to emigrate. From then onward, the concentration of Caribbean immigrants in the New York City area accelerated rapidly, particularly among persons coming from the English- and Spanish-speaking islands; the entry of Haitians into New York was a later development. By 1980, Caribbeans in New York totaled close to 464,000 persons, representing 19 percent of the state's and 29 percent of the city's foreign-born population. This figure accounted for one half of the Barbadian, Trinidadian, Haitian, Jamaican and Guyanese and three quarters of the Dominican immigrants residing in the United States in that year. As a regional proportion, the New York-based Caribbean immigrant community accounted for close to 40 percent of all Caribbean immigrants living in the country.

The growing importance of the Caribbean community in relation to New York City may best be appreciated with the information presented in Table 3.8. The growth patterns of different nationality groups residing in the city between 1960 and 1980 have been plotted, first by ranking each nationality group according to its 1980 population size and second by comparing this rank to the corresponding order assigned to each nationality group by their 1960 population base. The percentage change in the community size of each nationality group over the 20 year period is shown, depicting clearly the expansions and contractions that have taken place. Though Italian-born immigrants maintained their lead throughout the 1960–1980 period, other nationality groups such as Dominicans and Jamaicans, who were positioned 24 and 25 in 1960, had by 1980 moved up to rank second and third in numerical importance. The same process occurred with Haitians who moved up in rank from 42 to eight during the twenty-year interval.

Dominicans increased their presence in New York City thirteenfold, from 9,000 in 1960 to 120,600 in 1980, outgrowing all other nationality groups except the Italians. Jamaican immigration also skyrocketed during that period, increasing more than eightfold from 11,000 to 93,000. Significant gains in population were also noted among the Trinidadian and Tobagans, from 5,500 to 40,000, and later among Haitians whose initially small community of 3,000 increased sixteenfold to reach 50, 000 by 1980.

The concentration of Caribbeans in the New York area has persisted during the 1980s. In 1988 and 1989 the number of legal immigrants admitted from the Caribbean who selected residence in New York numbered more than 40,000 each year, with Dominicans and Jamaicans representing two thirds of the Caribbean inflow. As a proportion of the nationwide number legally admitted into the country in 1988 and 1989, New York absorbed in each of these years over 60 percent of all the Dominican immigrants, 50 percent of the Jamaican and 74 percent of the Guyanese. Overall, the number of Caribbeans in New York is much larger when the undocumented segment is included: some estimates place the

TABLE 3.8

COMPARATIVE DIFFERENCES IN THE NUMERICAL IMPORTANCE OF NATIONALITY
GROUPS AMONG FOREIGN-BORN RESIDENTS IN NEW YORK CITY, 1960–1980

Country of Birth	Rank in 1980	Number in 1980	Rank in 1960	Number in 1960	% Change 1960–1980
All Countries	—	1,675,160	—	1,562,478	+7
Italy	1	156,280	1	281,033	-44
Dominican Republic	2	120,600	26	9,223	+1,208
Jamaica	3	93,100	24	11,160	+734
USSR	4	87,360	2	204,821	-57
China[a]	5	85,100	15	19,769	+330
Poland	6	77,160	3	168,960	-54
Germany, West & East	7	60,760	4	152,502	-60
Haiti	8	50,160	42	3,002	+1,571
Cuba	9	49,720	11	28,567	+74
Ireland/No.Ireland	10	43,520	5	114,163	-62
Greece	11	41,760	12	28,882	+45
Colombia	12	41,200	34	4,766	+764
Trinidad-Tobago	13	39,160	32	5,495	+613
Ecuador	14	39,000	44	2,796	+1,295
Guyana	15	31,960	b	b	b
Austria	16	26,160	6	84,389	-69
England	17	22,720	8	40,769	-44
Hungary	18	22,660	7	45,602	-50
Yugoslavia	19	22,300	19	12,399	+80
India	20	21,500	54	1,243	+1,630
Philippines	21	21,260	39	3,997	+435
Panama	22	20,840	33	677	+2,978
Korea, North & South	23	20,380	59	562	+3,526
Barbados	24	19,680	b	b	b
Romania	25	17,560	14	24,784	-29
Total Countries Listed		1,231,900	—	1,249,541	-1
All Other Countries		331,620	—	305,835	+8
Not Reported		111,640	—	7,102	+1,472

Source: E. Bogen, *Immigration in New York.* (New York: Praeger, 1987). Table 3.2

Notes: [a] Includes Hong Kong and Taiwan.

[b] These figures are not available for 1960 because Guyana and Barbados were included in the total for the British West Indies.

ratio of documented to undocumented Caribbeans in the city at 1:1 (City of New York, Department of City Planning, 1985).

At the time of the 1980 census, New York ranked third (behind California and Hawaii) with respect to the size of its population who were of Asian origin or descent: these numbered 328,000 at the time and accounted for 9.4 percent of all reported Asians in the United States. New York was hosting 290,456 foreign-born Asians, or 11.4 percent of the total in the country. Close to 200,000 amongst these resided in New York City. There they represented 11.6 percent of the reported 1.7 million residents of foreign birth and 2.8 percent of all city residents. Estimates made for New York City's expansion during the 1980s had forecast a 35 to 50 percent increase in the city's Asian population by 1990.

Asian immigration into the United States was restricted until 1965 and the few pockets of Asian nationalities that did exist were mostly concentrated on the West Coast. The Chinese were the first Asian group to settle in New York. By 1980, the reported foreign-born Chinese community in the state, inclusive of those born in Hong Kong and Taiwan, totaled 96,000 with 85,000 (88%) residing in New York City, where their numbers exceeded the Chinese community of San Francisco (City of New York, Department of City Planning, 1985). Among New York's Asian immigrant community, the Chinese have historically represented the largest group.

The second largest nationality group in New York's foreign-born Asian population were Indians, totaling 33,434 in the state and 21,500 in New York City, followed by Filipinos, 27,500 and 21,260 respectively. Of the 27,000 Koreans in the state, 75 percent were New York City residents. Neither the Japanese nor the Vietnamese had a sizeable community in New York.

In the case of New York, it was not the Refugee Act of 1980, which had opened so many doors to Southeast Asians across the country, that acted as a catalyst for the expansion of the Asian community, but rather economically-based factors that brought nonrefugee Asian nationals into the state.

The Chinese, because of their initially larger population base, drew full advantage from the family reunification priorities established in the 1965 Immigration Act to replenish and expand their community base by continually bringing in newcomers. Of the 126,000 Chinese ethnics identified in New York City in 1980, close to 70 percent were foreign born. Asian Indians are latecomers to the United States; since their influx into the country in the mid-1970s they have shown a certain preference to reside in the New York-New Jersey area. In 1980, persons of Indian ancestry and birth totaled 48,860 in New York City and amongst these close to 50 percent were foreign born. However, Asian immigrants, including the Chinese, have established residence in other parts of the country as well, namely in California, Illinois and New Jersey. In 1988, the sum total of legally admitted immigrants coming from China, India, Korea, the Philippines and Pakistan and establishing residence in New York came close to 20,000 persons; in 1989 the corresponding total increased to 24,389. In relation to the nationwide entries of Asians in 1988, the New York-bound immigrant group represented only 5 percent of all the Filipinos admitted, between 11 and 15 percent of the Indians and Koreans, 20 percent of all Pakistanis and 27 percent of mainland Chinese. In 1989, the New York share in the Chinese and Indian admissions was slightly higher (33% and 14.6%), with few percentage point losses from among Koreans (15% to 12%). California at the same time absorbed a significantly larger portion of Filipinos (50%) and of Koreans (31%) compared to New York, also surpassing the state's share in the admission of Indians (19%).

Despite the geographical spread of most Asian immigrants across other parts of the country, their growing importance in the overall configuration of New York's foreign-born population should be given full attention. Among immigrants entering the United States prior to 1975 who resided in New York by 1980, China was the only Asian nation listed among the ten leading immigrant supplier countries. Among the 1975–1980 cohort, Korea and India appeared on the top list of immigrant suppliers to New York, ranking seventh and tenth in importance respectively. By that time, (mainland) China had strengthened its position to become the city's fourth largest supplier.

Recent Compositional Trends: 1980–1989

From the yearly admission statistics compiled by the immigration authorities, the records for 1983 through 1989 clearly show that Dominicans, Jamaicans, Chinese, Guyanese and Haitians continued to maintain their lead position as central immigrant suppliers to New York State (Table 3.9).

What is of particular interest, however, is that these countries did not dominate the nationwide or California immigrant flow in the late 1980s. This fact highlights some of the continuing distinctiveness of the New York experience. As shown in Table 3.10, the first and second largest supplier countries to New York (the Dominican Republic and Jamaica) were eighth and ninth in rank as nationwide suppliers and twenty-fifth and twenty-seventh in rank as immigrant sources to California. The fourth and fifth leading source countries to New York (Guyana and Haiti) were absent from the national list, appearing in the end section of the list for California. The combined number of entries from the four Caribbean countries in 1989 represented 6.7 percent of the nationwide admissions, 32 percent of the inflow to New York and 0.1 percent in the immigrant profile of California.

China ranked relatively higher as a supplier country to New York (third in rank) than to California (seventh in rank) an to the country as a whole (sixth in rank), but India ranked nearly equal in the three host sites. The Soviet Union

TABLE 3.9

TOP 8 COUNTRIES DOMINATING THE POST-1980 LEGAL
IMMIGRANT FLOW INTO NEW YORK STATE

Country of Birth	1983 No.	1983 & Total	1986 No.	1986 % Total	1988 No.	1988 % Total	1989 No.	1989 % Total
All Immigrants Admitted	93,159	(100.0)	110,216	(100.0)	109,259	(100.0)	134,766	(100.0)
Dominican Republic	—	—	17,379	15.7	17,570	16.0	16,500	12.2
Jamaica	10,132	10.8	10,468	9.4	10,471	9.5	12,370	9.2
Guyana	6,379	6.8	7,857	7.1	6,420	5.8	8,050	5.9
Haiti	4,836	5.1	7,029	6.3	6,558	6.0	6,546	4.8
China	7,075	7.5	7,663	6.9	7,722	7.0	10,602	7.8
India	3,914	4.2	4,208	3.8	4,059	3.7	4,558	3.4
Korea	3,316	3.5	4,016	3.6	3,912	3.5	4,282	3.2
Colombia	3,255	3.4	3,616	3.3	3,021	2.7	4,177	3.1
Other Countries	54,252	58.2	62,236	56.4	26,912	45.0	67,681	50.2

Source: U.S. Immigration and Naturalization Service, *Annual Report Statistical Yearbook File: 1965–1988.* (Washington, DC: U.S. Government Printing Office). Table IMM 5.2 and Table 16. (unpublished). U.S. Immigration and Naturalization Service, *1989 Statistical Yearbook of the Immigration and Naturalization Service.* (Washington, DC: U.S. Government Printing Office, 1990). Table 16.

TABLE 3.10

TEN LEADING IMMIGRANT SUPPLIER COUNTRIES TO NEW YORK STATE IN RELATION
TO THEIR IMPORTANCE TO CALIFORNIA AND THE UNITED STATES, 1989

Leading Countries	New York State Rank[a]	New York State % Share in Total	California Rank[a]	California % Share in Total	United States Rank[a]	United States % Share in Total
Dominican Republic	1	12.2	27	.0	8	2.4
Jamaica	2	9.2	25	.1	9	2.2
China	3	7.8	7	2.4	6	2.9
Haiti	4	5.9	26	.0	15	0.9
Guyana	5	4.8	28	.0	18	1.2
India	6	3.4	10	1.2	7	2.8
Korea	7	3.2	8	2.3	5	3.1
Colombia	8	3.1	20	.3	12	1.4
Philippines	9	2.5	3	6.2	3	5.2
Soviet Union	10	2.1	12	1.0	16	1.0
Others		45.8		86.5		76.9

Source: U.S. Immigration and Naturalization Service, *1989 Statistical Yearbook of the Immigration and Naturalization Service.* (Washington, DC: U.S. Government Printing Office, 1990). Table 16.

Note: [a] Ranking is based on the listing of the 28 countries of birthplace of legal immigrants admitted to the United States in 1989.

showed to be slightly more important to New York (tenth in rank) and to California (twelfth in rank) than nationwide (sixteenth in rank). The combined contribution of China, India and Korea to the 1989 group of immigrants who established residence in New York was 14.4 percent, the corresponding fraction in California was 6 percent, while for the country as a whole it was 9 percent. The gap is partly due to the nationality mix of immigrants admitted under the 1986 status legalization provisions which was heavily dominated by Mexicans and Salvadorans and thereby depressed the proportional representation of the Asian countries in some states. Legalization admissions affected the 1989 distributional profile of nationalities in the country as a whole and certainly in California, but had relatively little effect on New York.

It is the infusion of Caribbeans that is the most distinctive feature of New York's immigrant profile, not only during the 1980s but as a trend that has persisted since the 1970s. In 1989, the share of all Caribbeans in the nationwide immigrant flow was 7.8 percent; in the pool of legal immigrants arriving in the United States that year who selected to reside in New York State, the corresponding proportion was 33 percent. In California it was less than one percent.

Residential Choices of the Foreign Born in New York City

Throughout this study, the overwhelming concentration of foreign-born persons in the central city area of New York has been emphasized. This concentration has had significant demographic consequences for the nationality and ethnic composition of New York City, as well for the local communities within the metropolis. From comprising 40 percent of the city's population in 1910, the more recent foreign-born component was reported at 18.2 percent in 1970 and an estimated 30 percent in 1990 (see, Table 2.1).

Just as New York State immigrants selectively migrate to New York City, there also exist focused patterns of residential choices among the different nationality groups within the city. Ellen Kraly (1987) has documented these choices across the various boroughs of the city and the account presented below relies entirely on her work.

Two major trends are noticeable in the way that the immigrant population has spread throughout New York City: 1) showing consistency with the congregation and segregation patterns for earlier waves of immigrants and 2) demarcating a sharp variation between earlier and more recent immigrant streams. Earlier immigrant groups such as the Europeans and Soviets have concentrated in the larger New York-New Jersey metropolitan area (this is the case with Israelis as well); newer immigrants are heavily concentrated in the central city area—West Indians and South Americans are the most outstanding cases.

TABLE 3.11

DISTRIBUTION OF THE FOREIGN-BORN POPULATION OF NEW YORK CITY BY
BIRTHPLACE AND BOROUGH OF RESIDENCE, 1980 (NUMBERS IN THOUSANDS)

Area and Country of Birth	Total Number	Boroughs (%)				
		New York	Brooklyn	Queens	Bronx	Staten Island
Total Population	7,071.6	20.2	31.5	26.7	16.5	5.0
Foreign-Born Population	1,670.2	20.9	31.8	32.4	12.9	2.1
Europe	578.0	17.4	29.6	35.6	14.0	3.5
Germany	60.7	29.6	14.1	42.8	10.7	2.7
Ireland	41.4	17.6	15.9	32.9	30.5	3.2
Italy	156.4	5.5	39.7	31.6	17.1	6.0
Poland	78.1	13.6	46.2	25.4	13.5	1.3
United Kingdom	33.5	30.9	24.5	27.6	12.2	4.7
USSR	88.4	14.1	45.8	26.1	13.4	0.6
Asia	214.7	29.3	21.4	41.0	5.6	2.8
China	60.8	47.1	19.8	28.6	3.4	1.2
India	21.9	15.3	16.3	56.8	7.5	4.0
Japan	9.5	3.1	39.6	44.2	11.2	1.8
Korea	18.4	13.2	11.3	59.6	9.8	6.1
Philippines	20.2	23.5	17.5	44.7	6.5	7.8
Vietnam	3.4	24.6	27.9	36.8	9.5	1.2
North & Central America	494.6	23.0	39.2	22.5	14.6	0.7
Canada	15.9	32.0	27.2	27.1	9.1	4.6
West Indies	414.0	23.8	38.9	22.2	14.7	0.4
Cuba	46.9	34.1	15.8	38.3	10.9	0.9
Dominican Republic	124.1	51.6	16.0	18.8	13.4	0.2
Jamaica	90.8	6.2	44.9	21.3	27.3	0.3
South America	153.7	16.2	24.2	49.0	9.4	1.2
Africa	23.6	26.0	30.9	28.3	11.1	3.8
All Other Countries	2.2	57.3	14.3	18.6	4.5	5.2
Country Not Reported	115.0	23.5	30.3	26.1	18.7	1.4

Source: E. Kraly, "U.S. Immigration Policy and Immigrant Populations of New York." In *New Immigrants in New York City*. Edited by N. Foner. (New York: Columbia University Press, 1987). Table 2.9.

The distribution of the foreign-born population in New York City by birth-place and residential location across the five boroughs in 1980 is shown in Table 3.11. The borough of Queens houses the largest number of foreign-born New Yorkers (32.4%) and is the most ethnically diverse county, including large numbers of Italians, Chinese, Koreans, English-speaking Caribbeans and South Americans. It has grown to be the major area of concentration for Asians and South Americans (half of each of the Korean, Filipino, Indian, Colombian and Ecuadorian residents of New York live there). Brooklyn contains nearly as high a proportion of the foreign born (31.5%) as Queens, composed of Haitians, some Dominicans, English-speaking Caribbeans, and a relatively large proportion of Russians — just under 50 percent of the latter are located in this borough. The Bronx includes a 16 percent portion of the foreign born — both old and new immigrants — with large proportions of Italians, Irish and English-speaking Caribbeans. The borough of Manhattan is the major settlement area of the Chinese and the Dominicans. Typically one half of the population of each nationality are concentrated here and one third of Cubans, Canadians, English and Germans. Overall, the borough housed only one in every five immigrants in 1980. The Richmond-Staten Island borough included only 2 percent of the immigrant population in 1980. In relation to that minimum, the following three nationality groups were over-represented: Filipinos, Koreans and Italians (between 6% and 7%).

Accompanying Changes in Racial and Ethnic Diversity

Shifts in the national origin of immigrants establishing residence in New York since 1965 have had obvious implications for the racial and ethnic composition of the state. The difficulties lie in how to measure these implications in a meaningful way from the information available because of problems intrinsic to both the objective and subjective systems of data collection which form the basis of census reporting. One of the past difficulties (corrected in the 1990 census) pertains to the level of comparability in the categorization and classification of "race" between the 1970 and 1980 censuses.[5] The second problem, a more sensitive one that is (realistically) not correctable, relates to the "accuracy" of racial self-definition and consequent subjective (self) reporting among individuals whose "view of race" encompasses a multicategory continuum from white to black. Such a continuum bears little conformity to the bipolar racial dichotomization of "black" versus "white" as conceptualized and operationalized in the United States (Denton and Massey, 1989). Denton and Massey (1988, 1989) are to be credited for their sensitive analysis of this fundamental issue with respect to Caribbean Hispanics. The same problem they identify is probably confronting other multiracial nationality groups as well when asked to identify their race for the U.S. census or any other survey. In the particular case of Caribbean or other Hispanics, since race and Spanish origin are asked in separate questions, Spanish-descent persons are free to place themselves in any one of the racial categories they choose, but this in itself does not address the entire complexity of the problem. Given the "social meaning" attached to race (existing in societies other than the United States), any skewing in reporting that would occur will most likely be in favor of inflating the category of "whites," though some individuals "of color" may intentionally identify themselves as "black" as a form of political statement. In light of these limitations the following statistical reporting on race drawn from the census must be interpreted with caution.

The 1980 data reported the following racial/ethnic distribution of New York's foreign-born residents: 45.8 percent non-Hispanic white (European in origin); 18.4 percent non-Hispanic black; 11.7 percent belonged to the various Asian ethnic/racial groupings and 23.6 percent were of Spanish descent, both black and white. Table 3.12 examines the correspondence between shifts in the national origin of immigrants and their increasing diversity with respect to race and ethnicity characteristics by tracing the chronology of arrival of three cohorts. Among early cohorts arriving prior to 1965, three immigrants in every four reported themselves as "white," reflecting the European presence. Combined with Spanish-descent groups, the white population accounted for 90 percent of the pre-1965 migratory flow. Racial and ethnic diversity begins to appear with immigrants arriving after 1965, and this is manifested in the following patterns: 1) a substantial drop in the share of "whites" from 73 percent in the pre-1965 flows to 25.7 percent among those arriving between 1975 and 1980; 2) a corresponding threefold increase in the share of "blacks"—from 8 percent to 23.4 percent; 3) over a twofold increase in the share of Spanish-descent persons; and 4) between 1965 and 1980 a fivefold increase among Asian racial and ethnic groups—from a 4 percent share in the 1965–1974 immigrant group to a 22.2 percent share among the 1975–1980 cohorts.

Table 3.13 documents the self-reported race and ethnic identity of the foreign-born and American-born residents of New York State based on a 5 percent sample of the population enumerated by the census in 1980. This sample population forms the basis of much of the analysis presented in Chapters 4, 5 and 6 of this study. The distribution provides a tentative indication of the influence that international migration has had on the racial and ethnic transformation occurring in New York.

From what has been documented earlier regarding the changing nationality profile of New York's immigrants and based on the self-reported racial and ethnic identity of New York's foreign-born residents in 1980, it is clear that

TABLE 3.12

SELF-REPORTED RACIAL AND ETHNIC CATEGORIES OF U.S.-BORN AND FOREIGN-BORN RESIDENTS OF NEW YORK CITY BY PERIOD OF IMMIGRATION, 1980

Self-Reported Racial/Ethnic Categories	Total Population	U.S. Born	Total	Foreign Born by Period of Immigration		
				Pre-1965	1965–74	1975–80
Total	100.0	100.0	100.0	100.0	100.0	100.0
White (Non-Hispanic)	52.0	53.9	45.8	73.1	24.0	25.7
Black (Non-Hispanic)	24.0	25.7	18.4	8.4	27.9	23.4
Asian (Non-Hispanic)	3.6	1.1	11.7	4.3	4.1	22.7
Other (Non-Hispanic)	0.3	0.2	0.5	0.3	0.6	0.8
Hispanic	20.2	19.1	23.6	13.9	33.4	27.4

Source: E. Bogen, *Immigration in New York.* (New York: Praeger, 1987). Table 3.4.

TABLE 3.13

SELF-REPORTED RACIAL AND ETHNIC CATEGORIES OF THE U.S.-BORN AND FOREIGN-BORN RESIDENTS OF NEW YORK STATE BY REGION OF BIRTHPLACE, 1980 (POPULATION 16+)

Region of Birthplace	Number in Sample Population 100.0%	Self-Reported Racial/Ethnic Categories						
		White	Black	Chinese	Asian Indian	Other Asian	Spanish	Other
U.S. Born	540,675	86.2	12.4	0.1	0.01	0.1	0.9	0.3
Foreign Born	111,275	66.6	15.8	4.5	2.0	3.0	6.5	1.6
Africa	804	25.6	64.4	0.4	6.1	—	0.8	2.7
No. America[a]	3,430	94.1	2.5	0.7	—	0.1	—	2.6
So. America	6,747	67.6	2.6	0.2	0.2	0.2	25.7	3.4
Cen. America[b]	3,188	36.0	37.1	0.2	—	—	24.3	2.4
Caribbean	22,969	17.9	60.4	0.5	2.0	—	16.8	2.4
Asia	10,418	6.7	0.1	44.0	14.4	30.3	—	4.5
Middle East/ North Africa	2,911	97.5	0.5	—	0.5	0.1	—	1.4
N/W Europe	18,826	98.2	1.2	—	0.1	0.1	0.1	0.3
So. Europe	19,295	99.3	0.1	—	—	—	0.3	0.3
East. Europe	9,770	99.8	—	—	0.1	—	—	0.1
USSR	5,906	98.8	0.5	—	0.1	—	—	0.6
Other	6,998	57.4	21.2	3.0	1.0	1.2	11.9	4.3

Source: U.S. Bureau of the Census. *Census of Population, 1980: Public Use Microdata Sample.* Tape Documentation. (Washington, DC: U.S. Bureau of the Census, 1983).

Notes: [a] Includes Canada, Greenland and Bermuda.

[b] Includes Mexico.

continuing immigration from Asia, Africa, the Caribbean and Central and South America will further increase the racial and ethnic mix of New York. State residents born in European, Soviet, North Americans, Middle Eastern and North African regions in nine cases out of ten identified themselves as "white."

In the overall spectrum of the self-reported racial and ethnic characteristics of New York's foreign and American-born populations, can the impact of immigrants in further increasing the racial and ethnic heterogeneity of New York be delineated? Based on 1980 census information, the characteristics of the profile indicate that, in relation to the state level total of the population in each ethnic and racial category, foreign-born New Yorkers in 1980 accounted for 90 percent of all Asian Indians, 86 percent of all Asian Chinese, 59 percent of all Spanish-descent groups, 21 percent of all blacks and 14 percent of all whites.

Summary

To summarize past trends and highlight some of the identifiable dynamics occurring at the present, the following observations may be made regarding the evolving immigration scenario in New York.

Unless there are changes in the apportionment of entries, it is reasonable to expect a yearly influx of approximately 100,000 to 110,000 legal immigrants into the state over the 1990–2000-year period,[6] not taking note of how many initially entering New York will subsequently migrate to other states or enter and reside in the state "illegally."[7]

The lead supplier countries of the 1980s — Dominican Republic, Jamaica, China and Guyana — are expected to continue the same migration patterns in the 1990s. The numerically less significant presence of Indians and Koreans will continue and their growing importance in the demography of New York will be increasingly established. In the event that more migratory flows will come from East Europe and Soviet immigration to the United States increases, a notable portion of these population groups will settle in New York and enlarge the European component.

Black and Hispanic Caribbeans have been strongly entrenched in New York City since 1950, but their volume increased considerably after 1965. This has distinct implications for the racial mix of New York City. Among New York's ten largest immigrant suppliers during 1975–1980, black Caribbeans from Jamaica, Guyana and Haiti ranked fourth, fifth and sixth in numerical importance. In the 1980s, black Caribbeans ranked second, fourth and fifth in the supplier list.

Immigrants born in Asia have settled in New York selectively. Their numbers have increased and they will continue to make their presence felt, propelling further changes in racial/ethnic heterogeneity. Aside from the settlement of the Chinese, Indians and Koreans, Filipinos and Pakistanis are also expected to gain further in numerical importance, bringing greater racial diversity. During 1980-1986, Asian nationalities represented 25 percent of all legal immigrants settling in New York State.

The presence in New York of immigrants of Spanish descent is longstanding. They come mostly from Colombia, Ecuador and parts of Central America, and have become a major factor in the growth of New York's Hispanic community, merging and identifying in many cases with U.S.-born Hispanics. The extent to which foreign-born Spanish descent groups and their offspring are contributing to the growth of the U.S. Hispanic population projected for New York State is considerable. Foreign-born Spanish origin groups made up almost 60 percent of the overall Spanish/Hispanic population of the state. By both birth and descent, 9.5 percent of New York State's population and 20 percent of the city's population were Hispanic in 1980. Provisional data from the 1990 census count shows the corresponding proportions to have increased to 12.3 percent and 24 percent respectively.

NOTES

[1] All figures cited in this discussion, whether in reference to regions, nations or origins, designate the birthplace of the foreign-born/immigrant population rather than nationality or place of last residence.

[2] Between 1871–1965, only 16,000 Indians came to the United States. Between 1965 and 1975 alone, entries of Indians totaled 97,000.

[3] The 125,000 Cubans who entered the United States during the boatlift in 1980 became eligible for status adjustment in 1985–86. Over 40,000 adjusted to permanent resident status under this provision during 1985 and 1986.

[4] Central and North America were collapsed into one category and it was not possible to differentiate what portion of the 615,233 were born in Central America. In combined form the two regions accounted for 25.8 percent of all the foreign-born residents in New York State. This included Canada and Mexico.

[5] In 1970, the Census categories for race were limited to: White, Black, Other. Though "Other" theoretically included all other ethnic/racial groups, that procedure was not followed in the codification procedures. Asian Indians and Hispanics were coded as "White," Vietnamese and other Asians as "Other." In 1980, the Census categories had been expanded to 12, in response to the increasing diversity characterizing the immigrant flow to the United States and to pressures exerted from certain ethnic communities keen to preserve their identity.

[6] This figure is based on the number of legal admissions of immigrants between 1983 and 1988 who selected to reside in New York. They totaled 638,500 for the six-year period.

[7] The flow of nonimmigrants to the United States (nearly ten million in 1983) bears special significance to New York because of the inclusion of nationalities—Caribbeans, Colombians, Ecuadorians, Indians—which have strong roots in the state. Entering the United States as a nonimmigrant is often the chosen route among those planning to remain in the New York area in an undocumented immigration status. In fact, among several large ethnic groups in New York, that route has been an important means of reconstituting their families in the New York metropolitan area with little regard for the legal status of family members.

4

SOCIO-DEMOGRAPHIC CHARACTERISTICS OF NEW YORK'S FOREIGN-BORN RESIDENTS

Up to this point, the study has identified the various categories of immigrant status groups that compose the foreign-born population and delineated the transformation in the nationality, ethnic and racial composition of immigrant flows into New York that has taken place after 1965. This section and the two that follow examine the social, demographic, economic and labor force characteristics of foreign-born New Yorkers. Of immediate interest in the present discussion is a look into data related to the age composition of immigrants, their marital patterns and their educational attainments. Insofar as the data permit, comparisons will be drawn in the presentation with corresponding characteristics of American-born New Yorkers and with the foreign-born averages for the United States as a whole. The purpose behind such comparison is to explore whether there is a demographic and educational distinctiveness to foreign-born persons who select to establish residence in New York in relation to American-born residents in the state and to the characteristics of the foreign-born population nationwide.[1]

In organizing the framework for the discussion that follows it has also seemed important to differentiate the sociodemographic characteristics of foreign-born residents by the period of entry into the United States. The data available establish the dividing line between the pre-1970 early cohorts (unfortunately an open category) and the more recent cohorts designating those who arrived between 1970 and 1980. Marking this differentiation was prompted by two reasons: "recent arrivals," based on the 1970–1980 cohorts, typically represent the modality for future migratory streams into New York State and should therefore be analyzed in some detail; and early cohorts of immigrants have been somewhat neglected in the current immigration literature and not much is known about their life conditions — particularly those who are the elderly. The findings obtained from studying both groups should have some implications for policy, and for this alone deserve special attention.

Demographic Characteristics

The Age Composition

Characteristics of age are one of the proximate indicators of the "potential" role that an immigrant population can perform in the receiving society. The age structure determines whether a given population ranks high or low in youth and old-age dependency and the economic impact this bears upon state welfare and that portion in the population who are in the economically productive ages. The ratio of people of labor-force age represents the population within the fifteen to 64-year-old age range, and among those it is in particular the twenty to 44-year-old age bracket that is identified as the prime working age. Characteristics of age also indicate the immigrant potential for childbearing and its possible impact on population growth. The potential fertility impact is indexed by the proportion of women in the childbearing ages – typically fifteen to 44 years – though it is clear that actual reproductive behavior will always be mediated by social and economic circumstances.

Table 4.1 presents comparative data on the age distribution of New York's foreign-born and native-born residents alongside the corresponding averages in the national population. Though the median age of the 1970–1980 cohort of immigrants was virtually identical to that of American-born New Yorkers – 29.0 and 29.8 years respectively – there were internal differences in the weighting of specific age categories within the distribution between the two populations, and these are kept in mind throughout the discussion.

In terms of economic impact, New York's post-1970 foreign-born arrivals were characterized in 1980 by a high proportion of persons in the economically productive and biologically reproductive ages and a low proportion of persons in the dependent-age group "under age fifteen" and "65 years and above." Fifty-six percent of this immigrant population were in the prime working ages of twenty to 44 years; among native-born New Yorkers the proportion was only 36 percent. The fraction in the recent immigrant population who were "theoretically" in the dependent ages totaled 18.4 percent as compared to 25.2 percent among American-born residents. This is because the age composition of recent immigrants yielded a lower youth – age dependency than native-born residents (15% vs. 23.5%) and a lower percentage of elderly persons (3.7% as compared to 10.2%).

TABLE 4.1

AGE DISTRIBUTION OF THE U.S.-BORN AND FOREIGN-BORN RESIDENTS OF
NEW YORK STATE AND THE UNITED STATES, 1980

	New York State Population			United States Population		
		Foreign Born			Foreign Born	
Age Groupings	U.S. Born	Pre-1970 Arrivals	1970–80 Arrivals	U.S. Born	Pre-1970 Arrivals	1970–80 Arrivals
Total Population	15,169,134 (100.0%)	1,556,134 (100.0%)	832,804 (100.0%)	212,465,899 (100.0%)	8,519,543 (100.0%)	5,560,363 (100.0%)
< 5 years	7.3	–	2.5	7.5	–	3.9
5–9	7.4	–	5.5	7.6	–	7.9
10–14	8.7	0.9	7.5	8.3	1.4	8.3
15–19	9.7	2.5	10.4	9.5	3.6	10.2
20–24	8.9	3.4	12.0	9.4	4.8	14.2
25–34	15.7	10.7	28.7	16.2	12.3	28.6
35–44	11.1	15.0	15.7	11.0	15.7	13.7
45–54	10.5	15.3	8.4	9.9	15.2	6.5
55–64	10.2	14.8	5.3	9.6	13.8	3.6
65 +	10.2	37.0	3.7	10.6	32.9	3.1
Median Age	29.8	56.2	29.0	29.4	52.9	27.4

Sources: U.S. Bureau of Census, *Census of Population: 1980.* Vol. 1. Chapter D. Detailed Population Characteristics. Part 34. New York. Section 1. (Washington DC: U.S. Government Printing Office 1983). Table 196 A. U.S. Bureau of the Census, *Census of Population: 1980.* Vol. 1. Chapter D. Detailed Population Characteristics. Part 1. United States Summary. (Washington DC: U.S. Government Printing Office 1983). Table 255.

While the median age of the post-1970 immigrants was earlier identified as 29 years, this is a collective statistic that veils significant age differences among the various nationality groups. Country specific information indicates that Cuban and Chinese immigrants were considerably older than the typical newcomer to New York of the 1970s (median ages 40 years and 36 years respectively), followed by Filipinos (median age 33 years). The most youthful immigrants in New York were represented by the Canadians, Vietnamese and English (median age 25 years), followed closely by Dominicans, Jamaicans and Mexicans. Caribbean immigrants, in general, are known to emigrate in their early twenties (Chaney, 1985; Pessar, 1987).

While supplying New York with this youthful foreign-born population, overall immigration has also had an opposite effect on the demography of New York because of the age structure of the early immigrant group. These cohorts have, to a certain extent, contributed to the "aging" of New York and the state may, in fact, be hosting the oldest immigrants in the United States. In 1980, the median age of the early immigrant population residing in New York was 56.2 years, higher than the median age average of all the pre-1970 cohorts of immigrants in the country (52.9 years). The number of persons 65 years of age and over as a proportion of the pre-1970 cohorts was 37 percent in New York, but only 32.9 percent nationwide. In relation to the demography of New York, this 37 percent statistic is almost four times as high as the corresponding fraction of the 65-year-old and over in the population of American-born New Yorkers (10.2%).

Older immigrants in New York have produced a relatively high dependency ratio within their own cohort and in some way contributed to establishing New York as the "second oldest state" in the country (Florida is the first). In 1980, for example, cohorts of immigrants who arrived prior to 1970 accounted for only 9 percent of New York's total population. Among New York's overall elderly population (65 years and over) immigrants in that range represented 26.5 percent. One in every four elderly persons in the state is an immigrant and the majority among them are women.

Aside from being somewhat older than the nationwide average, New York's foreign-born residents in 1980 were not demographically distinctive with respect to age. They included a slightly larger proportion of dependents; the fraction of persons "under age fifteen" and "65 years and over" represented 37.9 percent of the immigrant population in New York; nationwide the corresponding percentage was 34.3.

Sex Ratio, Marital Patterns and Fertility

Historical patterns characterizing immigrant flows into the United States in general and into New York in particular have been selective of sex; as a consequence the sex ratios have been skewed at various times in different directions. Nationwide, the heavily male-dominated flow characteristic of the early immigrant waves gave way, since 1930, to a more equal sex distribution, though at times there have been distinct reversals in favor of women. In recent years, the legal streams showed to be more evenly distributed by sex. Among the 1970–1980 reported arrivals and immigrants legally admitted into the country during the 1980s, the sex ratio stood at 102:100 in favor of men. However, in the more marginal populations such as refugees, asylees, and undocumented, the male ratios have been high—130:100 among refugees and asylees and 113:100 in the estimated population of the undocumented reached by the 1980 census (Bouvier and Gardner, 1986).

New York State over the past decades and until the present appears to hold a particular appeal for the single woman immigrant. Among the 1970–1980 arrivals to New York the sex ratio was 100:95 in favor of women and women comprised 52 percent of all those legally admitted during 1978–1986 who established residence in New York. Even among the 234,000 undocumented aliens reached in New York in 1980, women were more highly represented than men. The 1980 census for New York State shows higher female ratios among foreign-born persons coming from the Philippines, Cuba, Jamaica, the Dominican Republic and Korea, in contrast to African-born residents where the sex distribution showed a 60 percent male majority component.

Patterns such as these are by no means accidental. They manifest themselves within a situational context influenced by political, economic and social factors which affect nationalities differently at different time periods. The migration history of the Chinese and Caribbeans in New York illustrates this well. Chinese immigration to New York has historically exhibited an excess of men over women in the most marriageable age groups, which in part was an outgrowth of the 1882 Chinese Exclusion Act. In 1890, the sex ratio in New York was 2,679:100 or 27 Chinese men for every woman. Prior to 1945, very few Chinese women and children could be seen in Chinatown, and it was only with the influx of Chinese war brides that the female population began, in the mid-forties, to gradually grow. But even by 1960, Chinese men in New York City outnumbered Chinese women 2:1. This imbalance was reflected in the marital statistics of Chinatown prior to 1970: 74.5 percent of Chinese women but only 59.4 percent of the men were married. Following the 1965 Immigration Act, the situation improved (Sung, 1987), though to date the ratios have not been fully balanced—in 1980 men outnumbered women 106:100.

Outmigration from the Caribbean prior to 1950 was selective of men. However, when these movements were later intensified, it was the women who came to dominate the migratory streams headed in the direction of New York. During the 1960s, 75 percent of the legally admitted Jamaicans establishing residence in New York consisted of women migrating on their own—in some instances followed later by husbands and children (Foner, 1987). This pattern was characteristic of two thirds of the legally admitted Dominicans as well, and the general perception is that Caribbean women equally represent a high proportion of the undocumented segment (Pessar, 1987). This particular migration pattern has been generated and sustained by strong demand factors in the U.S. labor market for services that Caribbean women can respond to, making it relatively easier for them rather than the men to obtain labor certification and find employment in the country mostly as middle-level professionals in the nursing area and in service-related jobs as private household workers, companions, childcare helpers, etc. As immigration progressed, larger percentages of Caribbeans qualified for immigrant status on the basis of family ties rather than by occupation; in 1981, for example, 93.5 percent of all Jamaicans granted immigration visas had family connections. Yet field studies among Caribbean immigrant communities in New York have shown that women continued to dominate the streams in the 1980s as well, and this is substantiated by the high female to male ratios in the marriageable ages — among Haitians 123, Jamaicans 114 and Dominicans 107 women for every 100 men (Chaney, 1985).

The legislative emphasis placed by the 1965 Immigration Act on family reunification has meant that legal admissions are highly selective of family members. In fact, the average allocation of entries on the basis of family relationships has totaled 80 percent over the past years, with priority given to children and spouses of U.S. citizens and permanent residents. An indirect outcome of the 1965 law has been to encourage residential propinquity among families and nationality groups, thereby strengthening ethnic bonds. This, in turn, has undoubtedly promoted the success of the family/ethnic-based small enterprise system.

Yet in what precise manner is the family reunification directive reflected in the marital status composition of foreign-born persons in New York who immigrated after 1965? The data presented in Table 4.2 provides separate entries for the marital distribution patterns of the early immigrant population and those who arrived during the 1970s. Data on the corresponding foreign-born averages for the entire United States are included for purposes of comparison. The conventional breakdown by marital category showed that in 1980 the "currently married" status applied to slightly over 50 percent of the post-1970 cohorts of men and women. Among the early group of immigrants, however, "currently married" was the modal status of men but certainly not for the women — 71 percent of the men but only 50 percent of the women were "currently married" at the time.

A glaring feature of the marital status profile of the foreign born in New York is the unequal way in which women are affected by marital disruption. This is true in the two cohorts, though brought about by different reasons. In the recently arrived population characterized by a median age of 29, 15.5 percent of the women but only 6.6 percent of the men were either separated, divorced or widowed. In fact, women were six times more likely than men to have lost their spouse through death and not remarried. Marital dissolution was experienced with greater frequency by immigrant women who arrived prior to 1970. In that population sex differentials in mortality had brought about a sex ratio of 100 women to 77 men, and only 50 percent of the women were married.

However, the particular marital composition of these early cohorts leads one to suspect that dynamics other than male mortality have been operating to produce some of the imbalance in marital patterns. For example, women were four times more likely to be widowed than men — 28 percent versus 7 percent — and when the proportions who were divorced, separated and widowed are collapsed, the result shows that 36 percent of the women but only 13 percent of the men were (technically) "partnerless." The extent to which this differential is brought about by earlier male mortality leaving an excessive supply of widowed women behind, or sociologically induced by immigrant women being left partner-

TABLE 4.2

MARITAL STATUS OF THE U.S.-BORN AND FOREIGN-BORN RESIDENTS
BY PERIOD OF ENTRY TO THE UNITED STATES, 1980

Location/ Status	U.S.-Born Population	Foreign-Born Popualtion Period of Entry/Sex			
		1970–1980 Arrivals		Prior to 1970 Arrivals	
		Male	Female	Male	Female
United States					
Single	20.3	38.0	25.3	15.7	11.2
Currently Married	65.5	56.0	62.3	71.6	60.0
Separated	—	2.1	3.2	1.7	2.3
Widowed	8.0	0.8	5.4	6.3	24.3
Divorced	5.8	2.4	3.6	4.5	6.1
New York State					
Single	32.3	36.3	29.7	15.0	13.0
Currently Married	51.7	56.9	54.6	71.4	50.3
Separated	3.4	2.9	5.1	2.4	3.5
Widowed	7.6	0.9	6.0	7.3	27.7
Divorced	5.0	2.8	4.4	3.7	5.3

Source: U.S. Bureau of Census, *Census of Population: 1980.* Vol. 1. Chapter D. Detailed Population Characteristics. Part 34. New York. Section 1. (Washington DC: U.S. Government Printing Office, 1983). Table 196 A. U.S. Bureau of the Census, *Census of Population: 1980.* Vol. 1. Chapter D. Detailed Population Characteristics. Part 1. United States Summary. (Washington DC: U.S. Government Printing Office, 1983). Table 255 B.

less because older immigrant men choose to marry native-born women while women of their immigrant cohort do not have or do not want the reciprocal opportunity to marry American-born men, would be an interesting subject to pursue. Currently there is little data available on intermarriage patterns among immigrants except for the findings noted by Bogen (1987) for New York City, which reported 22.3 percent of the spouses in households headed by immigrants to be American born.

"Within sex" comparisons between the post-1970 arrivals and American-born New Yorkers show great similarity in marital patterns among the men in the two populations, but not among the women (data not shown). Compared to the native born, more foreign-born women are married (54.6% vs. 48.7%); only one-half as many are likely to be widowed (6% versus 12%), and fewer have experienced marital dissolution (15% vs. 21%). However, some of these differentials are explained by internal differences in age-specific allocations between the two female populations. American-born residents are characterized by an age composition more heavily weighted towards the older age categories than recent immigrant women despite the nearly identical median age reported in the two populations. Thirty-one percent of native-born women, but only 17.4 percent among the 1970–1980 cohort, were 45 years and older in 1980, explaining in part the higher proportion in "current marriage" and lower proportion widowed among the foreign born.

In what way do the marital patterns of the more recently arrived immigrant women in New York compare to the corresponding average in the immigrant population nationwide? A comparison of the two marital status profiles reveals some distinctive features. New York's average immigrant woman tends to marry at a later age and with lesser frequency. When she does marry, the probabilities are greater that she will experience divorce and separation and when this happens she is less likely to remarry than immigrant women residing in other parts of the country. The statistical reporting of the comparative differences are shown in Table 4.2. The foreign-born New Yorker shows a lower proportion married (54% against 62% nationwide); a larger percentage in single status (30% vs. 25%), a higher incidence of separation and divorce (9.5% vs. 6.8%), but nearly equal proportions widowed (6%).

In reporting these marital statistics, a cautionary note must be introduced. To the extent that Caribbeans comprise a significant component of New York's immigrants, their reported marital patterns influence the shape of New York's foreign-born profile. Caribbean scholars (Chaney, 1985, in particular) have frequently mentioned that marital and family status of contemporary Caribbean immigrants are sometimes difficult to determine because of complex mating patterns, and that the conventional marital status categories identified in data collection systems may not reflect their social reality. Specifically, it is pointed out that marital status does not appear a reliable indicator to distinguish immigrants who may have left family behind from those who have not and that legal marriage is not the best test of family relationships because many Caribbeans live together for years, if not permanently, as man and wife, though in the reporting system they may appear as single, divorced or separated depending on past marital history.

Variations in marital disruption patterns, indexed by the conventional designations of divorce and separation, show to be disproportionately high in the immigrant population of Dominicans, Cubans and some South Americans. It is conceivable that some of the reportings on "separation" reflect the case of women who are principal migrants temporarily separated from their partners rather than the actual disruption of a union.

In 1980, twice as many households headed by immigrants arriving in New York during the 1970s contained "own children under age six" (39.8%) as compared to households headed by American-born New Yorkers (20.8%). The disparity between the two populations was not as great with respect to the percentage of households which included "own children under age 18" (66% vs. 51% respectively). But compared to the nationwide average of immigrant households, the New York-based immigrant households with "own children under six years" were relatively lower in proportion (39.8% vs. 44.5%). With respect to households with "own children under eighteen," the proportions in New York and nationwide were nearly equal among immigrant households – 66 percent and 68.5 percent respectively (Table 4.3). A more revealing 1980 statistic is that one in every eight children under age ten in New York State and one in every four in New York City were living in households headed by a recently arrived immigrant. A substantial proportion of New York's children were, in fact, the offspring of recent entrants into the country; moreover, the overwhelming majority of immigrant children residing in the state in 1980 were born in the United States (Alba and Trent, 1988).

Do these facts imply that immigrant women have higher fertility levels than American-born women? The fertility of native-born women in New York is generally low, but this is true of the state's immigrant population as well. Immigrant women arriving in New York during the 1970s who in 1980 were within the 25 to 34 age range reported an average of 1.32 children ever-born, nearly identical to the average number reported by American-born New Yorkers – 1.29 children. Cohorts of immigrant women within the 35 to 44 year age range reported the average number of children born to be 2.24; among a corresponding group of American-born women, the average was 2.47 (Table 4.4).

It is generally believed that immigrants sustain high fertility levels until such a time when economic and cultural adjustments are made to conform to the predominant family size norm (Bouvier and Gardner, 1986). This does not seem to be a necessary process for immigrants selecting to reside in New York. What is happening in the state, however, is that the recent immigrant female population is more heavily concentrated in the childbearing ages than American-born women (56.2% as compared to 36.3%, respectively, are within the twenty to 44 age range) and as a consequence bearing a substantially large proportion of New York's children (Alba and Trent, 1988). State level data for 1980 indicated that over 30 percent of the child population under age ten belonged to families headed by recent immigrants, while nearly one child in every four in the New York City population came from an immigrant household.

Fertility averages conceal important variations in reproductive behavior among nationality groups. The data in Table 4.4 provide some detail of fertility differences by region and country of origin. Highest fertility levels reported are linked to immigrant women from Italy and most of the Caribbean countries, except Cuba; lowest fertility levels are more characteristic of women from Asia, Europe (except Italians), Cuba and the Philippines. For internal contrasts within

TABLE 4.3

CHARACTERISTICS OF FAMILY-BASED HOUSEHOLDS BY NATIVITY OF HOUSEHOLDER AND PERIOD OF ARRIVAL TO THE UNITED STATES, NEW YORK AND THE UNITED STATES, 1980

Family-Based Household Characteristics	New York State Population			United States Population		
	Foreign Born		U.S. Born	Foreign Born		U.S. Born
	1970–1980 Arrivals	Pre-1970 Arrivals		Pre-1970 Arrivals	1970–1980 Arrivals	
Total Number Family-Based Households	565,846	206,298	3,695,887	3,054,964	1,257,419	54,877,750
% of All Households	67.4	78.0	70.4	70.3	73.6	73.6
% Households with Female Householder	20.1	22.0	22.0	17.0	14.6	16.8
% Female Householders/Husband Absent	16.3	17.0	18.1	14.0	11.6	13.9
% Single-Spouse Households	20.2	22.7	22.0	17.0	18.0	17.1
% With Own Children Under 18 years	40.5	66.0	51.2	43.7	68.5	51.8
% With Own Children Under 6 years	14.6	39.8	20.8	16.8	44.5	22.0

Source: U.S. Bureau of the Census, *Census of Population: 1980.* Vol. 1. Chapter D. Detailed Population Characteristics. Part 34. New York. Section 1. (Washington, DC: U.S. Government Printing Office, 1983). Table 196. U.S. Bureau of the Census, *Census of Population: 1980.* Vol. 1. Chapter D. Detailed Population Characteristics. Part 1. United States Summary. (Washington, DC: U.S. Government Printing Office, 1983). Table 255.

TABLE 4.4

CHILDREN EVER BORN OF RECENT IMMIGRANT WOMEN BY
NATIONALITY AND AGE GROUP, NEW YORK, 1980

Nativity/Region/Country of Birth	Average Number Born Per Woman at Ages	
	25–34	35–44
All Women		
New York State	1.3	2.4
U.S. Born	1.3	2.4
Foreign Born (pre-1970 arrivals)	1.5	2.2
Foreign Born (1970–1980 arrivals)	1.3	2.2
Europe	1.2	1.9
Italy	1.7	2.4
Greece	1.4	1.9
United Kingdom	0.9	1.5
Asia	1.1	2.0
China	1.2	2.5
India	1.3	2.0
Korea	1.1	2.2
Philippines	0.8	1.4
Caribbean		
Dominican Republic	1.6	3.0
Haiti	1.4	2.7
Jamaica	1.5	2.6
Cuba	1.0	1.9
South America	1.3	2.3
Africa	1.4	2.0

Source: U.S. Bureau of the Census, *Census of Population: 1980.* Vol. 1, Chapter D. Detailed
Population Characteristics, Part 34. New York. Section 1. (Washington, DC: U.S. Government
Printing Office, 1983). Table 196 A.

regions, compare the fertility levels of Cuban and Dominican immigrant women,
of Italian and Greeks and of the Filipino and Chinese, all of which point to the
importance of taking nationality differentials into consideration when discussing
regional averages.

Household Composition and Structure

The population census categorizes residential units into family-constituted
households, nonfamily households that include single person households and
group quarters. Household headship was found to be associated with family-
constituted households in 75 percent of the cases among the more recently
arrived immigrant population and in 67.4 percent among earlier immigrants.

Among American-born New Yorkers, household headship was linked to family-constituted house holds in seven out of ten cases.

One household in every five in which the household head was a recent immigrant and one in every three where the head was an early immigrant were not family constituted and in these female headship was relatively high — among the recently arrived immigrants, 30 percent; in units headed by an early immigrant it was 70 percent. This is understandable in light of the relatively large numbers of single, divorced and separated women in the younger immigrant group and the high percentage of widows among the early immigrant population.

Only a fraction of New York's immigrants were reported to be living in group quarters — 1.6 percent among the recent arrivals, 3.4 percent among the pre-1970 cohorts, as compared to 2.6 percent among American-born residents. The early immigrant population residing in group quarters had the largest proportion reported as "inmates of institutions" — 80 percent as compared to 20 percent among the recent arrivals living in group quarters.

It is worth describing family headship in more detail, for this provides useful background information regarding the more personal aspect of immigrants' living conditions.

From the status profile documented earlier, it was shown that a number of family-constituted households in New York do not conform in structure and composition to the traditional married couple unit. In 1980, close to one immigrant household in every four was headed by one-spouse, with either husband or wife absent from the home. How many of these households were single-parent or single-person households cannot be established from the data set.

Family-constituted households which were headed by foreign-born persons arriving in this country after 1970 were in 22 percent of all cases headed by a woman; in 17 percent of these units the husband was absent from the home. The woman-headed household "with no husband present" was more typical of immigrants arriving in the United States between 1965 and 1974. It was also closely associated with Caribbeans: 38.5 percent of all Dominican households, 30.5 percent of the Jamaican and 25.1 percent of the Haitian households were headed by women.[2]

There were also cases of family-constituted households headed by immigrant men "with wife absent" from the home, and these appeared to be closely linked to residential units headed by recent (1970–1980) arrivals. These could conceivably be households in which the male as principal immigrant has not as yet been joined by the wife or marital partner, a pattern not uncommon among Chinese immigrant men who experienced long years of separation from their spouses. Sung (1987) refers to these structures as "mutilated families" in her account of Chinese immigrants in New York.

Comparing immigrant and native-born residents of New York brings out greater similarities than differences with respect to family structure variables and female headship. Table 4.3 substantiates this.

The presence of single parent households among the native-born population has been influenced by the large American-born black and Hispanic minority populations residing in the New York area. Alba and Trent (1988) report that in 1980, 30 percent of all households headed by American-born blacks and 25 percent headed by United States Hispanics in New York involved women "with no husband present," and that most of these consisted of single mothers with dependent children. It is plausible that in certain cases the structural antecedents leading to apparent similarities in household structure between immigrant and U.S.-born populations may be different. In the case of some immigrants, what is reported as a woman-headed household "with no husband present" may represent a temporary adaptation to economic circumstances and not necessarily a broken family, as could be the case in native households headed by American-born residents.

Some information is available about the economics of the different types of households in the New York City area. Income differentials reported in 1980 by household type among American-born and foreign-born residents of New York point to married couple families as recipients of the highest median income when compared to other family types: $21,966 for native-born couples; $17,601 for the foreign born. Second highest income levels were reported in male-headed households "with wife absent" from the home (typically $17,000 in each population). Women heads-of-household "with husband absent" from the home are the most disadvantaged family type in the American-born population (the reported median income in 1980 was $8,402), but this was not the case in immigrant households headed by women, where the reported median income was $10,073. Among immigrants, it was the nonfamily constituted household that fared the poorest of all with a reported median income of only $6,918 (Bogen, 1987).

How does the family/household structure of New York's immigrants compare to immigrants nationwide? Table 4.3 presents comparative data for the United States to highlight the contrasts and similarities between the two populations. What appears to be the most striking difference between the two immigrant households is the higher incidence of female headship, single-spouse headship and "absence of husband" from the home in the immigrant population of New York. Of even greater interest is that it is these very same features that characterize the differences in household structure between American-born New Yorkers and the native born nationwide. To be specific, the proportion of native households headed by women in New York in 1980 was 22 percent; nationwide the corresponding proportion was only 17 percent. "Absence of husband" from the home was reported in 18 percent of native households in New York, but in only 14 percent nationwide; and single-spouse households described the family structure of 23 percent of native-born New Yorkers, but of only 18 percent in the national population.

The Changing Educational Profile

Serious questions have been raised concerning the educational resources and skill levels of immigrants coming to the United States in recent decades. The issue has become of vital concern even in the reformulation of immigration policy because of the importance it bears upon national productivity and the country's competitiveness in the international market. Borjas (1990) has presented strong arguments to the effect that recent immigrant waves show a "precipitous" decline in educational attainment (relative to natives). His analysis of nationwide trends over the 1960–1980 period indicate that whereas the typical immigrant arriving to the United States in the late 1950s had 0.3 years more schooling than the native born, the typical cohorts of the late 1970s had 0.7 years less. The author attributes this relative decline in educational attainment among successive immigrant waves to the changing national origin mix of the immigrant flow (today's major source countries are characterized by relatively little schooling) and to changing conditions in the U.S. immigration market leading it to become increasingly attractive to unskilled workers.

Though education is a key variable in the upward social mobility of immigrants and is tightly linked to higher earning potential, it alone is not a sufficient barometer of immigrant success. Many immigrants who come with academic degrees and prior employment experience in occupational specializations that require licensing in the United States are forced to take menial jobs, particularly when knowledge of English is weak. At the same time, immigrants with no or limited education can usually find work within the family-based/ethnic enclaves where certification and diplomas are not required nor, in many cases, is command of the English language (Papademetriou and Muller, 1987).

As an integral part of the social characteristics of foreign-born New Yorkers that are being examined, the discussion below addresses the question of immigrants' educational attainment, its changing patterns and trends over time, drawing comparisons with the educational characteristics of American-born New Yorkers and the educational average of all foreign-born residents in the country.

The Educational Profile of New York

Based on findings obtained from examining cross sectional data for 1980 which classifies immigrant cohorts according to period of arrival in the United States, and keeping in mind problems of equivalency and comparability between educational systems of different countries, it would appear that Borjas' thesis does not fully apply to the recent group of immigrants who have established residence in New York.

Educational attainment has not been high for earlier immigrants coming into the state. Among those who arrived prior to 1970, for example, 38 percent had eight years of schooling and less. What recent immigration has brought into New York is a bimodal inflow consisting of a large number of immigrants who parallel or actually surpass the educational achievement of American-born New Yorkers and even more strikingly the nationwide foreign-born educational average and of a contrasting small group of immigrants who are poorly equipped in formal educational resources.

One important source of variation among the foreign-born population is that individuals immigrate into the country at different times. Separating the 1980 data according to immigrant's time of arrival into the United States shows that the foreign-born population establishing residence in New York who rank equal to or surpass the educational attainment of native-born New Yorkers has been progressively on the increase with each successive cohort, while groups with little or no education have remained nearly stable over time. Whereas only 14 percent of the pre-1960 cohorts had completed four years of college, an average of 22 percent among those arriving after 1960 possessed college degrees. In 1980, the proportion with college degrees among the most recent (1975 to 1980) arrivals, 23.2 percent, was nearly equal to the educational average of American-born New Yorkers, which was 24.6 percent (Table 4.5). However, the incremental rise in educational attainment among recent immigrant flows into New York is most striking in regard to graduate education. Whereas among early (pre-1960) arrivals only 5.5 percent had attained five years or more of college, among the 1975–1980 cohort residing in New York 14 percent had attained/completed that level. Among native-born New Yorkers in 1980, the corresponding proportion was 10.3 percent.

When the proportions in the population who completed college only and those who attended/completed graduate educational levels are combined, the highest achievers are foreign-born persons who came to the United States after 1975 and were residents of New York by 1980. Their combined percentage totaled 37.2 as compared to 29.7 percent among the 1960–1969 cohorts and 19 percent among those arriving prior to 1960. The corresponding percentage for American-born New Yorkers in 1980 was 25.6 percent.

Differing from the foreign-born educational average nationwide as identified by Borjas, immigration into New York after 1970 appears to be associated with relatively higher educational attainment than in the past. The fact that a considerable number of recent immigrants, unlike their predecessors, have come into

TABLE 4.5

EDUCATIONAL ATTAINMENT OF U.S.-BORN AND FOREIGN-BORN POPULATION
AGES 25+ BY PERIOD OF ARRIVAL TO THE UNITED STATES, NEW YORK, 1980

Nativity/Year of Arrival	Total Number in Sample Population 100%	%				
		No Schooling	Completed Primary	Completed High School	Completed 4 Years College	Completed Graduate Level
U.S. Born	417,725	0.5	3.1	61.6	24.6	10.3
Foreign Born by Arrival	97,875	3.5	16.2	54.5	17.8	7.8
Pre-1060	49,428	4.3	16.6	59.5	14.0	5.5
1960–69	22,999	2.3	16.7	51.3	21.1	8.6
1970–74	13,579	2.8	16.1	49.6	21.6	9.7
1975–80	11,869	3.8	14.0	44.9	23.2	14.0

Source: U.S. Bureau of the Census, *Census of Population, 1980: Public Use Microdata Sample.* Tape Documentation. (Washington, DC: U.S. Bureau of the Census, 1983).

the state with substantive investments in education has been highlighted by other researchers as well (Papademetriou and Muller, 1987). The proportion coming to New York between 1970 and 1980 with four years or more of college totaled 20.8 percent, slightly higher than the corresponding statistic for American-born New Yorkers, 18.8 percent. More significantly, the proportion was considerably higher than that observed for the corresponding educational levels attained by immigrants who had come to the United States prior to 1970; only 12 percent reported four years or more of college education (Table 4.6).

However, international migration has also been bringing to New York an adult population with very little or no formal education reflecting the bifurcation of the educational distribution of immigrants manifested nationwide. Yet, contrary to the national profile which identifies increasing proportions of immigrants with limited schooling in each successive stream, in New York the proportion who are educationally disadvantaged in the immigrant population has more or less remained stable across the various cohorts. Among those arriving prior to 1970, the percentage with less than five years of schooling totaled 10 percent; it was 9 percent among the post-1970 arrivals, four to five times as high as the corresponding proportion among native-born New Yorkers, 2.2 percent.

The educational characteristics just described point to two very important trends. The first is that progressive increases in the proportion of immigrants coming to New York with higher educational qualifications outweigh the negative effect of those who enter with limited educational resources. The second is that

TABLE 4.6

COMPARATIVE DIFFERENCES IN EDUCATIONAL ATTAINMENT BETWEEN U.S.-BORN
AND FOREIGN-BORN RESIDENTS OF THE UNITED STATES AND NEW YORK, 1980

Population by Nativity and Period of Arrival	Educational Level Completed (Population Ages 25 +)		
	< 5 Years Primary	High School Graduate	4 Years or More of College
United States Population	3.6	66.5	16.2
U.S. Born	2.9	67.7	16.3
Foreign Born 1970–80 Arrivals	12.8	56.9	22.2
Foreign Born Pre-1970 Arrivals	11.1	51.5	13.2
New York State	3.6	66.3	17.9
U.S. Born Population	2.2	69.6	18.8
Foreign Born 1970–80 Arrivals	8.8	59.0	20.8
Foreign Born Pre-1970 Arrivals	9.9	49.0	12.0

Source: U.S. Bureau of the Census, *Census of Population: 1980*. Vol. 1. Chapter D. Detailed
Population Characteristics. Part 1. United States Summary. (Washington DC: U.S. Government
Printing Office, 1983). Table 255. U.S. Bureau of the Census, *Census of Population: 1980*. Vol. 1.
Chapter D. Detailed Population Characteristics. Part 34. New York. Section 1. Washington DC:
U.S. Government Printing Office, 1983). Table 196.

the bifurcation of the educational distribution of immigrants in New York is not
becoming more pronounced over time, as appears to be the case nationwide.
Fewer of the overall adult immigrant population with no schooling appear to
come to New York than go to other parts of the country. While their proportion
among New York's immigrants has remained stable, in the nationwide profile the
component with less than five years of schooling has increased slightly, from 11
percent to just under 13 percent (Table 4.6).

Comparative Differences in Educational Attainment among Regional and National-Origin Groups

The bimodal educational structure just described is not only a result of substantial
variations in educational attainment within the immigrant source countries but
of intracountry differences with respect to persons who choose to emigrate to the

the United States as well. In the overall educational distribution of immigrants residing in New York in 1980, Africans, followed by Asians, had attained the highest educational levels, out-ranking immigrants from all other regions and the native born. Over 38 percent of the African immigrant population and 30 percent of the Asian population held college degrees; 24 percent in each of the two populations had attained five years or more of college. Among native-born New Yorkers, the corresponding percentages in 1980 were 24 and 10 percent respectively. Third in rank with respect to educational attainment are immigrants from the Middle East and North Africa, 25.4 percent completed college and 15 percent had graduate level education (Table 4.7).

TABLE 4.7

DISTRIBUTION OF U.S.-BORN AND FOREIGN-BORN RESIDENTS AGES 25 + BY
EDUCATIONAL LEVEL COMPLETED AND REGION OF BIRTHPLACE, NEW YORK, 1980

Nativity/Region/ of Birthplace	Educational Level Completed				
	Never Attended School	Primary	High School	College	5 Years or More of College
U.S. Born	0.5	3.1	61.6	24.6	10.1
Foreign Born	3.5	16.2	54.5	17.8	7.8
Africa	1.6	3.3	31.6	38.4	24.8
North America[a]	0.3	6.5	65.4	20.6	7.1
South America	1.2	14.7	56.6	20.1	7.2
Central America & Mexico	2.0	19.0	55.0	19.6	4.4
Caribbean	1.8	16.2	58.5	18.8	4.5
Asia	6.8	10.2	29.7	30.3	23.0
Middle East/No. Africa	3.6	11.0	44.4	25.4	15.5
N/W Europe	1.1	6.2	65.3	19.9	7.4
So. Europe	5.5	34.4	48.9	8.0	3.0
East. Europe	5.6	14.8	57.0	14.5	7.8
USSR	7.5	13.0	51.4	17.0	11.0

Source: U.S. Bureau of the Census, *Census of Population, 1980: Public Use Microdata Sample.* Tape Documentation. (Washington DC: U.S. Bureau of the Census, 1983).

Note: [a] Includes Canada, Bermuda and Greenland.

The achievements of Asian immigrants are the most frequently documented and among several nationality groups have been impressive. In the larger metropolitan area in 1980, 61 percent of all Asian Indian men and women had college degrees, a rate exceeded only by recent arrivals from the Philippines among whom seven in every ten were college educated (Papademetriou and Muller, 1987). Many Asians come into the country equipped with a good command of English and a highly skilled technical education, and this combination often assures them above average earnings. In 1980, for example, the median earnings of the 2,541 Asian female physicians working full time in New York (they constituted 30% of all female physicians within the state) exceeded $30,000, 18 percent above the average median earnings of physicians in the state (Papademetriou and Muller, 1987).

Not much is known about the achievements scored by small-sized immigrant communities such as the Middle Eastern and the African. Yet their presence in New York is of importance because the human capital resources they bring to the state represent the top layers in their own countries. This is true of some of the English-speaking Caribbean immigrants as well who represent high educational ranks in the professions, management and in technical and skilled labor. This fact is not discernible in the collective educational profile of the region because of the predominance of Hispanic Caribbeans whose educational achievements are lower.

TABLE 4.8

EDUCATIONAL LEVELS COMPLETED BY THE POST-1970 FOREIGN-BORN RESIDENTS OF NEW YORK STATE BY SELECTED REGIONS/COUNTRIES OF BIRTH, NEW YORK, 1980

Region/Country of Birthplace	Educational Level Completed		
	Less than 5 Years Primary School	High School Graduates	4 or More Years of College
All Foreign-Born Residents			
Pre-1970 Arrivals	9.9	49.0	12.0
1970–80 Arrivals	8.8	59.0	20.8
Europe	10.9	53.9	19.0
Greece	8.6	39.5	9.0
Italy	20.8	27.9	6.0
Portugal	41.0	25.8	3.6
UK	1.1	88.6	33.7
Asia	8.2	73.2	40.6
China	22.1	44.8	16.4
India	1.9	87.3	60.8
Korea	4.4	83.5	45.7
Phillipines	2.2	88.9	68.2
Canada	1.1	79.4	38.8
Central America	12.1	45.7	8.1
Cuba	11.1	40.6	9.7
Dominican Republic	23.2	24.4	2.4
Haiti	6.8	64.2	9.5
Jamaica	4.2	58.4	8.2
Mexico	15.5	40.8	11.6
South America	6.1	56.7	10.8
Africa	1.7	86.9	41.5

Source: U.S. Bureau of the Census, *Census of Population: 1980*. Vol. 1. Chapter D. Detailed Population Characteristics. Part 34, New York. Section 1. (Washington DC: U.S. Government Printing Office, 1983). Table 196.

Alongside these high achievers there is a substantial number of recent entries with little or no schooling at all. Among the 1970–1980 cohort, the lowest achievers were immigrants from southern and Eastern Europe and from among Third World countries – the Caribbean collectively and Central America. Country-specific information on educational levels completed singles out the Portuguese with an astonishingly high percentage of newcomers with less than five years of schooling (41.0%), followed by Italians, Dominicans and the Chinese – roughly 21 percent of their 1970–1980 immigrant population fell into that category (Table 4.8).

Both Asia and Europe seem to represent source regions that export both the highest and the least qualified to New York. A detailed study of immigrants by individual country of origin is needed to identify further existing intraregional differences in human capital resources in order to understand the roots of the bifurcation of the educational distribution of the foreign born in the United States.

NOTES

[1] The data is by necessity limited to information obtained from the 1980 public-use micro-data file and the 1980 General Census of Population since the 1990 census count had not been released by the time this study was finalized. Whereas updated information on size, composition and residential distribution of post-1980 immigrants are available in the INS publications, information on family structure-related variables and on the educational resources of the most recent immigrants is practically nonexistent.

[2] Not all immigrant family units headed by women in 1980 contained single mothers raising minor children. While the majority probably did, female-headed families contain other configurations as well, such as older women living with grown married or unmarried children, grandchildren and other adult relatives (Alba and Trent, 1988).

5

ECONOMIC CHARACTERISTICS OF NEW YORK'S
FOREIGN-BORN RESIDENTS

This chapter examines several aspects of the economic status of New York's immigrant population having two objectives in mind. The first is to address a serious concern expounded by restrictionists regarding the detrimental impact of the immigrant presence on the economic health of the country (Borjas, 1990). Of importance to this study is the question of how this concern applies to the particular case of New York. Are foreign-born residents in the state economically unassimilated? Do they form a permanent underclass which could "further strain the provision of public revenues and exacerbate social problems of poverty already underway" in the state? From the perspective of the foreign-born community itself, the second objective is to examine what are the economic consequences of "being foreign," combined with race and gender as stratifying variables conditioning the economic prospects of immigrants in New York and their integration into the mainstream economy. The immigrant market not only determines who comes into the country but also controls long-term economic opportunities made available to each immigrant, at the same time that national origin groups manifest different incentives and aptitudes for adapting themselves to the United States (Borjas, 1990).

Three specific areas of inquiry are pursued in the following discussion: the incorporation of immigrant labor into the local economy relative to domestic labor; income attainment of the foreign born from wages and other sources of revenue; and immigrant exposure to poverty. The economic data drawn upon carry the limitations of age,[1] having been compiled in 1980 when New York was confronting a severe economic crisis.

Foreign-Born Workers in the Labor Market

Until the 1980s, virtually no systematic empirical research had been undertaken on the subject of immigrant labor in New York. Fortunately, the recent literature contributed principally by Papademetriou (1989); Papademetriou and Muller (1987); Lindsay-Lowell (1989); Marshall (1987, 1983) and Waldinger (1988, 1985, 1984) focuses their research on foreign-born workers in New York and makes use of a number of recently available data sets containing information on the labor market experiences of U.S. immigrants and on the role of their labor in the national economy (*see,* U.S. Department of Labor, 1989; Papademetriou and Muller, 1987). Data paucity still prevails in one of the most critical areas of labor force research and this is information on labor demand in specific industries and occupations at local or regional market levels. Without such information limitations are set as to what can be said regarding the role of the foreign-born resident in the labor market and his or her contribution to the productivity of the country (Meissner and Papademetriou, 1988).

Following World War II, there were radical shifts in the relationship between immigration and the structure of the U.S. economy resulting from the interaction between changes in labor demand created by new industrial growth in the country and an immigration policy that stressed social and humanitarian considerations more emphatically than the economic ones. The post-World War II demand for labor was not for special skills but for large supplies of unskilled workers at low wages. This the domestic working class did not fully respond to because by then American-born workers had job alternatives that enabled some to reject low factory wages and service jobs. Thus, large numbers of unskilled workers from abroad were welcomed, and the influx of immigrants into the U.S. economy no longer played the role of supplementing domestic labor supply (Bach and Papademetriou, 1989).

The 1965 Immigration Act increased the diversity of legal statuses under which immigrants were admitted and allowed to work in the United States, though only two of the seven categories of admission in the 1965 Immigration Act took labor market factors into consideration (*see,* Chart A, Appendix). During the 1970s, for the first time in half a century, immigrants comprised a substantial share of the growth in the U.S. labor force. Nationally, they represented 12 percent of all workers added to the national economy between 1970 and 1980,[2] but their importance was most evident in the highly urbanized areas of the nation. In the metropolitan area of Los Angeles, immigrants arriving during the 1970s comprised 69 percent of all new workers. In the New York City area, they added 338,000 workers to the labor force at a time when the employed population of the city decreased by 362,000 persons (Alba and Batutis, 1984).

Labor Market Conditions in New York

The 1970s marked a period of deteriorating economic conditions in the New York area preceding the nationwide recession of the early 1980s. New York's situation was undoubtedly influenced by the deterioration in the aggregate labor market conditions, yet the economic transformation experienced by this state was particularly traumatic because of the loss of what had been its economic power base for decades – the manufacturing production sector (Papademetriou and Muller, 1987). Unemployment rates were high (11.5 percent in New York City) and the total nonagricultural employment level in the metropolitan area fell below the 1960 level.

From the mid-1970s, manufacturing jobs had been declining sharply, particularly in New York City, and reduced earnings from this sector led to the loss of employment in retail trade. Growth of employment in the upcoming service sector at the time was not fast enough to offset the job loses incurred in manufacturing, and work participation rates declined affecting all social groups. Reactions against these deteriorating conditions led to the outmigration of approximately 800,000 predominantly white, American-born, young, college-educated New Yorkers from the city (Alba and Batutis, 1984).

Yet despite these circumstances, large numbers of immigrants continued to pour into the city. The state was absorbing 13 percent of all U.S. immigrants, with the foreign-born population increasing in size from 1.4 million in 1970 to 1.7 million in 1980. The reported foreign born share of the New York City population, which was 18 percent in 1970, reached 24 percent ten years later.

New York had a sizable immigrant presence of 596,000 workers prior to 1970, which included 267,000 women. Despite the restricted range of employment opportunities in the 1970s, 338,000 immigrants mostly from among the post-1970 arrivals obtained jobs in the New York metropolitan area in the late 1970s; in the early 1980s the number of reported immigrant workers in that area was placed at 1.2 million, or 26 percent of the total labor force (Marshall, 1987; Papademetriou and Muller, 1987). The most dramatic increases in new job attainments were for non-Hispanic Caribbeans and Asians – from 55,000 to 170,000 and from 31,200 to 108,000 respectively – while Central and South American immigrants increased their presence in New York's work force by 55 percent (Papademetriou and Muller, 1987). In 1980, one out of every twelve New York State workers and one out of every six in New York City was a recent immigrant (Alba and Trent, 1988); an estimated 38 percent of all workers in menial low wage sectors were immigrants and refugees (Marshall, 1983). Between 1980 and 1985, it is estimated that New York further opened up more jobs and that immigrants made up more than three fourths of this employment increase (Lindsay-Lowell, 1989).

It is not the case that immigrant groups took over the jobs vacated by the American-born population in the late 1970s, though some may have. Marshall (1987), in fact, points out little difference in the location of foreign-born workers during 1970 and 1980 despite differences in unemployment rates. The outmigration of the native born to a large extent led to a realignment of occupations creating new and more attractive job opportunities for domestic groups often outside of manual labor. Black men and women found employment opportunities in the public sector that offset their earlier losses in manufacturing; succeeding them were the recently arrived immigrants of the 1970s. By 1980, these immigrants came to account for 12 percent of the male and 23 percent of the female blue-collar sector, but for only 7 and 5 percent respectively of the white-collar sector (Lindsay-Lowell, 1989). New immigrants were also heavily over-represented in service occupations, and in a few years' time immigrant labor stimulated its own demand as employers came to increasingly depend on the immigrant flow.

By then the New York labor market had become sufficiently differentiated and broken increasingly into high- and low-wage sectors and into skilled and unskilled. Lindsay-Lowell (1989) writes:

> In short time immigrants created their own demand for labor
> in the leather and garment industries by utilizing labor intensive
> production processes — which held down wages — subcontract-
> ing, piece rate work and encouraging home labor, guaranteeing
> a niche of immigrant employment. (p. 68)

The mix of immigrants fitted well with this diversity of job opportunities. Hispanic and Caribbean immigrants of the 1970s gained ground in employment sectors in which black employment had declined; Asian immigrants gained across the board, particularly in skilled service sectors.

Employment and Unemployment Trends in 1980

The Population "At Work"

The profile drawn from the 1980 census identifies a reported total of 1,110,725 foreign-born workers in New York in 1980 — 632,890 men and 477,835 women. Collectively they represented 15 percent of the state's work force at the time. Foremost they were wage workers employed in the private sector (80%) — only 12 percent were public sector employees (one in every two among these worked in local government agencies) and just under 9 percent were self-employed and/or employees in their own corporations. Wage employment was less common for the American born (72%), but public service was more frequent (20%). The data do not show foreign-born workers to be more actively involved in entrepreneurial activities as compared to the native born when "self-employment" and "employee/own corporation" are taken as base indicators.

The profile of the New York population aged 16 years and older who were "at work" in 1980 indicates that the local economy had been able to absorb both its domestic and immigrant population by the end of the 1970s; among the men the participation rates were only slightly in favor of native-born residents (67.6% compared to 63.0%) (Tables 5.1 and 5.2). The gap was larger among the women: 39.1 percent among the immigrant population compared to 46.5 percent of the native born were actively "at work." The difference is partly accounted for by the relatively higher fraction of elderly individuals in the foreign-born population who, because of age, were outside the purview of the economically active seg-

TABLE 5.1

ECONOMICALLY ACTIVE AND INACTIVE MEN AGES 16+ IN NEW YORK STATE BY
NATIVITY, ETHNICITY AND REGION OF BIRTHPLACE, 1980

Nativity, Ethnicity and Region of Birth	Economically Active in Civilian Labor Force		Economically Inactive
	% at work[a]	% Unemployed	% Not Working
U.S. Born	67.6	5.3	26.5
White	69.8	4.8	24.8
Black	53.3	8.4	37.7
Hispanic	45.6	9.7	43.7
Foreign Born	63.4	4.2	32.1
Africa	62.8	5.8	31.3
North America[b]	58.0	3.7	38.0
South America	76.6	5.3	17.8
Central America[c]	75.1	5.3	19.4
Caribbean	69.5	7.2	23.0
Asia	73.3	2.9	23.3
Middle East/No. Africa	70.1	3.8	25.9
North/West. Europe	57.4	2.2	40.2
Southern Europe	60.8	3.7	35.5
Eastern Europe	56.2	3.2	40.4
USSR	43.7	3.1	53.1
All Other	56.5	5.0	38.1

Source: U.S. Bureau of the Census, *Census of Population, 1980: Public Use Microdata Sample.* Tape Documentation. (Washington, DC: U.S. Bureau of the Census, 1983).

Notes: [a] Includes those "with job" but not "at work" on designated day (roughly 1.5%).

[b] Includes Canada, Bermuda and Greenland.

[c] Includes Mexico.

TABLE 5.2

Economically Active and Inactive Women Ages 16+ in New York State
by Nativity, Ethnicity and Region of Birthplace, 1980

Nativity, Ethnicity and Region of Birth	Economically Active in Civilian Labor Force		Economically Inactive
	% at work[a]	% Unemployed	% Not Working
U.S. Born	46.5	3.4	50.0
White	46.9	3.1	49.8
Black	42.7	5.2	50.0
Hispanic	31.5	6.0	60.6
Foreign Born	39.1	3.3	57.5
Africa	42.0	4.5	53.3
North America[b]	34.8	2.3	62.8
South America	48.7	6.0	45.1
Central America[c]	53.8	5.1	41.0
Caribbean	53.7	5.3	40.9
Asia	53.8	2.5	43.5
Middle East/No. Africa	34.1	3.0	62.8
North/West. Europe	31.8	1.7	66.5
Southern Europe	29.0	2.7	68.3
Eastern Europe	27.9	2.5	69.5
USSR	20.7	2.6	76.6
Other	36.1	3.0	60.7

Source: U.S. Bureau of the Census, *Census of Population, 1980: Public Use Microdata Sample.* Tape Documentation. (Washington, DC: U.S. Bureau of the Census, 1983).

Notes: [a] Includes those "with job" but not "at work" on designated day (roughly 1.5%).

[b] Includes Canada, Bermuda and Greenland.

[c] Includes Mexico.

ment. In 1980, two thirds of the foreign-born work force was comprised of the pre-1970 cohorts of immigrants and among these close to one-third were elderly. The age structure of the post-1970 cohorts was much more favorable in maximizing labor force participation rates (*see,* Table 4.1) and new immigrants did, in fact, report higher work participation than domestic workers (Table 5.3), though they were not as frequently employed in full-time capacity all year when compared to American-born workers (55.3% vs. 62.3%).

Differences in the labor market behavior of the foreign born by region of origin showed to be dramatic. Among men, the proportions "at work" ranged from a low of 43.7 percent for the Soviets to a high of 76 percent among immigrants born in Central and South America. Women born in the Soviet Union and Eastern

TABLE 5.3

LABOR FORCE STATUS OF RECENTLY ARRIVED IMMIGRANTS
RESIDING IN NEW YORK STATE BY SEX, 1980

	Native-Born Population		Foreign-Born Population (Entry into U.S. between 1970–80)	
	Male	Female	Male	Female
Number Employed	3,565,140	2,764,903	233,171	170,227
Activity Rate	67.5%	45.8%	70.7%	48.0%
Number Unemployed	281,425	206,623	19,762	18,212
Percent of Civilian Labor Force	7.3	7.0	7.8	9.7

Source: U.S. Bureau of the Census, *Census of Population 1980*. Vol. 1. Chapter D. Detailed Population Characteristics. Part 34, New York. Section 1. (Washington, DC: U.S. Government Printing Office, 1983). Table 196.

Europe showed the lowest participation rates (20 to 27%), while Central American, Caribbean and Asian women surpassed their counterparts in all other regions, averaging an active work participation rate of 53 percent.

Without controlling for differences in demographic and skill-level characteristics, the variations in labor force behavior among New York's foreign-born residents and how these compare to American-born residents may be highlighted as follows:

—Men from Third World countries show the highest percentage "at work." With the exception of persons born in Africa, the employment rates of all Third World men were higher than those of U.S.-born men.

—With the exception of the Soviet Union, foreign-born men from all regions report employment rates that are consistently and considerably higher relative to U.S.-born black and Hispanic men.

—Foreign-born women follow the same employment pattern as their men with the exception of those born in Africa and the Middle East/North Africa region who report lower employment rates. In all other cases, foreign-born women exceed the employment rate of all groups of women born in the United States.

—The relatively low employment rate of African and Middle Eastern-born women parallels the rate of U.S.-born black and Hispanic women, but this is probably due to different structural reasons.

The Unemployed

Whether or not a local economy is capable of absorbing the available labor supply — both foreign and domestic — is reflected most particularly in the incidence of open unemployment. In 1980, unemployment rates for foreign-born men collectively (4.2%) were similar to those of American-born white men (4.8%), and this pattern held true for the women as well — 3.3 percent and 3.1 percent respectively.

American-born ethnic minorities reported the highest incidence of unemployment as compared to American-born whites and to the foreign born of each region. The chance of being unemployed in New York in 1980 was twice as high for an American-born minority male and almost 2.5 times as high for a minority woman compared to all other groups. Do these statistics suggest a process of labor displacement among minority workers resulting from the presence of immigrants in the state? This issue would need to be further investigated with a different methodology and data base.

There were significant differences in unemployment rates among immigrants which signal to the economic vulnerability of certain foreign-born groups over others in the New York area. Women and men born in the Caribbean, and Central and South America reported the highest unemployment rates (between 5 to 7%); Asians, Europeans, North Americans and Soviets reported the lowest. The highest unemployment rate reported by any foreign-born group (7%) was lower than the unemployment rate of U.S.-born black and Hispanic men. Women born in the Caribbean and in South and Central America had the highest unemployment rates of all foreign-born women and paralleled the high incidence of unemployment reported by black and Hispanic women born in the United States.

Differences in unemployment rates between immigrant and native-born populations are often examined in relation to occupation and industry-specific sectors of employment; when these are held constant, the general finding is that immigrant unemployment levels do not differ substantially from that of other workers (Papademetriou and Muller, 1987). In that context, the high unemployment rates reported among Caribbean, Central American and South American immigrants in 1980 could be in large part associated with the demise of the manufacturing sector in New York which has historically been the largest immigrant employer.

The Timing of Arrival

The labor market experience of the foreign born in New York also differed according to the timing of their arrival to the United States. This is shown in the data presented in Table 5.4 where labor force status is classified by birthplace and period of immigration: only one-third among the early cohorts (the age

TABLE 5.4

1980 LABOR FORCE STATUS OF FOREIGN-BORN RESIDENTS AGES 16+ BY PERIOD OF IMMIGRATION TO THE U.S. AND BIRTHPLACE

Labor Force Status/ Region of Birthplace	Period of Immigration			
	< 1960	1960–69	1970–74	1975–80
All Foreign-Born				
At Work	34.6	62.6	61.5	51.2
Unemployed	2.0	4.6	5.2	5.7
Africa				
At Work	42.8	73.0	63.4	41.2
Unemployed	—	5.1	6.7	6.5
North America				
At Work	36.5	59.8	64.3	54.1
Unemployed	2.5	5.0	2.7	1.3
Latin America				
At Work	53.8	63.2	60.2	52.3
Unemployed	3.7	5.7	6.0	5.9
Central America				
At Work	56.5	64.4	64.2	52.1
Unemployed	3.5	5.7	5.1	5.9
Caribbean				
At Work	50.0	63.2	58.5	52.3
Unemployed	3.0	5.5	7.0	8.0
Asia				
At Work	56.6	70.8	68.8	52.5
Unemployed	2.2	2.3	2.4	3.4
Middle East/No. Africa				
At Work	42.0	60.5	61.4	45.1
Unemployed	2.4	3.1	4.7	4.6
North/West. Europe				
At Work	35.0	63.7	63.3	53.2
Unemployed	1.5	2.9	3.4	3.0
Southern Europe				
At Work	31.5	60.8	62.4	53.9
Unemployed	2.2	4.5	4.8	4.8
Eastern Europe				
At Work	32.3	59.7	64.3	61.3
Unemployed	2.2	4.2	4.4	6.0
USSR				
At Work	22.6	50.9	59.4	41.4
Unemployed	1.2	5.4	3.2	7.7

Source: U.S. Bureau of the Census, *Census of Population, 1980: Public Use Microdata Sample.*
Technical Documentation. (Washington, DC: U.S. Bureau of the Census, 1983).

factor) and one half of the post-1975 arrivals (the recency factor) were reported "at work" in 1980, as compared to nearly two thirds of the 1960 to 1974 cohorts who were a more established group. It was the foreign born in the more recently arrived groups — those who emigrated after 1970 — who faced the greatest risk of being unemployed in 1980.

It is not possible to infer from the above information, however, whether it is duration of stay, the resourcefulness of certain cohorts, the outmigration of the unsuccessful, or propitious labor market conditions at a given time that account for these employment differentials. Two explanations have been offered in the literature to account for variations manifested between the pre-1970 and post-1970 arrivals. The first is the more conventional. It contends that productivity, growth and some assimilation and adaptation into the U.S. labor market takes place as a cohort ages; this implies that early immigrants (to the extent that they are still economically active) are more likely to be in the work force, less likely to be unemployed and more likely to have higher wages. The second explanation is more controversial. It maintains that the demographic characteristics and skill levels of persons who chose to migrate to the United States after 1970 are not as favorable as those of earlier immigrants and this makes it difficult for them to find employment (Borjas, 1990). It is this notion that has mobilized some political circles to seriously question the economic consequences of further immigration into the country under the current provisions.

A number of important trends and differences may be summarized from the findings reported: at the aggregate level, the 1980 labor market profile of New York signaled to the presence of an economically motivated immigrant population and the overall capacity of the local labor market structure to absorb the post-1970 influx of immigrants into the city despite the serious economic situation confronted in the state. Nevertheless, certain nationality groups in the foreign-born population fared worse than all others and give cause for concern because of their relatively low employment and high unemployment rates: Caribbeans, Central and South Americans and Africans. The fact that immigrant women originating from these regional areas manifested the same high incidence of unemployment as American-born black and Hispanic women may not be coincidental and should be explored in greater detail. The low employment rate of African immigrants is particularly disturbing given that their reported educational attainment at college and graduate levels surpasses other immigrant groups.

In instances where a process of labor absorption has taken place, two central questions must be addressed. Was this absorption achieved through incorporating foreign-born workers into the mainstream of the labor market structure or has it merely meant an annexation in numbers with (some) workers placed marginally on the fringe of the economy? Has labor incorporation been made possible through the restructuring of certain sectors of the economy in New York and, if so, what are the consequences of this for future immigrants? It is questions such as these that deserve continuing attention in immigration research.

Questioning the Quality of Immigrant Labor

Borjas (1990) has argued that the composition of immigrant flows entering the United States in the past two to three decades has deteriorated significantly (relative to earlier waves of immigration and to the U.S.-born population) with respect to socioeconomic background characteristics, formal educational attainment, skill qualification and productivity output. On the basis of national time-series data, the author maintains that post-1970 cohorts manifested a precipitous decline in education attainment, lower success levels in their labor market integration, and significantly lower entry wages and earning potential. Factors contributing to the consolidation of these differences in skill sorting are attributed to the particular national origin mix of the post-1970 flows, the criteria set forth in immigrant admission and the changing attractiveness of what the United States has to offer in the immigration market over time. It is changes in the latter most particularly, according to Borjas, that have attracted a different type of immigrant than the one arriving in the 1950s.

In the particular context of New York, it has been contended by independent sources that the immigrant labor supply provided to compensate for population losses incurred during the 1970s was not as qualified as its domestic predecessor, and that with the entry of immigrant workers the New York labor force shifted toward less-skilled blue-collar jobs (Alba and Batutis, 1984). Emphasis has also been placed on the widening mismatch between new job demands and immigrant skills with the restructuring of the New York economy away from a production base toward a technologically sophisticated service sector (Waldinger, 1988).

There is no systematically and empirically derived data base available to respond to either one or the other of these contentions. In the absence of a systematically compiled/comprehensive listing of existing labor shortages in New York it is difficult to assess whether or not the mismatch between labor needs and immigrant resources has actually widened. Neither have systematic evaluation studies undertaken by the industry sector on the quality performance of their work force been publicized. By way of statistical reporting, the only macrolevel indicator available to assess the "quality" of immigrant resources, qualifications and skill levels is formal education attainment. This information has limited use. It can tentatively suggest whether immigrants are qualified to hold positions in managerial, professional, technical and white-collar sectors, but is certainly not fully indicative of qualifications necessary to produce quality workmanship in technical production-related skills and service-related work. Accepting these limitations, what can the available data report on the resources of immigrant workers?

The 1980 information available on recent immigrants establishing residence in the New York area does not confirm the particular trends singled out by Borjas (1990) in his nationwide analysis of immigrant flows (see, Table 4.6). The extensive analysis of the role of immigrant labor in New York undertaken by Papademetriou and Muller (1987) clearly indicates that "it is not the poorest, the least well equipped or less resourceful U.S. immigrant who typically comes to settle in New York" (pp. 28–29). The authors describe the recent arrivals as being "of middle-class origin and professional background. As a result the immigrant profiles in education and labor force status are from the upper socioeconomic reaches of the immigrant origin countries" and "with information, the educational tools and the monetary means to leave deteriorating or downward spiralling economies in favor of better opportunities in the United States" (p. 29).

In 1980, the educational distribution of New York's foreign-born population ages 16 years and above who were reported as actively "at work" showed that 52.2 percent had completed high school, 24 percent held college degrees and 11 percent had attended or completed graduate studies. An additional 11 percent had very limited formal schooling and 2 percent had no schooling at all. The corresponding profile of the American-born worker in New York showed a higher representation of college graduates (31%) and near absence of workers with primary schooling only (1%). With respect to the percentages with high school education and graduate level studies, the relative proportions were similar between the two worker populations.

Of greater relevance to the discussion is the information provided in Table 5.5, showing changes in educational attainment by labor force status according to year of arrival to the United States. With each successive cohort who were "at work" in 1980, the percentage having completed college remained stable, while the proportion with graduate level education increased among recent immigrants arriving between 1975 and 1980. What is somewhat troubling, however, is that this same cohort reported a high percentage with graduate education in the category of the "unemployed" (7%) relative to earlier cohorts (4.6% among the 1970 and 1974 arrivals). This would suggest that even the highly educated immigrant may not have always found it easy to obtain employment in New York during the latter part of the 1970s. On the other hand, the data in no way indicate a decline over time in the percentage of workers with limited schooling.

To pursue the relationship between "quality" of immigrant resources (indexed by formal education level) and their employment in greater detail, a special analysis was made of all the subcategories of occupations listed in the labor force profile of New York State in 1980 which had the highest concentration of foreign-born workers. For each of these, the education attainment of all Ameri-

TABLE 5.5

DISTRIBUTION OF FOREIGN-BORN RESIDENTS AGES 16+ BY LABOR FORCE
STATUS AND EDUCATIONAL ATTAINMENT ACCORDING TO YEAR OF ARRIVAL
IN THE UNITED STATES, NEW YORK, 1980

Labor Force Status and Year of Arrival	Educational Attainment				
	Never Attended School	Completed Primary	Completed High School	Completed College	Attended/ Completed Graduate Levels
Total Population 16+	3.2	14.8	56.0	18.7	7.1
At Work					
<1960	1.1	8.8	56.1	23.1	10.8
1960–69	1.3	12.3	50.7	25.3	10.2
1970–74	1.8	12.5	50.7	24.3	10.4
1975–80	2.7	11.4	48.7	24.1	13.0
Unemployed					
<1960	1.7	15.9	60.0	16.6	5.7
1960–69	0.5	17.0	58.5	20.1	3.7
1970–74	1.6	13.9	60.0	19.1	4.6
1975–79	2.1	12.4	60.5	17.7	7.1
Not in Labor Force					
<1960	6.1	20.9	61.2	9.1	2.5
1960–69	3.6	18.3	58.3	16.8	2.8
1970–74	3.6	15.5	58.9	18.2	3.7
1975–80	3.6	11.6	55.4	21.9	7.4

Source: U.S. Bureau of the Census, *Census of Population, 1980: Public Use Microdata Sample.* Tape Documentation. (Washington, DC: U.S. Bureau of the Census, 1983).

can-born and foreign-born workers was plotted separately and compared for the purpose of examining the educational differentials between the two worker populations.

Table 5.6 maps out the findings and these highlight the following: in upper skill level occupations (executive, managerial, professional, technical, sales) the percentage of workers with graduate education is generally higher among foreign-born workers relative to American-born workers. The educational advantage of the foreign born in professional specialties, health technology and registered nursing is particularly striking. In sectors where the percentage of foreign-born workers with graduate education does not surpass the American-born average, immigrants maintain an education attainment commensurate to their native-born counterparts.

TABLE 5.6

PERCENTAGE OF FOREIGN- AND U.S.-BORN WORKERS WITH COLLEGE
DEGREES AND GRADUATE EDUCATION IN SELECTED OCCUPATIONAL
SUBCATEGORIES, NEW YORK, 1980

| | Foreign-Born | | U.S.-Born | |
Occupations	College Degree	Graduate Education	College Degree	Graduate Education
Executives, Adm. Managers	37.2	17.2	44.4	18.8
Management Related	53.3	24.0	54.8	18.4
Engineers, Architects & Surveyors	39.3	50.8	55.7	27.5
Math/Computer Scientists	48.3	44.4	57.3	24.8
Natural Scientists	29.6	66.2	45.4	45.2
Health Diagnosis	6.2	92.7	8.2	90.4
Registered Nurses	59.7	16.8	79.4	9.8
Health Asses./Treatment	38.1	37.4	47.1	35.1
Teachers	30.2	55.3	29.1	64.2
Health Technicians	47.1	17.0	55.6	6.7
Other Technicians	48.1	27.3	53.8	13.1
Sales	29.7	5.5	35.3	4.9
Administrative Support	33.6	5.1	31.1	2.8

Source: U.S. Bureau of the Bureau, *Census of Population, 1980: Public Use Microdata Sample*. Tape Documentation. (Washington DC: U.S. Bureau of the Census, 1983).

In the skilled/precision production sector, the percentages of workers with high school diplomas and college degrees were very similar in the two worker populations among those located in the mechanical and electrical repair sectors. Within the ranks of construction and overall precision-production workers, immigrants begin to lose their educational advantage. This is even more noticeable in the semiskilled category of workers—85 percent among the American born but only 60 percent among the foreign born completed high school. More significantly yet is the presence of foreign-born semiskilled workers with very limited or no schooling at all (Table 5.7).

To the degree, then, that formal education is recognized as a resource that bears a positive influence on quality of work performance, it can be stated that the immigrant presence has not lowered the quality of managerial, executive, professional and white-collar work nor of work in selected areas of skilled precision and repair production. At other levels, particularly in the semiskilled sector, it is likely that the entry of immigrant workers may well have had an adverse effect on the quality of workmanship and lowered the skill level of some blue-collar jobs. Such findings need to be subjected to on-the-job evaluations of worker performance to be given full credibility.

TABLE 5.7

PERCENTAGE OF FOREIGN- AND U.S.-BORN WORKERS AGES 16+ AT DIFFERENT
EDUCATIONAL LEVELS IN SELECTED AREAS OF PRECISION PRODUCTION AND
REPAIR AND SEMISKILLED LABOR CATEGORIES, NEW YORK, 1980

	Foreign Born			U.S. Born		
	Restricted Education	High School	College	Restricted Education	High School	College
Precision Production, Repair						
Mechanical Repair	11.8	71.6	15.1	2.0	81.7	15.9
Electrical Repair	7.0	68.7	21.2	1.3	74.5	23.0
Construction	19.1	67.1	11.4	2.0	77.5	19.0
Precision Production (Except Food)	16.0	63.7	15.7	1.6	72.4	23.2
Precision Production (Food)	20.7	67.7	9.8	2.4	80.3	16.3
Operators, Fabricators, Laborers						
Machine Operators	15.7	65.8	15.7	2.2	82.1	14.7
Metal, Wood, Plastic, Textile Operators	37.8	56.2	5.0	6.3	87.8	5.8
Transport, Material Movers	13.7	67.6	16.1	2.9	82.6	13.5
Handlers, Laborers	27.2	61.5	10.0	3.8	80.9	14.5

Source: U.S. Census Bureau, *Census of Population, 1980: Public Use Microdata Sample.* Tape
Documentation. (Washington DC: U.S. Bureau of the Census, 1983).

Linked to poverty in educational resources is the question of immigrants'
language skills. In 1980, only 60 percent of foreign-born New Yorkers who were
16 years of age and older indicated command of the English language: 33.5
percent in this group spoke English only and the rest spoke it "very well." Yet 18
percent in New York's adult foreign-born population spoke "little" or "no
English at all." However, speaking little or no English at all did not appear to be
closely associated with problems of employability. It is true that individuals not
knowing "any" or "only little" English appeared with more frequency among the
unemployed (23%) than in the population as a whole (18%); yet among those
actively "at work" in 1980, 16.5 percent spoke "little" or "no English at all." At
the same time, 30 percent of those who spoke English only, and 23 percent among
those who spoke English "very well" were searching for work (Table 5.8).

That absence of formal schooling and lack of command of the English language have not prevented the insertion of some immigrants into gainful employment is evidence of the bimodal occupational structure of New York City. Parallel
to and in direct contrast with the technologically sophisticated skilled-service

TABLE 5.8

SELF-REPORTED PROFICIENCY IN ENGLISH OF NEW YORK'S FOREIGN-BORN
RESIDENTS AGES 16+ BY LABOR FORCE STATUS, 1980

Proficiency Level in Speaking English	Total 16+	Employed (N = 53,586)	Unemployed (N = 4,185)	Not in Labor Force (N = 51,348)
Only Language Spoken	33.5	32.9	30.1	34.5
Very Well	26.8	28.9	23.3	24.8
Well	21.6	21.7	23.7	21.5
Not Well	12.8	12.4	16.2	13.0
Not At All	5.3	4.1	6.7	6.2
Total	100.0	100.0	100.0	100.0

Source: U.S. Bureau of the Census, *Census of Population, 1980: Public Use Microdata Sample*. Tape Documentation. (Washington DC: U.S. Bureau of the Census, 1983).

sector and the growth of professional specialization that has developed in New York, jobs are still available in the larger metropolitan area for the untrained and unskilled in the service industries. These absorb not only immigrants with limited educational resources but qualified immigrants as well who are ready to accept low-skill jobs as entry points (Cafferty *et al.*, 1983). Since the erosion of the manufacturing production sector which historically provided low-skilled immigrants with work placement and security, absorption into low-level service jobs has become a predominant trend and served to neutralize what otherwise could have built up into a community of displaced workers.

The educationally less resourceful immigrant has also been absorbed by the family and ethnic-based entrepreneurial system. Established by resourceful immigrants as a route for entry into the local economy, the small-scale immigrant-owned business has shown to be not only profitable, but an important employment outlet for newcomers who lack the qualifications and resources to become absorbed in the wider New York labor market. Ethnic businesses are unique in their use of "cultural barriers" and "ethnic affinities" to gain privileged access to markets and labor sources (Wilson and Portes, 1980). These include ethnic preferences in hiring, sustained patronage by co-ethnics and the use of ethnic resources in business. More importantly, they represent a system of larger social and economic relations with well-defined reciprocal personal and professional obligations (Papademetriou and Muller, 1987).

Does the presence of small-scale ethnic-based activities have negative effects on New York? The general sentiment is that the economic recovery of New York City in the 1980s has been fueled by the growth occurring in the small business sector, particularly in the area of food services, construction, apparel—all sites of heavy immigrant entrepreneurship.

The larger question that needs to be posed, however, concerns the impact that this duality in the structure of the labor market bears upon the future mobility of the less resourceful immigrant in New York. Some have viewed ethnic entrepreneurship and the benefits it provides to their co-ethnics as positive developments. Others, however, have expressed concern about the "pre-capitalist" and paternalistic relationships that are engendered in the employer and employee relationship (Bonacich, 1973). Though this alternative sector undeniably reinforces stable social and economic relationships, there is some danger that it could, on a continuing basis, restrict the insertion of young immigrants into the mainstream economy, while at the same time providing considerable benefits to owners and employers.

The Marginalization of Immigrant Workers in the Labor Market

The literature has established that ethnicity and race are important labor market differentiating variables in the national population. The question raised here is whether immigrants face the repercussions of similar problems because they are foreigners. Hirschman and Kraly (1988) have suggested that immigrants occupy the same marginal positions in the economic structure parallel to that of the American-born ethnic minorities in relation to the white majority. They propose, in fact, that the standard framework for the analysis of the economic progress of immigrants be similar to the perspective applied to study American-born ethnic minorities.

The information presented in Tables 5.1 and 5.2 provides some indication of the economic marginality of American-born ethnic minorities and of some foreign-born nationality groups in New York. Data presented in Table 5.9 detail further the linkages observed between birthplace, race, gender and labor force status. The percentages computed represent ethnic/race-specific activity rates by sex for foreign- and American-born New Yorkers, indicating in each case the proportions within each race and ethnic group who were "at work," "unemployed" and "outside the labor force" in 1980.

The findings are listed below, but should be interpreted with caution since no statistical analysis has been introduced to control for employment-related variables.

> —Being a nonwhite foreign-born person is not a deterrent to obtaining work in New York State. All nonwhites in the foreign-born population reported higher employment rates than foreign-born whites. Within the nonwhite group of immigrants, the general patterning points to Asians reporting the highest work participation rates, Spanish descent groups reporting the lowest, with black immigrants in between.

TABLE 5.9

RACE/ETHNIC-SPECIFIC LABOR FORCE RATES OF FOREIGN- AND U.S.-BORN
RESIDENTS OF NEW YORK STATE BY SEX, 1980

Labor Force Status, Sex, Nativity	All Persons	White	Black	Chinese	Indian Asians	Other Asians	(Write-in) Spanish
At Work: Men							
Foreign Born	63.4	60.3	67.3	69.9	81.6	75.2	68.3
U.S. Born	67.6	69.8	53.2	64.7	49.2	66.9	45.8
At Work: Women							
Foreign Born	39.1	32.0	57.4	57.5	50.8	53.3	43.1
U.S. Born	46.5	46.9	44.7	57.8	30.1	58.8	33.2
Unemployed: Men							
Foreign Born	4.3	3.4	7.4	3.0	4.0	2.2	7.0
U.S. Born	5.3	4.8	8.4	4.1	1.5	6.5	9.8
Unemployed: Women							
Foreign Born	3.3	2.7	5.2	2.1	4.5	2.3	5.6
U.S. Born	3.4	3.1	5.2	3.4	3.0	3.1	6.0
Outside Labor Force: Men							
Foreign Born	32.1	36.1	25.0	26.9	14.2	22.4	24.4
U.S. Born	26.5	24.8	37.7	30.8	49.2	26.0	43.9
Outside Labor Force: Women							
Foreign Born	57.5	65.2	37.2	40.0	44.5	44.3	51.2
U.S. Born	50.0	49.8	49.9	38.7	66.8	38.0	60.6

Source: U.S. Bureau of the Census, *Census of Population, 1980: Public Use Microdata Sample.* Tape Documentation. (Washington DC: U.S. Bureau of the Census, 1983).

—The 1980 unemployment profile shows foreign-born black men and women of Spanish descent to be at a greater disadvantage relative to other racial/ethnic groups: roughly 7 percent of the foreign-born men and 5.5 percent of foreign-born women who reported themselves as black and of Spanish descent were seeking work, followed by foreign-born Asian Indian men and women—4 percent each. White and Asian ethnics (excluding Indians) showed the lowest incidence of unemployment: only 3 percent of the men and 2.5 percent of the women were affected.

—Foreign-born black men and women report considerably higher employment rates than U.S.-born blacks; the differential is approximately 13 percentage points higher. It is also 23 percentage points higher for foreign-born men of Spanish descent and 10 percentage points higher for women of Spanish descent, compared to U.S. Hispanics.

—The relationship between race, ethnicity and labor force status is different for U.S.-born New Yorkers. White men report higher employment rates than the nonwhite. Employment rates in 1980 were particularly low (under 50%) for U.S.-born Asian Indians and Hispanics. U.S.-born Chinese and Asian women (excluding Indians) reported higher employment rates than white women, while U.S.-born Indian and Hispanic women showed lowest participation in the work force. There were almost twice as many U.S.-born Chinese and other Asian women (excluding Indians) working compared to U.S.-born Indian and Hispanic women. For U.S.-born women and men alike, the incidence of unemployment is greatest for blacks and Hispanics.

—There is an unexplainable inconsistency in labor force behavior between U.S.-born and foreign-born Asian Indians. Those born abroad report an employment rate of 81 percent, compared to only 49 percent for Indian men born in the United States. The corresponding rates for Indian women are 50.8 percent and 30.1 percent. Further research is needed to explain why foreign-born Indians appear to have less of an option to not work compared to their counterparts born in the United States.

Combining the information presented in Tables 5.1 and 5.2 with the data in Table 5.9, it is possible to identify those foreign-born persons who in 1980 were least integrated into the labor market by birthplace, race and ethnicity. They are, by region of birthplace, Caribbeans, South and Central Americans and Africans; by race and ethnicity, blacks and Spanish descent groups.

Nevertheless, the economic marginality observed to characterize these particular immigrant groups in no way parallels the disadvantaged labor market position of American-born blacks and Hispanics. This disparity is often accounted for by the educational advantage that black and Hispanic Caribbeans, South and Central Americans and black African immigrants have over native-born blacks and Hispanics. Since appropriate controls have not been introduced into the findings presented in Table 5.9, no definitive statement may be made · regarding differences in human capital resources between the two groups. But it may also be the case that differences in employment status between the races and ethnics in these populations result from unobserved residuals, which are neither quantifiable nor measurable, that enable some foreign-born groups, regardless of race and ethnicity, to be more compatible with the U.S. labor market than some native ones (Papademetriou, 1989).

The findings identified in this discussion, though tentative, strongly suggest that variables of race and ethnicity in immigrant populations need to be identified and treated as stratifying variables in labor market studies and other areas of immigration research. Whether factors of race and ethnicity have different meanings and consequences depending on whether the individual is native or foreign born is an extremely important body of information and one that is necessary to explore in order to gain a comprehensive understanding of how and under what circumstances discrimination operates. It is also essential to study the internal differentiation within racial and ethnic populations to demonstrate the complexity and variety within groups such as the black (or the Hispanic), which are often treated as if they were monolithic (Bryce LaPorte, 1977). This complexity is obscured by the current practice in most federal and state agency reporting systems to collapse native- and foreign-born populations and disaggregate them by racial and ethnic characteristics only without specifying birthplace, making it thereby impossible to detect whether or not these variables present different outcomes according to nativity.

Income Attainment among New York's Foreign-Born Residents

After accounting for the incorporation of the various immigrant groups into the labor market of New York, the discussion now turns to the economic assimilation of the foreign born from the perspective of the income they have attained.

Three lines of interest guide the organization of this discussion: identify the different sources of income to which the foreign-born population has access; compare the income position of the foreign born relative to native-born residents; and single out divergences among nationality groups within the foreign-born community in respect to income attainment. Major emphasis is placed on labor earnings, for though not the only meaningful index of economic integration, wage/salary income is the best single indicator of success.

Total Income

Table 5.10 presents information showing the fraction of individuals in the foreign and American-born populations aged 16 years and over who had access to the different sources of income identified in the 1980 census based microdata file and the total value received from each source. The percentages are computed on

TABLE 5.10

MEDIAN INCOME OF FOREIGN- AND U.S.-BORN PERSONS AGES 16+ FROM
"ALL SOURCES" FOR THOSE WHO ARE INCOME RECIPIENTS, NEW YORK, 1980

Income Source	Median Income Foreign Born (U.S.$)	% in Pop. 16+ Receiving this Source	Median Income U.S. Born (U.S.$)	% in Pop. 16+ Receiving this Source
Wages/Salary	9,675	51.8	10,005	62.0
Self-Income: Non-farm Sources	8,505	4.0	6,755	4.1
Property Income: Interest, Dividend, Rentals	1,005	25.0	505	29.9
Public Assistance	2,365	5.3	2,405	4.7
All Sources[a]	7,405	81.9	8,705	84.2

Source: U.S. Bureau of the Census, *Census of Population, 1980: Public Use Microdata Sample.* Tape Documentation. (Washington DC: U.S. Bureau of the Census, 1983).

Note: [a] "All Sources" represents, in addition to the above sources, income that foreign-born persons 65+ received from Social Security during 1979 which had a median value of $3,485 per person and reached 75.3% of the population 65+. U.S.-born persons, in addition to the above sources, received a median income of $3,605 per person from Social Security during 1979, paid to 79.9 % of the population 65+, as well as self-income from farm sources and from "other" sources such as compensations, pensions, alimony, child support, etc. which were not reported for foreign-born residents. In all cases the median value for income "all sources" has taken into account negative income (losses) incurred in self-employment income and property income.

the basis of the numbers of persons who were actual income recipients of one, several or all sources of income, and not on the total population ages 16 and over. The data in Table 5.11 differentiate the income attainment by source and gender to identify disparities between male and female income patterns.

As a collective, 81.9 percent of New York's foreign-born residents as compared to 84.2 percent among the American-born population received income from at least one source in 1980. The median income attained from all income sources during that year totaled $7,415 for the foreign born and $8,705 for the native-born resident. Comparisons within gender across the two populations showed little differences in the percentages who were income recipients: 91 percent of the men in each population and 76 percent of the women reported income from at least one source. The value of the total income received, however, differed significantly among the men and between gender groups. Whereas the typical male immigrant in New York attained a median income of $10,215, American-born men had access to $13,500. Among the women, the total median

TABLE 5.11

MEDIAN INCOME OF FOREIGN- AND U.S.-BORN MEN AND WOMEN AGES 16+ FROM
"ALL SOURCES" FOR THOSE WHO ARE INCOME RECIPIENTS, NEW YORK, 1980

Income Source	Median Income Foreign Born (U.S. $)		% in Pop. 16+ Receiving Income		Median Income U.S. Born (U.S. $)		% in Pop. 16+ Receiving Income	
	Men	Women	Men	Women	Men	Women	Men	Women
Wages/Salary	12,005	7,005	63.7	42.2	14,005	7,005	72.6	52.8
Self-Income: Non-farm Sources	10,005	5,005	7.0	8.1	9,005	3,005	6.8	1.9
Property Income: Interest, Dividends, Rentals	1,005	925	31.7	19.7	505	515	37.0	23.8
Public Assistance	2,255	2,405	3.4	7.0	2,165	2,505	2.9	6.3
All Sources	10,215	5,105	90.5	75.0	13,500	5,745	91.7	77.7

Source: U.S. Bureau of the Census, *Census of Population, 1980: Public Use Microdata Sample.* Tape
Documentation. (Washington DC: U.S. Bureau of the Census, 1983).

incomes reported were very similar—$5,105 and $5,745 respectively for the
foreign- and American-born—but were significantly lower than male income. Sex
differentials in income attainment were highest among native-born New Yorkers:
women's total income represented about 42 percent of male total income; among
immigrants the equivalency level was 50 percent.

Recently arrived immigrants, as expected, reported a lower median income
than other cohorts, though it is still difficult to establish the time period after
which they are expected to reach parity in income with the native born. Income
assimilation has generally shown to proceed at different paces and certainly
varies by nationality groups. In the case of New York, time of entry into the United
States accounted for the following differences: arrivals during the 1970s averaged
median incomes totaling $11,475 for the men and $6,972 for the women. Those
who came prior to 1970 reported $15,221 and $7,329 respectively, paralleling the
averages of American-born men and women in 1980—$15,673 and $7,643 respectively. But since the pre-1970 cohort is an open category, it is not possible to
establish from this information the time period required for parity.

Income in the form of rentals, dividends and interest were reported by one
foreign-born resident in every four and by approximately one in every three
among the native born, with significant differences in the value received between
the two. Foreign-born New Yorkers received twice as high a median income from
investments in 1980 ($1,000 yearly) as compared to American-born residents

($505). Property income was more closely associated with persons from northwestern Europe, North America and the Soviet Union (most probably the older established population) and least frequently among those born in the Caribbean and South and Central America.

Income from self-employment showed to be an important source of income, but available to only a small fraction of New York's population: only 4 percent in each of the two populations reported revenues from self-employment. The median value attained showed to be substantially higher for the foreign born ($8,505) as compared to the native-born resident ($6,755) signaling the importance of small-scale ethnic entrepreneurship in the economic life of select immigrant communities. Self-employment was more closely associated with earlier immigrants and, among those who were post-1970 arrivals, Asians and Europeans headed the list. The least likely nationality groups to be linked to self-employment were Caribbeans and Central and South Americans.

The differences among native-born and foreign-born residents who were public assistance participants in New York in 1980 was insignificant (4.7% vs. 5.3% or a 0.6 differential), with women being major recipients (Table 5.11). The New York figures were considerably lower than the national welfare participation rate which was 9 percent among the foreign born and 8 percent among American-born persons at the time (Borjas, 1990).

The general perception has been that immigrants are less welfare prone than American-born minority groups because they can count on strong supportive networks. This may be too broad a generalization and most likely drawn from a specific refugee experience. Certainly, it is not the case for immigrants coming from the Caribbean and South and Central America. The representation of these three regions in the listing of foreign-born public assistance recipients in New York was shown to be disproportionately high, particularly among women, as compared to other national origin groups. Immigrant women heading households with 'husband absent from the home' had a visible presence among public assistance recipients, though they showed less dependency on welfare than women heads-of-household born in this country.

Income from Labor

The data underlying the wage and salary profile of New York's foreign and native-born workers provide a measure of the labor market assimilation rate of its immigrant population. A smaller fraction of persons in the foreign-born population (52%) were wage/salary recipients than native-born workers (62%). This is in part explained by the older age structure of immigrants, which kept some out of the work force, and the lower work participation of adult youths ages 16 to 24 among foreign-born New Yorkers as compared to the native born.

Wages and salaries earned in New York in 1980 were slightly more favorable to the American-born male worker — the median value reported was $10,005 as compared to $9,675 for the foreign born. Immigrant men were typically earning wages/salaries equivalent to 85 percent of the median labor income of American-born men. Among women workers, however, there were no corresponding differences in annual earnings — $7,000 in each case. Several factors may account for the lower earnings among immigrant men. They were concentrated in occupational and industrial sectors where wages were depressed because of the economic recession (Papademetriou and Muller, 1987) and were less likely to be year-round full time employed compared to the native born. Among women the situation was reversed. Female immigrant workers reported year-round full-time employment more frequently than American-born workers.[3]

The earning power of immigrants varied by birthplace, gender, race and ethnicity, and the patterns that describe these variations reflect one measure of the differential labor market assimilation rate among immigrants at the same time that they provide an index of economic inequality among this group. Tracking differences in the earning power of immigrants shows that national origin does play a role in conditioning income assimilation, but this is not in the absence of powerful variables such as educational attainment and occupational background.

In 1980, immigrants from northwestern Europe, Eastern Europe, the Middle East and North Africa reported the highest wage/salary incomes — the median value of earnings ranged from $12,005 to $16,005 and exceeded the reported labor earnings of American-born workers (Table 5.12). The lowest median incomes from wages/salaries were reported for immigrants born in South and Central America and the Soviet Union — the values were under $9,000. Labor earnings of North American and southern European immigrants converged with the median wage/salary income of native-born residents ($10,005) and exceeded that of the Asian-born worker ($9,675).

Whether or not race and ethnicity factors operated as a stratifying variable to influence the wage and salary income of immigrants in New York was looked into tentatively, and the findings obtained from classifying regional-origin groups by race and ethnicity in relation to labor earnings are shown in Table 5.13. The observations made are from data which have not been standardized for education and occupation.[4]

Among white ethnics, those born in Asia showed to have highest earnings from wage/salary income — $12,505; those born in Central America reported the lowest — $7,805. Among black ethnics, those born in Central America reported the highest wage and salary income — $10,005; those from South America had the lowest — $8,005. Ethnics of Spanish descent consistently show to be the most disadvantaged group. Those born in the Americas and in the Caribbean report the lowest earnings from labor relative to all other groups, ranging between $6,505

TABLE 5.12

MEDIAN WAGES AND SALARY INCOME PER PERSON AGES 16+ BY
NATIVITY AND REGION OF BIRTHPLACE, NEW YORK, 1980

Nativity/ Region of Birthplace	Median Wages/ Salary Income (U.S. $)
U.S. Born	10,005
Foreign Born	9,675
Africa	9,005
North America[a]	10,005
South America	8,005
Central America[b]	8,305
Caribbean	8,670
Asia	9,165
Middle East/North Africa	11,005
Northern/Western Europe	12,005
Southern Europe	10,005
Eastern Europe	11,005
USSR	8,900

Source: U.S. Bureau of the Census, *Census of Population, 1980: Public Use Microdata Sample*. Tape Documentation. (Washington DC: U.S. Bureau of the Census, 1983).

Notes: [a] Includes Canada, Greenland and Bermuda.

[b] Includes Mexico.

TABLE 5.13

MEDIAN WAGE AND SALARY INCOME PER PERSON AGES 16+ RECEIVING WAGES
AND SALARY BY NATIVITY, SELECTED REGIONS OF BIRTHPLACE,
RACE AND ETHNICITY, NEW YORK, 1980

Nativity/ Region of Birthplace	Median Wage/Salary Income				
	All Persons (U.S.$)	White (U.S.$)	Black (U.S.$)	Spanish (U.S.$)	Asian (U.S.$)
Foreign Born	9,675	10,005	9,125	7,005	9,005
Africa	9,005	10,005	8,505	2,165[b]	—
South America	8,005	8,805	8,005	7,235	10,445[b]
Central America[a]	8,305	7,805	10,005	7,805	—
Caribbean	8,670	9,005	9,185	6,505	8,305[b]
Asia	9,165	12,505	10,545[b]	8,865[b]	9,005
U.S. Born	10,005	10,005	9,145	6,400	9,015

Source: U.S. Bureau of the Census, *Census of Population, 1980: Public Use Microdata Sample*. Tape Documentation. (Washington DC: U.S. Bureau of the Census, 1983).

Notes: [a] Includes persons born in Mexico.

[b] Universe is too insignificant to have validity.

to $7,500 yearly. Spanish Caribbeans averaged $2,660 less than black Caribbeans; Spanish Central Americans averaged $2,200 less than black Central Americans, and Spanish South Americans close to $800 less than black South Americans. The disadvantage holds true for the U.S.-born Hispanic population as well. Comparing the earnings of blacks and whites across the various regional-origin groups indicates that among Africans, the differential flowed in the expected direction: white ethnics reported a $1,500 advantage in median income over blacks. This was true of South Americans as well except that the differential was of lower magnitude — $800. In Central America, however, the situation was reversed. Black ethnics reported wage and salary incomes $2,200 above those of white ethnics from that region. Among Caribbeans, black ethnics also held an advantage over white ethnics, but considerably less than might have been expected.

Income attained from wages/salaries showed generally to be responsive to educational attainment and occupation. When the expected relationship between the variables did not hold true, it was more likely in reference to immigrants and to women.

Differences in earnings by gender were substantial in the two populations (Table 5.14). Immigrant women earned the equivalent of 58 percent of the wage/salary income of immigrant men; American-born women fared worse, their earnings represented one half of the male earnings. The disparities are partly accountable for by the lower frequency of full-time year-round employment among both groups of women: only 23.3 percent of the pre-1970 cohorts, 36.3 percent of recent arrivals and 23.7 percent of native-born women were within that category.

In Table 5.14, the relationship of educational attainment and labor earnings is examined separately by gender. Higher education is definitely associated with higher earnings, but does the positive association persist when immigrants are compared to the American-born worker and when women are compared to men?

The data suggest that at commensurate levels of education attainment, foreign-born men do not earn as much as American-born men; the women generally do. At equivalent levels of education, the median value of the wage/salary income of foreign-born men in 1980 represented between 90 to 93 percent of the earnings of American-born men. The one exception was persons who had attained primary schooling only. Their median earnings were roughly the same in the two populations. By contrast, the median wage/salary income of foreign-born women exceeded the earnings of their American-born counterparts at all educational levels except the graduate. Barring the latter, immigrant women earned the equivalent of 110 to 117 percent of the earnings of their American-born counterparts, whereas at the graduate level their wage/salary income represented a corresponding fraction of only 92.8 percent. One possible factor at the root of this

TABLE 5.14

MEDIAN WAGES/SALARY INCOME PER PERSON AGES 16+ IN THE WORK FORCE BY
NATIVITY, EDUCATIONAL ATTAINMENT AND SEX, NEW YORK, 1980

Educational Level Completed	Median Income for Men 16+			Median Income for Women 16+		
	Foreign Born (U.S.$)	U.S. Born (U.S.$)	Foreign Born as % of U.S. Born	Foreign Born (U.S.$)	U.S. Born (U.S.$)	Foreign Born as % of U.S. Born
No Schooling and Less than Primary Completed	8,005	7,535	106.2	5,005	5,005	100.0
Primary	10,005	10,005	100.0	5,725	5,205	109.9
Secondary	10,895	12,005	90.7	6,670	6,005	111.0
College	14,005	15,005	93.3	9,150	7,835	116.7
5 Years or More College	20,005	22,005	90.9	13,005	14,005	92.8

Source: U.S. Bureau of the Census, *Census of Population, 1980: Public Use Microdata Sample.* Tape Documentation. (Washington DC: U.S. Bureau of the Census, 1983).

disparity is that graduate specializations pursued by native-born women may be more closely linked to higher paying occupations. The association between higher education attainment and higher earnings is stronger among native men as compared to the foreign born. Among women this association is uneven.

Completion of secondary schooling did not act favorably in increasing the earnings of immigrant workers over those holding primary certificates only; for American-born men, however, it did, raising their median wage/salary income from $10,080 to $12,000. Attainment of a college degree also raised the earning power of foreign-born women substantially, from a median income of $6,670 to $9,150 – a $2,480 jolt in median earnings that was not matched by American-born women; obtaining a college degree increased their median earnings by only $1,830. Graduate level education, however, was more highly rewarded for American-born men and women as compared to the foreign born. The increases in median earnings between college completion and graduate level education were $6,000 and $4,000 respectively for the two groups of women. For the men, the rewards were even more dramatic, raising earnings by $6,000 among immigrants and $7,000 among the American-born.

Gender appeared to operate more sharply in the American-born population as a stratifying variable influencing the association of higher education attainment and higher earnings. This trend is evident when gender differences in earnings are compared between immigrant and native-born New Yorkers in relation to education attainment. The 1980 median earnings of foreign-born women represented 60 percent of the earnings of foreign-born men at commensurate post-primary levels of education including the graduate. The earnings of American-born women were equivalent to only 50 percent of male earnings at all pre-graduate educational levels; at the graduate level their earnings increased in equivalency level to represent 63 percent of male earnings. The disparity could be explained by possible differences in the occupational specialization of American-born men and women holding graduate degrees.

Variations in labor earnings in relation to occupation are documented in Table 5.15, and the relationship between these two variables, as mediated by birthplace and gender, is expanded in Table 5.16. Six distinctive patterns are immediately discernible from the information presented.

1) For all but the immigrant woman worker, the association is consistent between earnings and the ranking of occupational categories. When these are ranked by wage/salary levels from highest to lowest, they appear in the following order: managerial/professional; skilled precision and repair production; technical, and nonprofessional white-collar jobs; semiskilled operators, fabricators and laborers; and service-related occupations.

2) The above association presents itself differently to the immigrant woman. In her case, it is the technical/nonprofessional white-collar sector (and not skilled production) that offers her the second highest earnings and service-related occupations, (not semiskilled blue-collar jobs) that offer her the third highest earnings.

3) Foreign-born men do not fare as well in their earnings in most occupational groupings when compared to American-born men. Except for service-related occupations, their earnings represented 90 percent of the earnings of U.S.-born men. Professional, executive and managerial positions operated as best equalizers: foreign-born men earned the equivalent of 95 percent of the wages and salary income of American-born men.

4) The earnings of foreign-born women exceed those of U.S.-born women in managerial and professional groupings; technical and nonprofessional white-collar jobs and service-related occupations. In the first two categories, their earnings were equivalent to anywhere between 109 and 112 percent of the earnings of U.S.-born women. In service-related occupations,

the equivalency was 179 percent. They fare the worst in skilled precision and repair production where their earnings are equivalent to 82 percent of the earnings of the American-born woman worker.

5) Gender differences in earnings by occupation are greater in the native population as compared to the foreign born. The median wage/salary income of U.S.-born women, overall, represents 53 percent of male earnings. The exceptions are managerial positions and the professions in which the corresponding equivalency is 63 percent, and service-related jobs where women earn 40 percent of what their men earn.

6) Foreign-born women's earnings are equivalent to 68 percent of their men's earnings in managerial positions and professional specializations, nonprofessional white-collar jobs and service-related occupations. The most significant gender differential in immigrant earnings appeared in skilled precision and repair production and semiskilled labor where immigrant women earned only 40 percent and 50 percent respectively of male earnings.

TABLE 5.15

MEDIAN WAGES/SALARY INCOME PER PERSON AGES 16+ IN THE WORK FORCE BY
BROAD OCCUPATIONAL CATEGORY, NATIVITY AND FOREIGN- AND
U.S.-BORN INCOME DIFFERENTIALS, NEW YORK, 1980

| Occupational Category | Median Wages/Salary Income | | Income of Foreign Born as % of U.S. Born |
	Foreign Born (U.S.$)	U.S. Born (U.S.$)	
Managerial and Professional	16,005	16,005	100.0
Technical, Sales, Administrative	9,185	8,705	105.5
Precision Production, Craft, Repair	12,005	14,915	80.4
Service Occupations	7,505	4,895	153.3
Operators, Fabricators, Laborers	7,005	9,505	73.6
Unemployed[a]	5,005	5,005	100.0

Source: U.S. Bureau of the Census, *Census of Population, 1980: Public Use Microdata Sample.* Tape Documentation. (Washington DC: U.S. Bureau of the Census, 1983).

Notes: [a] Represents people who were unemployed with previous work experience, but who have not worked in the five years preceding the census. The questionnaire asked for information on the last occupation for people who worked since 1975.

TABLE 5.16

MEDIAN WAGES/SALARY INCOME PER MEN AND WOMEN AGES 16+ IN THE
WORK FORCE BY BROAD OCCUPATIONAL CATEGORY, NATIVITY AND FOREIGN-
AND U.S.-BORN INCOME DIFFERENTIALS, NEW YORK, 1980

| | Foreign Born | | U.S. Born | | Income of Foreign Born as % of U.S. Born | |
Broad Occupational Category	Men	Women	Men	Women	Men	Women
Managerial and Professional	19,005	13,015	20,005	11,965	95.0	108.7
Technical, Sales, Administrative	12,005	8,005	13,505	7,145	88.8	112.0
Precision Production, Craft, Repair	13,360	6,605	15,005	8,005	89.0	82.4
Service Occupations	8,845	6,035	8,005	3,365	110.5	179.3
Operators, Fabricators, Laborers	10,005	5,620	11,185	6,005	89.4	93.0
Unemployed[a]	5,145	3,805	5,505	4,005	93.4	95.5

Source: U.S. Bureau of the Census, *Census of Population, 1980: Public Use Microdata Sample.* Tape Documentation. (Washington DC: U.S. Bureau of the Census, 1983).

Note: [a] Represents people who were unemployed with previous work experience who have not worked in the five years preceding the census. The census questionnaire asked for information on the last occupation for people who worked 1975.

Poverty among New York's Foreign-Born Residents

The prevalence of immigrant poverty is now examined as part of the economic profile of the foreign-born New Yorker. Two data sets are examined: the 1980 poverty rates of the different national origin groups and the proportions within the population who reported incomes "200 percent and more above the poverty threshold."[5] Both are indicators of existing economic inequality in the state.

The poverty rate represents the fraction of the population where household income is below the officially defined poverty line—the latter being calculated on the basis of family size, family income and household position.[6] Because the poverty rate summarizes the influence of all these factors on the economic welfare of foreign-born families, it is considered by some to be a much more encompassing indicator of economic well-being than the measure of labor absorption and income earned from labor (Borjas, 1990). The proportion within the population in the income bracket "200 percent and more above the poverty threshold" documents the other side of the polarity. When viewed in conjunction with poverty rates, this measure indicates tentatively which particular national origin groups in the foreign-born population tend to be more visibly characterized by individuals representing a mix of economic resources and, conversely, those who appear to be economically the more homogenous on one or the other side of the polarity.

On the basis of nationwide data, it has been argued that while overall poverty rates in the United States declined slightly between 1970 and 1980, the poverty of immigrants increased over the same time period, exceeding the national trend (Borjas, 1990). In 1980, for example, the fraction of individuals below the poverty line nationwide was 11.7 percent in the native-born population, but 15.2 percent among immigrants. More critically, a comparison of the poverty rates of various cohorts of immigrants over the 1970 and 1980 period showed substantial increases in poverty among successive immigrant waves. The 1965–1969 cohort indicated a poverty rate of 18 percent soon after arrival (in 1970), whereas the cohorts of the late 1970s reported (in 1980) a corresponding rate of 29.0 percent (Borjas, 1990). Borjas attributes the source of this increasing evidence of poverty "to changes in the national origin composition of immigrant flows along with the impact of these changes on skills and on the labor market attachment of immigrants" (p. 148).

What is the position of the immigrant population residing in New York State in relation to the nationwide findings? In 1980, the fraction of individuals who were living below the poverty line in New York State was 14.2 percent in the foreign-born population and 12.5 percent among American-born residents. The differences in relation to nationwide trends was minuscule (one percent and less in the two populations). The New York data do show that in foreign-born poverty groups, the women are the most vulnerable.

Length of stay in the United States showed to be conducive to reducing the incidence of poverty among the different cohorts (Table 5.17). Those who arrived in the late 1970s reported poverty rates in 1980 which were almost four times higher than those reported by the pre-1960 cohorts and more than double the rate of the 1960–1969 cohorts. Based on these data alone, however, it cannot be surmised whether the higher incidence of poverty among the recently arrived immigrants is to be attributed to the recency of their entry into the country or poverty in human resources and skills as Borjas (1990) suggests.

Age and Gender

Data inclusive of all foreign-born residents grouped by age and gender show that in relative terms to their numbers the largest single category of individuals living below the poverty line in 1980 were infants, children, teenagers and young adults. On the average, between one in every four or one in every five immigrants in the various age groupings under age 25 was living in poverty (Table 5.18). The immigrant poverty rate declines after age 25 and continues to recede until immigrants reach age 65. From that age onwards, the population is once again at

TABLE 5.17

FRACTION OF INDIVIDUALS LIVING BELOW POVERTY LINE AND THOSE WITH
INCOMES 200% AND MORE ABOVE THE POVERTY THRESHOLD BY SEX AND
PERIOD OF ARRIVAL TO THE UNITED STATES[a], NEW YORK, 1980

Period of Arrival to the U.S.	Fraction Living Below Poverty Level		Fraction with Incomes 200% Plus Above Poverty Threshold	
	Men	Women	Men	Women
All Foreign Born	12.3	15.8	64.1	58.3
Arrival < 1960	6.5	11.8	72.9	62.5
Arrival 1960–69	10.8	14.6	68.3	63.4
Arrival 1970–74	14.1	18.0	59.4	54.7
Arrival 1975–80	24.0	25.5	48.4	44.8

Source: U.S. Bureau of the Census, *Census of Population, 1980: Public Use Microdata Sample.* Tape Documentation. (Washington DC: U.S. Bureau of the Census, 1983).

Note: [a] Includes all persons except inmates of institutions, persons in military group quarters or in college dormitories or unrelated individuals under 15 years of age.

TABLE 5.18

POVERTY DIFFERENCES IN THE FOREIGN-BORN POPULATION[a] BY
AGE AND SEX, NEW YORK, 1980

Age Groups	Total Number in Population Sample (120,102) = 100.0%	Fraction of Individuals Below Poverty Line		Fraction of Individuals 200% and More Above Poverty Line	
		Men	Women	Men	Women
0–4	1,086	25.8	29.6	43.4	44.2
5–9	2,426	28.0	28.0	43.2	40.2
10–15	5,333	23.1	23.3	43.9	43.1
16–24	12,914	20.5	22.9	48.6	46.4
25–34	20,401	13.3	16.8	63.4	59.8
35–44	18,300	10.3	13.2	68.4	64.7
45–54	15,509	8.4	10.5	74.7	71.2
55–64	13,627	7.3	12.3	78.6	68.6
65 +	30,506	8.4	14.3	58.2	46.2

Source: U.S. Bureau of the Census, *Census of Population, 1980: Public Use Microdata Sample.* Tape Documentation. (Washington DC: U.S. Bureau of the Census, 1983).

Note: [a] Includes all persons of all ages except inmates of institutions, persons in military group quarters or in college dormitories or unrelated individuals under age 15.

high risk. Though women are consistently more visible in the poverty population than men at all ages, it is in particular the elderly immigrant woman in New York who is the most poverty prone. Among pre-1960 cohorts, the incidence of poverty was almost twice as high among women (11.8%) as among men (6.5%).

Columns 3 and 4 of Table 5.18 show corresponding data for foreign-born persons declaring incomes valued at "200 percent and more above the poverty threshold." The proportions who are recipients of these income levels vary by life cycle stage: close to one in every two is between the ages 16 and 25, and about three in every four are within the 45–64 age bracket. In older populations 65 years and above, these proportions decline, as expected, but more so among women than men. Whereas 58 percent of the men are still within this income range, the proportion among the women is only 48 percent.

National Origin

The incidence of poverty lies not only with factors associated with age and gender, it is manifested as well in and through certain national origin groups. The link between region of birthplace and immigrant poverty is illustrated in Table 5.19, which documents the considerable variation in poverty levels.

Poverty rates in 1980 tended to be highest for immigrants born in Africa, the Caribbean, the Soviet Union and Central America, and in many of these cases were closely associated with unemployment or withdrawal from the labor force. The incidence of poverty was lowest for immigrants who came from Europe and the Middle East/North Africa regions. European nationality groups reported a 9 percent poverty rate, Africans, Caribbeans, Central Americans and Soviets reported rates twice as high. The findings on poverty among Africans are particularly surprising given the high educational resources reported for this immigrant group.

The proportions in the population reporting income levels valued at "200 percent and more above the poverty threshold" totaled 61 percent among foreign-born residents and 70 percent among the American born. These income levels were attained by over 70 percent of the northwest European and North American immigrants; 65 percent of those from southern and eastern Europe, the Middle East and North Africa and Asia. Regional groups with the lowest visibility in this income bracket were the Caribbeans and Central Americans (48% and 52% respectively).

Race and Ethnicity

How race and ethnicity factors are reflected in the poverty rates of immigrants in New York is addressed in Table 5.20, with special data sets prepared to reflect

TABLE 5.19

POVERTY RATE DIFFERENCES AMONG NATIONAL ORIGIN GROUPS[a], NEW YORK, 1980

Region of Birthplace	Fraction Living Below the Poverty Line		Total Fraction of Individuals Below the Poverty Line	Fraction of Individuals with Incomes 200% Plus Above the Poverty Threshold
	Below 75%	Between 75–99%		
Foreign Born	9.2	5.0	14.2	61.0
Africa	15.1	5.3	20.4	58.7
North America[b]	5.7	3.5	9.2	70.9
South America	10.1	5.5	15.6	55.7
Central America[c]	12.9	5.8	18.7	49.6
Caribbean	13.3	6.4	19.7	52.0
Asia	9.1	4.1	13.2	63.3
Middle East/No. Africa	11.4	4.8	16.2	63.8
Western/No. Europe	4.6	3.4	8.0	72.2
Southern Europe	5.7	4.3	10.0	64.4
Eastern Europe	5.8	4.4	10.2	67.1
USSR	12.0	7.0	19.0	54.0
U.S. Born	8.4	4.1	12.5	69.8

Source: U.S. Bureau of the Census, *Census of Population, 1980: Public Use Microdata Sample.* Tape Documentation. (Washington DC: U.S. Bureau of the Census, 1983).

Notes: [a] Includes all persons except inmates of institutions, persons in military group quarters or in college dormitories, or unrelated individuals under 15 years of age.

[b] Includes Canada, Greenland and Bermuda.

[c] Includes Mexico.

TABLE 5.20

RACE AND ETHNIC-SPECIFIC POVERTY RATES OF FOREIGN- AND U.S.-BORN PERSONS[a] BY SELECTED REGIONS OF BIRTHPLACE, NEW YORK, 1980

Nativity/Region of Birthplace	All Persons	White	Black	Chinese	Indian	Other Asian	Spanish	Other
U.S. Born	12.5	8.5	30.4	10.6	11.0	8.6	48.5	42.0
Foreign Born	14.2	11.7	17.7	16.4	11.0	10.4	29.3	24.8
Africa	20.4	6.3	24.4	–	8.6	–	–	–
South America	15.6	14.0	16.8	–	–	–	18.5	16.4
Central America	18.7	15.0	19.5	–	–	–	23.4	6.0
Caribbean	19.7	17.3	16.2	5.3	18.9	–	33.7	23.6
Asia	13.2	21.6	–	16.1	7.0	10.3	–	17.2

Source: U.S. Bureau of the Census, *Census of Population, 1980: Public Use Microdata Sample.* Tape Documentation. (Washington DC: U.S. Bureau of the Census, 1983).

Note: [a] Includes all persons except inmates of institutions, persons in military group quarters or in college dormitories, or unrelated individuals under 15 years of age.

variations in the race and ethnic-specific poverty rates between foreign-born and native-born New Yorkers. The findings point to relatively high poverty rates among the foreign-born Spanish descent nationalities. Close to 30 percent were living below the poverty line in 1980 as compared to only 17.7 percent among foreign-born blacks and 16 percent among foreign-born Chinese ethnics. Lowest poverty rates, 11 percent, are associated with foreign-born Asian Indians and white ethnics.

The most significant finding in Table 5.20 is the contrasting experience in poverty among black and Spanish ethnics across the foreign-born and American-born populations. American-born black and Hispanic minority groups showed to be at an extreme disadvantage compared to the poverty levels of foreign-born persons who were of black and Spanish descent. Among native-born blacks, the poverty rate totaled 30 percent; it was only 17.7 percent among black immigrants. Among Hispanic ethnics the differential was even more dramatic: 48.5 percent of American-born Hispanics as compared to 29.3 percent among the foreign-born Spanish-descent population lived below the poverty level.

Comparisons of other ethnic groups across the foreign-born and U.S.-born population did not show such large variations. Poverty levels reported for American-born Asians, Asian Indians and white ethnics were very similar to those of their ethnic counterparts born abroad. The Chinese ethnics were the exception. American-born Chinese reported a lower incidence of poverty (10.6%) as compared to the foreign-born Chinese in New York—16.4 percent.

NOTES

[1] Extensive use has been made in this inquiry of the 5 percent public use microdata sample of 1980 which yields a population of 111,257 foreign-born and 540,675 U.S.-born persons for New York State within the ages of 16 years and above. This population constitutes the universe for most of the data presentation and discussion pursued in this section. In addition to state-level data, special labor force data sets for the larger metropolitan area of New York and independent data for New York City have been reviewed.

[2] It is estimated that during that decade, one to 2 million undocumented workers not counted by the census were probably added to the U.S. labor force, with the heaviest concentration in California and the Southwest.

[3] Among post-1970 arrivals, the proportion of workers who were year-round employed full time in 1980 was 52.1% for men and 36.3% among women as compared to 53.2% and 29.7% respectively for U.S.-born workers. Persons who arrived in the United States before 1970 reported year-round full-time employment in 44.7% of the cases for men and 23.3% for women.

[4] Hirschman and Kraly (1988) warn against drawing conclusions from comparisons of regional/ethnic differences in median income to indicate economic inequality among immigrant populations in the United States. Their cautionary note draws upon the finding that patterns observed may be

products of disproportionate inclusion or exclusion of some groups or an overrepresentation in economic sectors where cash incomes tend to be low.

[5] Poverty thresholds are updated yearly to reflect changes in the Consumer Price Index, based on national rather than regional/state figures. The poverty status of a person who is a family member is determined by the family income and its relationship to the appropriate poverty threshold established according to family size and occupation. That of the unrelated individual is determined by his/her own income in relation to the appropriate poverty threshold.

[6] Incomes below the poverty level are divided into two categories: those below 75% of the poverty level which include no income at all and those between 75% to 99% of the poverty level. Incomes above the poverty line fall into five categories: between 100 to 124% above; 125 to 149% above; 150 to 174% above; 175 to 199% above; and 200% plus above.

6

THE CONTRIBUTION OF FOREIGN-BORN WORKERS TO THE ECONOMY OF NEW YORK

This part of the study focuses on the way foreign-born workers fit into the industrial and occupational structure of New York and on what their particular contribution to the local economy has been. Three issues are of particular interest: to identify the labor market allocation of foreign-born workers in specific industrial sectors and occupational subcategories as compared to American-born workers in New York; to single out comparative differences and similarities between the various nationalities in respect to their location in the local economy with a view toward developing a typology of immigrant supplier countries based on the human capital characteristics that each region of birthplace supplies; and to tentatively examine the influence of background factors as they relate to the distribution of immigrant workers across occupational groupings.

The discussion concludes with a brief reference to the occupational characteristics of an additional human capital resource acquired by the state through the immigration process which is not included in the body of the 1980 data presented. This is by way of immigrants admitted during the 1980s under the category of third and sixth preference workers who selected to reside in New York.

Earlier, the unfavorable economic circumstances characterizing New York in the 1970s were reviewed. In the structure of employment the occupational categories affected the hardest during that period were: the managerial and professional — a net loss of 100,000 persons (representing one third of New York's total loss of labor force members); service-related occupations — a loss of 34,000; sales related occupations — 46,000 losses; and administrative support — 57,000 losses. Highly skilled labor lost 37,000 workers, but the less-skilled blue-collar sector only lost 10,000 jobs. The most serious losses were felt in the professions and related services — 83,000; sales and retail trade — 71,000; and in construction — 27,000. Manpower loss in the manufacturing sector was relatively small — only 28,000 workers, mostly from the ranks of the highly skilled (Alba and Batutis, 1984).

Despite the worsening of labor market conditions, large-scale immigration from South and Central America, the Caribbean and China continued to flow into New York and, notwithstanding the highly restricted employment opportunities, more than 338,000 legal immigrants and refugees — predominantly from among the ranks of recent arrivals into the country — were able to obtain employment in the state before the end of the 1970s.

The general contention has been that though large in scale, this labor absorption was not accompanied by significant increases of immigrants into the high wage sector and that the majority among them continued to remain concentrated in industrial and occupational sectors providing predominantly low-skilled manual jobs and low pay (Alba and Batutis, 1984; Papademetriou and Muller, 1987; Marshall, 1987). This description does not represent the totality of the immigrant labor experience in New York as evidenced in the findings on income attainment by occupation reported in Tables 5.15 and 5.16. It is true, nevertheless, that the data in those tables show reported labor earnings of immigrants in the technically skilled sector and in blue-collar jobs to be on the average equivalent to 75 percent of the corresponding native earnings. Whether this gap is in any way linked to the exclusion of immigrants from union membership is a subject that demands further investigation.

At the outset of 1980, the reported human capital resources available to New York State from its foreign-born residents included 632,890 male workers and 477,835 female workers. Combined they represented 15.2 percent of the state's work force. These figures do not take fully into account the large numbers of actively employed undocumented workers residing primarily in the New York City area and whose population in the mid-1980s was estimated to total between 500,000 to 600,000 persons. The immigration literature has identified the tendency for the undocumented population in New York to have background characteristics quite similar to those of legal immigrants; namely, they are of urban lower middle to middle-class origin; have prior employment history and favorable human capital resource characteristics — including a relatively high overall educational average and an age structure strongly skewed to the prime years of economic activity (Papademetriou and Muller, 1987). Research has also shown that the undocumented in New York become incorporated into the urban labor market in a manner "not readily distinguishable" from that of legal immigrants (Bailey, 1986; Waldinger, 1986). Studies conducted prior to the implementation of the 1986 IRCA employer sanctions by Papademetriou and DiMarzio (1986), Bach and Seguin (1986), Grasmuck (1984), Gurak and Kritz (1982), Perez (1981), Badillo et al. (1979) on the various types of immigrants and refugees in

New York concur that all immigrants, almost without regard to immigration status, played markedly similar labor market roles in the economy. Though differences in gross wage rates between legal and undocumented workers were discerned (Papademetriou and DiMarzio 1986; Grasmuck, 1984), these were attributable more to gender and length of stay in the United States than to legal status, ethnicity or significantly different human capital resources (Papademetriou and Muller, 1987).

The significance of the immigrant labor supply is even more striking when looked at in relation to the larger New York metropolitan area. It is estimated that with the rapid growth of the immigrant population in the 1970s—legal and undocumented—combined with the exodus of native-born New Yorkers, the foreign-born component in the New York metropolitan work force in the early 1980s had reached 26 percent (Papademetriou and Muller, 1987).

The precise manner in which immigrants, the legal and undocumented, incorporated themselves into the various sectors of New York's economy during the structural upheaval of the 1970s through replacing American-born workers cannot be fully captured by the 1980 census. Researchers specializing in New York's immigrant labor have placed selective emphasis in their writings on the substitution of natives by foreign workers in manual labor, and for this particular sector the process of replacement and substitution have been well documented (Alba and Batutis, 1984; Marshall, 1987). Very little is known, however, of substitution processes taking place in other sectors—in the professional, managerial, technical and white-collar categories, for example.

In the absence of more precise and updated information, the labor force statistics collected by the 1980 census and analyzed in the public use microdata file serves as the basis for the discussion that follows.[1]

Industrial and Occupational Distribution:
An Overview

Tables 6.1 and 6.2 compare the internal distribution of the reported foreign-born and American-born work force in New York State in 1980 across the different industry sectors and broad occupational categories. The last column in these two tables singles out the importance of the foreign-born worker component in each sector of the employment structure.

The economy of New York naturally determines the distributional patterning of each sector. What is of immediate interest in the comparative distribution of

TABLE 6.1

PERCENT DISTRIBUTION OF FOREIGN- AND U.S.-BORN WORKERS AGES 16+ BY
INDUSTRY SECTOR, NEW YORK, 1980

Industry Sector	All Workers	Foreign Born	U.S. Born	% of Total Who Are Foreign Born
All Industry Workers	469,103	71,596	397,507	15.2
	(100.0%)	(100.0%)	(100.0%)	
Agriculture, Forestry	1.3	0.5	1.4	6.7
Mining	0.1	—	0.1	7.7
Construction	4.1	4.0	4.1	15.0
Manufacturing	20.2	25.2	19.3	19.0
Transportation Communication	7.7	6.2	8.0	12.3
Wholesale Trade	4.2	4.4	4.2	16.0
Retail Trade	16.0	16.0	16.0	15.0
Financial, Real Estate	7.6	8.2	7.5	16.4
Business	5.1	5.3	5.1	15.8
Personal Service	3.3	5.6	2.9	25.6
Entertainment, Recreational	1.6	1.0	1.7	10.2
Professional & Related Services	22.7	19.5	23.2	13.1
Public Administration	5.2	2.9	5.6	8.4
Unemployed	0.4	0.5	0.4	17.8

Source: U.S. Bureau of the Census, *Census of Population, 1980: Public Use Microdata Sample*.
Tape Documentation. (Washington, DC: U.S. Bureau of the Census, 1983).

TABLE 6.2

PERCENT DISTRIBUTION OF THE WORK FORCE AGES 16+ BY BROAD
OCCUPATIONAL CATEGORY, AND NATIVITY OF WORKERS, NEW YORK, 1980

Broad Occupational Category	All Workers	U.S. Born	Foreign Born	% of Total who are Foreign Born
All Occupations	469,103	397,507	71,596	15.2
	(100.0%)	(100.0%)	(100.0%)	
Managerial/Professional	23.6	24.1	19.5	12.9
Technical, Sales, Administrative	33.9	35.1	27.6	12.4
Precision Production, Craft, Repair	9.9	9.6	11.7	17.9
Service	14.9	4.1	18.9	19.3
Farming, Forestry, Fisheries	1.5	1.6	0.7	7.2
Operatives, Fabricators, Laborers	15.8	15.1	20.9	20.0
Unempolyed[a]	0.4	0.4	0.5	17.9

Source: U.S. Bureau of the Census, *Census of Population, 1980: Public Use Microdata Sample*.
Tape Documentation. (Washington, DC: U.S. Bureau of the Census, 1983).

Note: [a] Unemployed are persons with previous work experience who have not worked in the 5
years preceding the census. The census questionnaire asked for information on last occupation for
people who worked since 1975.

workers in the two populations is the manner in which the profile of the immigrant worker "deviates" from that of the American-born worker. These deviations are important because they demonstrate the way in which human resources acquired through immigration may actually differ from those supplied by native resources and/or signal to the particular manner in which foreign human capital resources are utilized or allowed to perform in the receiving economy. By the same token, where allocation patterns are similar between the two populations of workers, or in proportional terms equal to the total employed in any one sector, one can denote areas where employment between American- and foreign-born workers is competitive. The fact that in 1980 immigrants in New York were over-represented in some sectors while the native born were not, points to the importance of economic options available to each population at that point in time (Marshall, 1987). This is not to negate that noneconomic factors related to the background characteristics of workers were operative as well in shaping the configuration of particular patterns of distribution and concentration.

The Industries

Though immigrants were concentrated in most industry sectors, their presence in the manufacturing industries was particularly high, both in relation to their average representation in the work force (19% vs. 15.2%) and when compared to the allocation of American-born workers in that sector (25.2% vs. 19.3%). Immigrant presence in manufacturing has been historically high — a fact considered to be strongly indicative of differential access to the nonmanual labor market (Marshall, 1987). Similar trends were noted in the personal services sector as well, where the proportional representation of immigrants is even higher — one worker in every four in the services was foreign born in 1980. At the same time, immigrant representation in professional and related services (13.1%) was only slightly lower than in the total work force (15.2%); one foreign-born worker in every five was allocated to this sector in the distribution. A third sector of selective importance for the foreign born was retail trade. In this sector, the allocation of workers in the internal distribution of the two populations was equal (16%) and the immigrant share in the overall sector was commensurate to their representation in the total work force (15%). The foreign born were noticeably underrepresented in public administration, mining and agriculture (Table 6.1).

The literature has singled out the role of immigrants in the manufacturing industry of New York for special scrutiny, tending to associate foreign-born labor almost exclusively with manual employment in the textiles and apparel industries. And it is true that labor concentration in this area has been traditionally high. In 1980, post-1965 immigrants held 50,000 jobs in manufacturing, 43,000 of which were in apparel, and these represented 55 percent of all jobs in that particular subsector.[2] However, the immigrant participation in the New York economy does not end there. As shown in Table 6.1, 16 percent of the human resource allocation in each of financial and real estate, wholesale trade, and business and related services and 15 percent in each of construction and retail trade were foreign-born workers.

A breakdown of the manufacturing sector into industry type further showed that immigrant workers were not only active in textiles and apparel, but in the food, paper, chemical and durable industries as well, accounting in each of these for roughly 15.5 percent of the entire work force. In addition, the cross classification of workers by industry and occupation indicates that immigrant participation in the industries was not limited to manual labor. A growing number among them have highly skilled jobs and many more hold professional and white-collar positions in the industries. In 1980 alone, close to 4,000 recently arrived immigrants were employed in a professional capacity in the manufacturing sector (Papademetriou and Muller, 1987).

Occupations

The occupational distribution in New York State in 1980 was strongly bimodal in structure: managerial, executive, professional positions, together with technical and nonprofessional white-collar jobs, accounted for 58 percent of all occupations; skilled labor in precision production, craft and repair represented a 10 percent share; service-related occupations employed 15 percent; and the category of semiskilled operators, fabricators and laborers made up for 16 percent of the state's work force.

Foreign-born workers tended to reinforce this pattern, with some internal differences in the allocation of workers across sectors. Close to 50 percent of the foreign-born work force was concentrated in the professional, managerial, technical and nonprofessional white-collar sectors and in skilled labor employment; 40 percent were in services and in lesser skilled blue-collar employment. The single most highly concentrated sector was the nonprofessional white-collar category, including the technical (27.6%); the second highest was in the less skilled category of jobs — operators, fabricators and laborers (20.9%). Proportionally, foreign-born labor allocated to manageriai and professional employment (19%) was equal to that allocated to service-related jobs.

How did the particular occupational distribution of immigrant workers compare to the allocation of American-born workers in these different categories, and how important was the presence of foreign-born workers in the overall structure of occupations in New York?

As shown in Table 6.2, the comparison based on the 1980 labor force data indicated the following:

— Immigrant workers showed to be less visible than native-born residents in professional and managerial specialties and in nonprofessional administrative and technical occupations (47% vs. 59%).

— Immigrants were somewhat more likely than native-born workers to be located in semi- and low skilled occupations in the blue-collar sector (21% vs. 15%).

— Immigrants were overwhelmingly more likely than the native born to be employed in service-related jobs (19% vs. 4%).

— In respect to categories of work related to skilled craftsman-ship, the percentage distribution was nearly equal between immigrant and native-born workers (12% and 10%).

In the absence of information related to prior employment, it is very difficult to assess whether this distribution truly reflects the skills immigrants bring to the New York labor market. In other contexts it has been noted that resources brought in by professional immigrants through high levels of education do not translate easily into commensurate positions because of language barriers and lack of job-seeking experience (Portes and Rumbaut, 1990). The high concentration of New York's immigrants in the service sector, for example, could reflect temporary points of entry for some immigrants who are qualified to do much better jobs or, in other instances, denote the exclusion of better qualified immigrants from upper employment sectors. The two possibilities would activate a downward trend in occupational placement.

Based on the information reported, the importance of immigrants in the overall structure of occupations may be surmised as follows: they accounted for 13 percent of all executive, managerial and professional positions and a nearly equal (12.4%) proportion of all workers in nonprofessional white-collar fields including the technical. Proportional representation in these two groupings was slightly below the average of immigrants in all occupations, which was 15.2 percent. This average was surpassed, however, in the proportional representation of immigrants in skilled crafts (17.9%), service-related jobs (19.3%) and manual labor (20%).

Subsectors in the Occupations with High Immigrant Labor Concentration

The above categories are somewhat general because the data are based on broad occupational groupings which are all-inclusive. A better understanding of the occupational role of immigrants in New York is gained from information classifying worker participation in the subcategories of occupations. These total 890 entries and are made available in the public use microdata file. In the subcategories in which the foreign-born presence was most noticeable the following were the most salient findings:

— In the top ranks of executives, managers and administrators, immigrants accounted for 28.2 percent of all managers in property and real estate, 16 percent of all financial managers and officers and 15 percent of all accountants and purchasing agents.

— In the professional specialties, the most outstanding contribution was in the health sector, though other areas of professional specialization reported the presence of immigrants as well. Professionals of foreign birth represented 29 percent of all those involved in health diagnosing, including 36 percent of all physicians and 14 percent of all dentists.[3] One in every five registered nurses and one in four health technologists and technicians were of foreign birth as well. The foreign born also accounted for 20 percent of all natural scientists, 16 percent of all architects and engineers, 21 percent of all nuclear engineers and 56 percent of all foreign language teachers in New York.

— In areas related to skilled craftsmanship — precision production, craft and repair — foreign-born workers averaged 16 percent of the work force in construction, 15 percent in electrical and mechanical repair, 22 percent in general precision production and 23 percent in food production.

— In the lesser skilled blue-collar jobs, immigrant labor was over represented among operators and fabricators working in textiles, apparel and furnishings in which their numbers accounted for 54.4 percent of the work force. Foreign-born New Yorkers were also economically active in metal work, plastic processing and wood work; in each subsector they accounted for 14 percent of all workers.

—In service-related occupations, 78 percent of all laundry work, 59 percent of domestic cooking and 40 percent of house-keeping, butlering, cleaning and domestic help were in hands of foreign-born workers. In jobs related to the preparation and servicing of foods, 29 percent of all supervisors and 26 percent of all cooks were foreign born. So were 23 percent of nurses aides and 17 percent of the health aides in the health service area. In the servicing and cleaning of buildings, foreign-born labor was particularly visible in work related to pest control (they represented 40% of the total in that area).

Stratifying Immigrant Supplier Regions by Human Capital Characteristics Exported

This discussion has, for the most part, emphasized New York's immigrant work force as a collective without taking fully into account the wide diversity and mix of international wealth represented in the human resource supply made available to the state. The distribution of this resource is not equal for all regions of birthplace, and immigrant suppliers are characterized by a stratifying order of their own with respect to the human capital resources each exports to the labor market in New York. This stratification may be ordered along two dimensions. The first addresses the question of the volume of immigrant labor supplied, indexed by differences in the sheer number of immigrant workers coming from each region of birthplace; the second dimension centers around the "quality" of the human capital resource brought into New York by each region. This is indexed by the reported location of immigrants in the occupational hierarchy.

Volume of Immigrant Labor Contributed

There are substantial differences between supplier regions regarding the number of workers each contributes to the New York immigrant work force (see, Table 6.3). The Caribbean islands top the list, supplying one in every four immigrant workers, followed by the northwestern and southern subregions of Europe which combined contribute an additional one third of the total immigrant work force. Asia, Eastern Europe and South America each supply between 7 and 11 percent, while Africa reported its share at less than one percent of the total.

Most of these variations are a function of the size of the different immigrant communities in New York, with few exceptions. For example, immigrants from Eastern Europe and the Soviet Union are underrepresented in the work force

TABLE 6.3

DISTRIBUTION OF THE FOREIGN-BORN RESIDENT POPULATION AGES AGES 16+
AND OF FOREIGN-BORN WORKERS IN THE OCCUPATIONS
BY REGION OF BIRTHPLACE, NEW YORK, 1980

Region of Birthplace	Persons in the Occupations	Residents
Foreign-Born Persons	71,596	111,257
	(100.0%)	(100.0%)
Africa	0.8	0.7
North America[a]	2.9	3.0
South America	7.3	6.1
Central America[b]	3.4	2.8
Caribbean	24.6	20.7
Asia	11.1	9.4
Middle East/North Africa	2.7	2.6
Western/Northern Europe	14.5	17.0
Southern Europe	15.6	17.4
Eastern Europe	7.6	8.8
USSR	3.7	5.3
Other Areas	5.8	6.2

Source: U.S. Bureau of the Census, *Census of Population, 1980: Public Use Microdata Sample.* Tape
Documentation. (Washington, DC: U.S. Bureau of the Census, 1983).

Notes: [a] Includes Canada, Greenland and Bermuda.

[b] Includes Mexico.

relative to their community size, whereas workers born in the Caribbean and
Central and South America are overrepresented. The age factor plays a major
role in explaining the differences. In the first instance, one is dealing with early
cohorts of immigrants with a declining number of members still able to be
economically active, while the latter case reflects the typical situation of nationality groups who are recent immigrants to the United States, arriving in the prime
productive ages with fewer options to not work.

Skill-Level of Resources Exported

An alternative profile of occupational diversity is obtained by ranking immigrant
source regions by the "skill level" of the human capital resources each supplies
independent of the number of workers exported. This diversity has been indexed
in Table 6.4 according to a broadly constructed typology of "upper skill" and
"lesser skill" resources developed from the occupational location reported by
immigrants at the time of the 1980 census count. Upper skill level occupations

TABLE 6.4

INTERNAL DISTRIBUTION OF FOREIGN-BORN WORKERS FROM
DIFFERENT REGIONS INTO OCCUPATIONAL GROUPINGS RANKED
ACCORDING TO SKILL LEVEL, NEW YORK, 1980

	Upper Skill Level			Lesser Skill Level		
Region of Birthplace	Managerial, Professional, Technical, White Collar	Precision Production and Repair	% of Total in Upper Skills	Service	Labor[a]	% of Total in Lesser Skills
All Foreign Born	47.3	11.7	59.0	18.9	20.9	39.8
Africa	64.4	4.8	69.2	15.6	14.1	29.7
North America[b]	59.2	10.8	70.0	13.6	14.2	27.8
South America	37.4	11.6	49.0	20.3	29.6	49.9
Central America[c]	38.4	10.0	48.4	25.1	24.8	49.9
Caribbean	40.7	9.2	49.4	25.1	23.8	48.9
Asia	61.4	4.3	65.7	16.3	17.4	33.7
Middle East/No. Africa	66.4	10.5	76.9	10.5	11.7	22.2
North/West Europe	60.6	12.2	72.8	16.0	9.7	25.7
Southern Europe	30.5	19.8	50.3	18.6	28.9	47.5
Eastern Europe	53.3	15.5	68.8	12.6	17.3	29.9
USSR	56.5	14.6	71.1	10.7	17.2	27.9
U.S. Born	59.2	9.6	68.8	14.1	15.1	29.2

Source: U.S. Bureau of the Census, *Census of Population, 1980: Public Use Microdata Sample.*
Tape Documentation. (Washington, DC: U.S. Bureau of the Census, 1983).

Notes: [a] Refers to Operators, Fabricators and Laborers.

[b] Includes Canada, Greenland and Bermuda.

[c] Includes Mexico.

include three categories: executive, managerial and professional specialists;
nonprofessional administrative and technical workers; and skilled craftsmen
classified in precision production, craft and repair. Lesser skill resources cover
all levels related to service occupations and semiskilled manual labor classified
as operators, fabricators and laborers.

The introduction of birthplace as a differentiating factor in the immigrant
labor market makes it possible to stratify supplier regions according to this
typology and the information noted in Columns 3 and 6 of Table 6.4 highlights
the sharp differences in human resources brought into New York according to
immigrant origin. As a collective, 59 percent of the immigrant work force were
classified in the upper skill level categories in 1980; the remaining 40 percent were
almost equally divided between lesser skill service jobs and manual labor. Among

American-born New Yorkers, the corresponding distribution along the upper skill and lower skill typology was in the approximate ratio of 7 to 3.

The data provided in columns 1 and 2 of Table 6.4 indicate that in proportions relative to the internal occupational distribution specific to each supplier region, the Middle East, Africa, Asia and northwest Europe were the most prominent in exporting top level resources in executive, managerial and occupational specialties and in nonprofessional white-collar and technical skills. In 1980, over 60 percent of the worker population coming from these four regions were holding positions in those two sectors with North American and Soviet-born immigrants falling closely behind. The weakest suppliers in these two upper skill areas were southern Europe, Central America and South America.

The geographical configuration of Third World countries along this typology is not surprising: the Middle East, Africa and Asia (excepting the Chinese) represent nationality groups with a relatively recent history of immigration. They have gained entry into the United States on the basis of their education and professional qualifications rather than family relations. They represent the first wave of the well-educated, professionally qualified urban elite emigres from these regions who will be followed in later years by a growing number of lesser educated/nonprofessional countrymen gaining admission as family members of established residents. Such a decline in standards has been noted among several nationality groups who first immigrated in the early 1960s (Borjas, 1990). The early influx of Dominicans, Caribbeans and South Americans are perfect examples of immigrant groups constituted overwhelmingly in the initial immigration period by well-educated and professionally trained persons. By the late 1970s and in the 1980s, however, their composition increasingly included many more persons with much lower educational standards — a trend that is reflected in the New York typology as well (Sassen-Koob, 1979). Similar declines are beginning to appear among some of the Asian nationality groups.

The supply of human capital resources in skilled craftsmanship was most closely associated in 1980 with southern and Eastern Europe and the Soviet Union (averaging about 17% of the immigrant work force of each region). The regions weak in supplying this particular skill were Africa and Asia (4% of their total in each case).

Regions most noticeable for supplying resources for the lesser skill category of occupations were South and Central America, the Caribbean and southern Europe: one worker in every two born in each of these regions was employed in either the service sector or in manual labor, in contrast to one in five born in the Middle East and approximately one in four among the other supplier regions. Collectively, the distribution of all immigrant workers was nearly equal between the service and manual labor sectors. This showed to be true at the level of most individual supplier regions, with four exceptions. Lesser skill workers supplied by South America, southern Europe and the Soviet Union showed a stronger presence in manual labor while northwest European workers had a higher proportion in the service sector.

To best summarize the typology illustrated in Table 6.4, the following points must be emphasized. Immigrant labor suppliers to New York are basically of two types: one exporting predominantly human resources filling the upper skill categories of occupations; the other which supplies a mix of human resources filling positions at both the upper and lesser skill levels. In 1980, the first type was represented by immigrants from the Middle East/North Africa region, northwest Europe, the Soviet Union and North America (between 70 to 77% of the workers were in upper skill level occupations). The second type of supplier was represented by South and Central America, the Caribbean and Southern Europe. In 1980, the immigrant worker population born in these four regions was equally divided between categories of occupational groupings ranked as upper skill and lesser skill.

Factors of Gender, Race and Ethnicity in Employment Distribution

Within the range of economic alternatives available to immigrants in New York in 1980, the pages that follow examine whether the clustering of immigrants around particular occupational sectors or their absence from others is associated with gender and race differences and, if so, whether such patterns are manifested in a similar way among foreign-born and American-born workers.

Gender Differences

The data presented in Table 6.5 makes it possible to compare sex patternings along occupational lines in the two worker populations as well as to examine differences and similarities in occupational composition within gender across the native and foreign-born population.

Among immigrants, the 1980 distribution patterns by sex showed the following: men were distributed with greater frequency than women in the managerial and professional categories (23 vs. 16%), but there was a much heavier concentration of women around the technical and nonprofessional white-collar jobs (36% vs. 20%). Disparities in distribution were not so significant with respect to service-related occupations (16.8% for the men and 21.2% for the women) and least evident in lesser skill blue-collar jobs where men and women were allocated in nearly equal proportions (20% and 22% respectively). There was a difference,

TABLE 6.5

SEX DISTRIBUTION OF U.S.-BORN AND FOREIGN-BORN WORKERS AGES 16+ INTO
BROAD OCCUPATIONAL CATEGORIES AND PROPORTION IN ALL OCCUPATIONAL
CATEGORIES WHO ARE WOMEN, NEW YORK, 1980

| | U.S.-Born | | Foreign-Born | | % in Total Occupational Categories Who Are Women | |
Occupational Category	Men	Women	Men	Women	U.S. Born	Foreign Born
All Ocupations	100.0	100.0	100.0	100.0	46.6	46.0
Managerial/Professional	25.5	22.4	22.9	16.4	43.5	37.9
Technical, Sales, Adm.	22.2	49.7	20.2	36.1	66.0	60.4
Precision Production						
Craft, Repair	16.7	1.5	18.8	3.4	7.6	13.5
Farm, Forestry, Fishing	2.6	0.6	1.1	0.2	17.1	14.9
Service	12.1	16.5	16.8	21.2	54.3	51.7
Operatives, Fabricators,						
Laborers	20.4	8.8	19.8	22.1	26.9	48.8
Unemployed[a]	0.3	0.5	0.4	0.6	58.1	58.5

Source: U.S. Bureau of the Census, *Census of Population, 1980: Public Use Microdata Sample.* Tape
Documentation. (Washington, DC: U.S. Bureau of the Census, 1983).

Note: [a] Refers to persons with previous work experience but who have not worked in the 5 years
preceding the census.

however, in employment related to skilled labor: only 3 percent of immigrant
women workers as compared to 19 percent of male workers were holding jobs in
this particular sector.

American-born women and men were almost equally distributed in the professions (22% vs. 25%); slightly less so in service-related jobs (16% vs. 12%). In
nonprofessional white-collar employment, the distributional differences were
striking — 50 percent of the women but only 20 percent of the men were allocated
to this sector. By contrast, women had a weak presence in the ranks of skilled
labor and semiskilled blue-collar jobs — only 1.5 percent were classified in precision production, craft and repair and 9 percent as operators and fabricators, in
contrast to their male counterparts who reported proportions of 17 and 20
percent respectively in the two sectors.

Within-gender comparisons showed considerable convergence in distribution
patterns among the men but not among the women. Typically, 45 percent of the
men in the two populations were employed in professional and nonprofessional
white-collar areas and 35 percent in the lesser skilled categories of occupation.
The women differed among the groups. Whereas immigrant women showed

considerable diversity in their occupational locations, having a visible presence in all groupings except the skilled labor category, American-born women were heavily clustered around professional and nonprofessional white-collar occupations. These two employment sectors absorbed 71 percent of the entire native born female work force in 1980; whereas among immigrant women, they accounted for only 51 percent. Women workers also differed with respect to their representation in the less skilled blue-collar sector: nine women in every 100 in the American-born work force as compared to 20 percent in the immigrant group were employed as operators, fabricators and laborers.

The traditional concentration of immigrant women in the manufacturing industries and other lesser skilled service and blue-collar jobs accounts for a major difference between the employment pattern of the American- and foreign-born woman worker. In 1980, over 50 percent of the women holding semiskilled jobs in the manufacturing industries of the larger New York metropolitan area were immigrants and immigrant women filled close to 40 percent of all those positions. The inclusion of undocumented women workers would raise the proportion to 50 percent. A second clustering occurs in "private household employment," inflating the presence of immigrant women in service-related jobs. Whereas factory work is heavily dominated by Dominican and, to a lesser extent, South American women, private household employment is associated with English Caribbean women who are principal migrants. Though many among them are qualified to take more prestigious jobs, non-Hispanic Caribbeans generally consider service-related work in private households as an acceptable entry point.

The above should not detract from the strong representation of immigrant women in the upper skill level occupations. In 1980, 46 percent of all foreign-born workers in New York were women, and women filled 38 percent of all managerial and professional positions and 60 percent of all the technical/nonprofessional white-collar jobs held by the foreign born in New York. This statistic needs to be underlined because of the popular perception that immigrants, most particularly women, are all located at the bottom of the occupational ladder in the bimodal structure of New York's employment base.

Race and Ethnicity in Relation to Occupational Location

In Chapter 5 the economic consequences of race and ethnicity as a stratifying variable in labor market absorption, income attainment and exposure to poverty were examined. In that context, the overall disadvantaged position of immigrants of Spanish descent was noted. Though variables related to human capital characteristics were not introduced to account for the differences in economic circumstances identified, the data available showed that while foreign-born blacks did experience some economic disadvantage relative to white and Asian ethnics, in the overall their economic status in 1980 did not manifest the unfavorable conditions characterizing the foreign-born Spanish descent groups.

The information presented now seeks to relate the race and ethnicity factor to the particular way in which foreign-born workers are distributed across the occupations. Data provided in Tables 6.6, 6.7, 6.8 and 6.9 have classified foreign-born workers by occupational grouping, sex, race and ethnicity. Gender has shown to be an important variable to consider in relation to race and ethnicity in order to explore whether racial distinctions among immigrant workers become less of a differentiating factor in regard to women as compared to men. This type of "blurring" has been noted in national labor market studies with respect to American-born minority groups.

The data presented in these tables have been organized to indicate whether immigrants are distributed across the various categories of occupations by race and ethnicity in the same manner that they are distributed in the overall work force. The purpose is to identify whether there are occupational areas that show either an overrepresentation or underrepresentation of certain racial and ethnic groups; and, if so, how does this differ by the geographical point of origin.

From the data presented, several observations can be made. Among male immigrants there was no indication of a blatant discrimination barring any one racial/ethnic group from any of the occupations. However, Spanish descent groups appeared disadvantaged because of their underrepresentation in upper skill level occupations relative to their distribution in the overall occupational structure by race and ethnicity and overrepresentation in lesser skilled jobs (Spanish descent groups born in South America were the exception). There were wide regional variations in the distribution of black men across the occupations. African-born black men were underrepresented in the managerial/professional ranks and overrepresented in jobs of lesser skill. This was not the case of blacks from Central America who were overrepresented in upper skill level white-collar jobs and underrepresented in the less skilled labor jobs. The occupational distribution by race and ethnicity was the most balanced among Caribbeans. Black Caribbean men had a relatively higher presence in technical and white-collar jobs and in skilled labor than in managerial and professional positions, though their presence in these sectors was visible. The occupational location of white ethnics was diversified as well. Those born in Africa, South America and the Caribbean showed relatively greater visibility in managerial and professional level positions. White ethnics from Africa were also highly represented in skilled labor. Those born in Central America were overrepresented in the less skilled blue-collar jobs, while the South American and African whites were underrepresented in service-related jobs. Asian ethnics showed to be highly stratified along occupational lines. Overall, Chinese men showed to be overrepresented in service-related jobs and less so in the semiskilled blue-collar

TABLE 6.6

OCCUPATIONAL DISTRIBUTION OF FOREIGN-BORN MALE WORKERS FROM SELECTED
REGIONS OF BIRTHPLACE BY RACE/ETHNICITY, NEW YORK, 1980

Occupational Category	White	Black	Ethnic Spanish	Other Incl. Asian
Africa				
Distribution by Race/Ethnicity in All Occupations	20.8	70.8	–	8.4
Managerial/Professions	23.5	64.2	–	12.3
Tech./Sales/Adm.	18.4	73.1	–	8.5
Skilled Labor	33.3	62.5	–	4.2
Service Jobs	16.0	76.0	–	8.0
Lesser Skilled Labor	19.6	78.8	–	1.6
Latin America				
Distribution by Race/Ethnicity in All Occupations	67.2	2.7	26.3	3.8
Managerial/Professions	78.3	1.8	16.4	3.5
Tech./Sales/Adm.	69.5	4.0	22.3	4.2
Skilled Labor	67.9	1.2	28.9	2.0
Service Jobs	62.3	3.3	29.3	5.1
Lesser Skilled Labor	62.3	2.7	31.2	3.8
Central America[a]				
Distribution by Race/Ethnicity in All Occupations	32.6	33.4	23.1	10.9
Managerial/Professions	36.8	42.7	17.1	3.4
Tech./Sales/Adm.	25.5	56.8	15.0	2.8
Skilled Labor	36.6	29.5	29.5	4.4
Service Jobs	34.6	32.0	30.4	3.0
Lesser Skilled Labor	40.2	27.0	29.7	3.1
Caribbean				
Distribution by Race/Ethnicity in All Occupations	18.6	59.0	16.7	5.7
Managerial/Professions	27.6	56.8	10.0	5.6
Tech./Sales/Adm.	17.0	64.5	12.7	5.8
Skilled Labor	14.8	66.4	13.6	5.2
Service Jobs	19.6	55.2	20.5	4.7
Lesser Skilled Labor	17.4	55.5	22.0	5.1

Source: U.S. Bureau of the Census, *Census of Population, 1980: Public Use Microdata Sample.*
Tape Documentation. (Washington, DC: U.S. Bureau of the Census, 1983).

Note: [a] Includes Mexico.

TABLE 6.7

OCCUPATIONAL DISTRIBUTION OF FOREIGN-BORN ASIAN MALE
WORKERS BY ETHNICITY, NEW YORK, 1980

Occupational Category	White	Chinese	Asian Indian	Other Asians	Other
Distribution by Ethnicity in All Occupations	6.1	43.6	18.0	26.8	5.5
Managerial/Professional	8.1	29.0	27.9	30.1	4.9
Technical/Sales/Adm.	8.2	19.3	32.4	35.1	5.0
Skilled Labor	6.2	43.0	11.3	28.9	10.6
Service Jobs	2.2	76.5	5.5	12.6	3.2
Lesser Skilled Labor	6.4	55.2	9.8	23.6	5.0

Source: U.S. Bureau of the Census, *Census of Population, 1980: Public Use Microdata Sample.*
Tape Documentation. (Washington, DC: Bureau of the Census, 1983).

sector. The Chinese were clearly underrepresented in managerial, professional, technical and white-collar positions. Asian Indians were overrepresented in technical and white-collar jobs and in managerial and professional specialties with a low visibility in the blue-collar service sectors. "Other" Asian ethnics were distributed fairly equally across the occupational groupings except for service-related jobs where they were hardly visible.

Among women immigrants, race and ethnicity appeared to mediate differently for women as compared to men. Black women, in general, were characterized more frequently than their men by a bimodal occupational distribution: those born in Central America and in the Caribbean were overrepresented in the upper skill level occupations (excepting skilled labor) relative to their distribution in the overall occupational structure. At the same time, black women, regardless of birthplace, were also overrepresented in service-related jobs. Black women from Africa were underrepresented in upper skill level occupations and were the only black group to be overrepresented in semiskilled blue-collar work. Women of Spanish descent were heavily underrepresented in managerial, professional, technical and white-collar occupations and overrepresented in the lesser skill level jobs. Hispanic Caribbeans were twice as heavily represented in skilled labor and in the semiskilled blue-collar category of jobs relative to their presence in the occupations as a whole. White women from Africa and South America were overrepresented in upper skill level occupations, but those born in Central America were underrepresented in this category. White Caribbeans were underrepresented in service-related jobs but overrepresented both in skilled labor and in semiskilled blue-collar jobs. Among Asians, Chinese women were overrepresented in the blue-collar category of jobs and underrepresented in the professions. They were more evenly distributed across the other occupational

TABLE 6.8

OCCUPATIONAL DISTRIBUTION OF FOREIGN-BORN WOMEN WORKERS FROM
SELECT REGIONS OF BIRTHPLACE BY RACE/ETHNICITY, NEW YORK, 1980

Occupational Category	White	Black	Ethnic Spanish	Other Incl. Asian
Africa				
Distribution by Race/Ethnicity in All Occupations	28.9	54.9	—	16.2
Managerial/Professions	36.8	52.6	—	10.6
Tech./Sales/Adm.	31.9	45.8	—	22.3
Skilled Labor	—	—	—	—
Service Jobs	25.0	68.1	—	6.9
Lesser Skilled Labor	12.5	62.5	—	25.0
Latin America				
Distribution by Race/Ethnicity in All Occupations	68.0	2.8	25.1	4.1
Managerial/Professions	78.7	—	15.3	6.0
Tech./Sales/Adm.	73.8	3.5	18.7	4.0
Skilled Labor	66.1	—	26.6	7.3
Service Jobs	64.7	4.5	25.7	5.1
Lesser Skilled Labor	61.1	—	33.7	5.2
Central America[a]				
Distribution by Race/Ethnicity in All Occupations	35.8	35.9	20.6	7.7
Managerial/Professions	34.7	50.3	13.4	1.6
Tech./Sales/Adm.	29.5	50.2	17.7	2.6
Skilled Labor	50.0	25.0	25.0	—
Service Jobs	34.5	44.9	19.3	1.3
Lesser Skilled Labor	45.6	17.0	35.4	2.0
Caribbean				
Distribution by Race/Ethnicity in All Occupations	15.8	65.1	14.5	4.6
Managerial/Professions	14.5	77.3	5.2	3.0
Tech./Sales/Adm.	15.6	69.8	9.4	5.2
Skilled Labor	26.4	36.7	34.2	2.7
Service Jobs	7.5	83.1	6.7	2.7
Lesser Skilled Labor	26.6	31.2	35.3	6.9

Source: U.S. Bureau of the Census, *Census of Population, 1980: Public Use Microdata Sample.*
Tape Documentation. (Washington, DC: U.S. Bureau of the Census, 1983).

Note: [a] Includes Mexico.

TABLE 6.9

OCCUPATIONAL DISTRIBUTION OF FOREIGN-BORN ASIAN WOMEN WORKERS BY
ETHNICITY, NEW YORK, 1980

Occupational Category	White	Chinese	Asian Indian	Other Asians	Other
Distribution by Ethnicity in All Occupations	4.6	45.2	12.6	33.6	4.0
Managerial/Professional	5.2	24.1	19.5	45.9	5.3
Technical/Sales/Adm.	5.8	38.1	15.7	36.9	3.5
Skilled Labor	15.9	55.6	1.1	25.0	2.4
Service Jobs	5.2	31.8	8.9	44.2	9.9
Lesser Skilled Labor	1.1	80.7	3.8	13.1	1.3

Source: U.S. Bureau of the Census, 1983, Census of Population, 1980: Public Use Microdata Sample.
Tape Documentation. Washington, DC: U.S. Bureau of the Census.

groupings relative to Chinese men. Asian Indian women showed a concentrated presence in managerial work and the professions specialties, followed by technical and white-collar employment. They had a low visibility in all other occupational groupings. Other Asian women were highly visible at both extremes of the occupational ladder — in the professions and in service-related jobs — but noticeably underrepresented in the semiskilled blue-collar sector.

Additional Human Capital Resources Available to New York During the 1980s

Occupational Background of the Post-1980 Immigrants

The Statistical Branch of the Immigration and Naturalization Service has now made available tape documentation which identifies the occupational characteristics of permanent residents admitted to the United States during 1978 and 1986 by state of intended residence. With additional information on file regarding the class of admission of newly arrived immigrants, it is possible to single out the legal immigrant population settling in New York State throughout the 1980s who were admitted under the work provisions established for third and sixth preference categories.[4] With these new data sets it is possible to expand information on the occupations of foreign-born residents beyond the 1980 census and tentatively identify human capital resources made available to New York in recent years.

Between 1980 and 1986, 660,951 persons from among the total number admitted into the United States as permanent residents during that period declared intent to establish residence in New York State. This figure includes persons of all ages. Sixty thousand persons among these arrivals were admitted under the third and sixth preference "worker provision" especially earmarked in the 1965 Immigration Act for domestic labor market needs. Table 6.10 identifies the occupational background characteristics of the 660,951 New York-bound immigrants.

Some caution is required in interpreting these data. The information on occupations was compiled from administrative records, mainly immigrant visas and labor certification applications, and can refer to a job held in the country of origin, country of last residence or job intended in the United States for which labor certification has been granted in the case of those admitted as third and sixth preference principals.

The format of these records include categories assigned to aliens who are "not in the labor force" or "non-employed" (e.g., homemakers, students, unemployed

TABLE 6.10

OCCUPATIONAL COMPOSITION OF IMMIGRANTS ADMITTED AS
LEGAL PERMANENT RESIDENTS WITH INTENDED SETTLEMENT IN
NEW YORK STATE, 1980–1986 (ALL AGES)

Occupational Category	Year of Admission						
	1980	1981	1982	1983	1984	1985	1986
Number Settling in New York	80,148	80,590	85,048	93,159	107,056	104,734	110,216
	(100.0%)	(100.0%)	(100.0%)	(100.0%)	(100.0%)	(100.0%)	(100.0%)
Prof./Technical	3.4	3.1	3.1	6.4	4.9	5.3	5.2
Manag./Admin.	4.9	4.3	4.3	3.5	3.6	3.3	3.3
Sales Workers	1.3	1.2	1.1	1.6	2.1	2.2	2.2
Clerical & Kindred	7.1	7.4	6.1	5.8	4.2	4.3	4.3
Craftmen & Kindred	5.5	5.4	4.8	6.4	6.6	6.2	6.2
Operatives	7.7	7.3	5.9	( )	( )	( )	( )
Transp. Equipment & Operatives	1.5	1.5	1.2	(8.2)	(7.6)	(7.5)	(7.5)
Laborers	2.2	2.4	1.7	( )	( )	( )	( )
Service Workers	4.8	4.1	4.1	( )	( )	( )	( )
Private Household Workers	3.3	3.2	3.3	(9.9)	(10.0)	(9.9)	(9.9)
Housewife, Children & Others	56.3	57.8	62.0	56.0	58.0	58.0	58.0
Others (Farm)	2.0	2.2	3.6	–	–	–	–

Source: U.S. Immigration and Naturalization Service, *Immigrants Admitted into the U.S. As Legal Permanent Residents.* FY 1978–1986. Tape Documentation. (Washington, DC: Statistical Analysis Branch, 1987).

persons, the retired and children). In the case of the New York-bound groups arriving during 1980 and 1986, the proportion "outside of the labor force" averaged about 58 percent of the yearly admissions.[5] Nationwide findings have shown, however, that the high incidence of family relations declaring "no occupation" or outside the labor force on entry to the United States severely understates the subsequent labor force behavior of these immigrants. Discrepancy between the numbers of those declaring to be non-employed or outside the labor force at entry and of those subsequently entering the labor force is most striking among the women.[6] The general trend is for immigrant men to report an occupation upon entry much more frequently than immigrant women. The wife who is a derivative beneficiary of her husband's visa classification may list herself as "housewife" under the occupation entry, even if she has worked before or fully intends to work after entering the country.

Keeping in mind problems of inaccuracy and completeness of information regarding occupational background and intent to work, the reported profile of the post-1980 New York-bound immigrant who did state an occupation upon arrival — 42 percent of the total — pointed to the following categories as occupational resources potentially available to New York State:

Executive, Managerial	3.4 percent
Professional Specialty	5.4 percent
(with engineers outranking health professionals)	
Technical, Administrative Support and Sales	7.7 percent
Precision Production, Craft and Repair	6.6 percent
Service-related occupations	9.1 percent
Operators, Fabricators, Laborers	7.8 percent

These percentages represent averages for the 1980–1986 entries and naturally obscure fluctuations that may have occurred from one year to the next. It should be noted that during the latter part of the 1980–1986 period there was a relative increase in the number of new immigrants with a background in the professions and in service-related jobs and a relative decline of those who had technical, administrative support and sales experience.[7] The proportions in all other occupational groupings remained more or less stable.

Immigrants Admitted Under the Worker Provision

During 1980–1986, 60,071 new immigrants of the 660,951 who expressed intent to settle in New York were admitted under the third and sixth preference categories. This figure, however, includes not only the principal reference person who applied and received labor certification from the United States but his or her immediate family as well.

To the extent that a comparative statement may be made about the characteristics of this potential resource available to New York on the basis of statistics that include principals and their dependents, the 1980–1986 information points to two trends. The first is an increase in the absolute number of immigrants coming to New York who were admitted under the worker provision: from 6,935 in 1980 to 9,353 in 1983 and to 10,050 in 1986. The second is a significant change in allocation between third preference and sixth preference workers entering and settling in New York. Whereas during 1980 and 1981 third preference admissions earmarked for professionals and persons of exceptional talent comprised only 18 percent of the total admitted under the worker provision; by 1982 this proportion had increased to 27 percent and by 1986 to 33 percent (*see,* Table 6.11). To what extent was this occupational shift a response to a real or perceived favorable labor market situation for professional specialties in New York is not known. Certainly by 1982 the process of New York's economic recovery was just beginning to get underway.

In further examining the geographic origin of the post-1980 supply of human capital resources, some interesting trends became discernible:

—National origin groups from Asia outranked all others in supplying New York with additional immigrant workers, followed by Caribbeans and northwest Europeans.

TABLE 6.11

NUMBER OF PERSONS LEGALLY ADMITTED TO THE UNITED STATES
UNDER THE WORK PROVISION WITH INTENDED RESIDENTIAL SETTLEMENT IN
NEW YORK STATE[a], 1980–1986

Year of Admission	Total Number Admitted	Third Preference	Sixth Preference
1980	6,935	1,269	5,666
1981	5,901	1,018	4,883
1982	8,978	2,436	6,542
1983	9,353	2,625	6,728
1984	9,783	2,829	6,954
1985	9,071	2,639	6,432
1986	10,050	3,284	6,766
Total	60,071	16,100	43,971

Source: U.S. Immigration and Naturalization Service, *Immigrants Admitted into the U.S. As Legal Permanent Residents. FY 1978–1986.* (Washington, DC: Statistical Analysis Branch, 1987).

Note: [a] These figures include immediate family of the reference person applying to enter the country under the work provisions.

—Over the 1980 to 1986 period between 40 to 50 percent of admissions under the third preference category of workers came from Asia, followed by northwestern Europeans (20 to 25%). The proportion of Caribbeans among the third-preference category of workers increased from 2 percent in 1980 to 10 percent in 1986: while among northwest Europeans the proportion had declined from 25 to 19 percent respectively. Middle Eastern/North African immigrants contributed a small but stable fraction of individuals to the professional category of workers (7%); African immigrants contributed about 5 percent.

—Caribbean immigrants accounted for one third of all the sixth preference category of workers coming to New York; South and Central Americans combined accounted for 20 percent. The numbers of Asians admitted under this category increased from 20 percent in 1980 to 30 percent in 1986, while that of northwest Europeans declined from 9 to 5 percent. Middle Eastern and North African immigrants supplied 7 percent of all sixth preference workers; African immigrants were not represented in this category.

NOTES

[1] The universe for most of the data presentation and discussion is the worker population in the age range 16 years and over identified in the sample population of the 1980 public use microdata file. This included 38,661 foreign-born men and 32,935 foreign-born women, and 214,653 U.S.-born men and 182,853 U.S.-born women.

[2] Women immigrants are highly concentrated in the lesser skilled blue-collar jobs in manufacturing. In the larger New York metropolitan area, over 50% of the women in semiskilled jobs in the manufacturing sector were immigrants in 1980, and they held close to 40% of all semiskilled jobs in that sector. Extensive research on the undocumented worker suggests that if undocumented women workers were included in the count the immigrant female representation in this sector would rise to 50%. Male immigrants are more diversified in their industrial sector employment.

[3] Though recognition has been given to the importance of immigrants in the health field, the reference made is almost always to health care service workers in hospitals and nursing homes, nursing aides, orderlies and attendants. The presence in New York of a large number of immigrants who are professionals and specialists in the health area has not been mentioned in the literature.

[4] The 1965 Immigration Act legislated 7 categories to regulate the admission of immigrants into the country. Two of these, the third and sixth preference categories, were earmarked for the benefit of labor market needs. The third preference refers to persons in the professions and of exceptional talent and ability; the sixth preference refers to skilled and semiskilled workers who are in demand

in the labor market. Both categories require labor certification and are not to exceed 10% of the yearly entries allocated to immigrants.

5 Nationwide admission statistics for 1985–1987 showed that among persons entering under family reunification provisions, 65% of the men and 36% of the women reported having an occupation. The rest were listed as nonemployed or outside the labor force.

6 In 1980, for example, 51% of immigrant women in the United States were in the labor force as compared to only 34% who declared an occupation at the time of their entry into the country.

7 The proportion in the professions was 3.2% among 1980–1982 arrivals and 5.3% among 1985–1986 arrivals; service occupations accounted for 7% of the total during 1980–1982 and 10% among those entering during 1983 and 1986. The white-collar category declined from 8.5% of the total during 1980–1982 to 6% for those who arrived between 1984 and 1986.

7

CONCLUSION:
CONSEQUENCES OF FUTURE
IMMIGRATION FOR NEW YORK

Mainstream immigration research has generally proceeded at three interrelated levels—the macro, midrange and micro—viewing immigration respectively in a worldwide context of international inequality, analyzing the adaptability or assimilation of specific immigrant groups to the host society and, at the sociopsychological level, emphasizing the need to view the migration experience from the subjective viewpoint of the migrant himself or herself. Each of these levels has incorporated various methodological approaches (Couch, 1979; also *see,* Bryce-LaPorte, 1979).

This study may be broadly classified as midrange in level. Its motivation has been to develop a research design that would examine the current status of the international migratory flow and the direction of its trends and changes over time, within a context that captures the particular experience of one locality in which immigrants are heavily concentrated—in this instance studying the mode in which the migratory process has manifested itself in New York State since 1965.

In the pages that follow brief consideration is given to some of the consequences of continuing immigration and to basic data gaps in the area of immigration which flow from this study. In the concluding remarks, a call is made for future immigration research to be more explicitly directed to policy-relevant concerns, and for the desirability that New York State assume greater responsibility in initiating data collection and generating research to assess the impact of international migratory flows upon the different localities within its boundaries.

Consequences of Immigration

Sustaining Population Growth

On the national level, population growth has been declining since the 1950s and since 1972 fertility levels have been below replacement level. In the late 1950s the average annual population growth had peaked at 1.8 percent; since 1982 it has been below one percent.[1] If the current low fertility schedule persists, the forecast is that the United States will have a negative rate of increase by the year 2030; in the absence of further international immigration, the country's population could dwindle to 100 million people within two centuries. Today, natural increase is still the prime factor in population growth, but the proportion of growth contributed by immigration has been on the rise: from an estimated 16.6 percent in the 1970s to 27 percent in 1990, with an expected increase to 35 percent by the year 2005 if current trends continue. If fertility levels do not increase dramatically during the forthcoming decades to offset the tendency of the nation's population to decline, the role of immigration will no longer be to add to existing population growth, but to makeup for fertility deficits (Edmonston, 1989).

Provisional data released from the 1990 census figures show a 2.8 percent growth rate for New York compared to 33 percent for Florida, 26 percent in California, 20 percent in Texas and 10.2 percent nationwide. This means losses for New York on several fronts: a "greying" of the population, shortage of labor supply and decline in political power and federal aid. The state has already lost three House of Representative seats as a result of the decline. These three factors alone could entice New York State to welcome a larger number of new immigrants into its borders.

On the basis of its track record from 1983 to 1988, New York has been receiving an average inflow of 106,000 legal immigrants yearly. Though migratory trends have shown an upward trend since 1984 following the state's recovery from the recession of the late 1970s, it is highly unlikely that New York will ever recapture its rank as number one host state. New York City, though, is expected to retain its magnetism as the favorite immigrant center. If New York continues to uphold the 18 percent share it averaged in the nationwide total of immigrant entries during the 1980s (1989 excepted), the new admission ceilings contained in the 1990 Immigration Act would raise the state's influx to approximately 122,000 admissions yearly. Whether or not the post 1990 flow will be headed in this direction depends in large part on New York's economic prospects. Should the economy soften, the flow may soften too.

The demographic impact of immigration upon the state depends not only on the sheer volume of entries, but upon the age structure, sex ratios, fertility and mortality patterns of immigrants once in New York, as well. Overall, immigrant mortality rates have shown to be comparable to the American-born population, while immigrant fertility needs to show one child or more than the resident population to make a noticeable impact on a population (Edmonston, 1990). The age structure of the 1970–1980 flows into New York showed to be much more favorable to childbearing than that of native-born New Yorkers, but there are also differences in immigrant childbearing patterns according to country of origin that need to be considered. New York immigrants of Spanish and Caribbean origin report higher than average fertility while Asian immigrants report much lower levels. However, changes in the nationality mix of future migratory streams as a result of the 1990 provisions may reshape the immigrant fertility profile.

Complementing Labor Market Needs

It was mentioned earlier that the nation is confronting both a demographic shortfall and an educational and skill deficit in the working-age population. An era of long-term labor deficits has been predicted based on the discrepancy between job openings and growth in the working-age population: between 1985 and 1990, eleven million new jobs opened while the total working-age population grew only by 5 million.[2] The problem is compounded by the fact that internal resources that are available do not offer the qualifications that are in demand.

Nationwide Educational and Occupational Demands

National projections for the short-term structure of employment indicate that as many as 40 percent of all new jobs to be created between 1988 and 2000 will be in the managerial, professional and technical occupations and another one-third will be in skilled service jobs. Low skilled categories of operators, fabricators and laborers are expected to contribute less than 2 percent to the new jobs even though they represent nearly 15 percent of current workers (Vernez and Mc Carthy, 1990). According to the Department of Labor, the new employment profile signals to increases of 30 percent in technical personnel, 24 percent in professional specialties and 22 percent in executive positions (Papademetriou, 1990). Whereas today 22 percent of the jobs in the country require a college degree, by the end of the century the corresponding requirement will total 30 percent (Richman, 1990). The demand for science and engineering PhDs is projected to double by the year 2000 while the supply of U.S.-born PhDs in these fields are expected at best to remain stable. At present, only one half of the slots in graduate schools specializing in technical and science areas in the country are filled by Americans.[3]

New York's Demand for Specialized Manpower

The State and City of New York mirror national trends and face even more severe problems related to the immense disparity between New York's human capital resource supply and the direction of the local economy. Compared to other areas in the tri-state region, New York City is predicted to experience a slower economic growth (Levine, 1990) at the same time that it confronts a critical shortage in specialized manpower. Having transformed its power base from a production-based economy to one that is highly sophisticated in professional specialties and technical services, the availability of a highly educated and occupationally specialized supply of labor is vital for the very existence of New York.

According to the Bureau of Labor Statistics for the Mid-Atlantic region (U.S. Department of Labor, 1990), recent employment growth in New York City has been concentrated at the higher end of the occupational and technical scale. Managerial and professional specialties and technical occupations not only accounted for two thirds of new employment growth in New York City between 1983 and 1987, but are projected to further increase by 24 percent by the year 2000. In other occupational sectors, the projected increases are no more than 12 percent.

A major portion of the resident working-age population of New York City is poorly equipped to meet this highly specialized demand. Netting out arrivals and departures, the growth of the city's labor force population has been dominated by Hispanics, blacks and other racial minorities who combined totaled 1.7 million in 1990. For the first time in the economic history of New York City, these "minority" groups have come to represent 50.3 percent of the resident working-age population (U.S. Department of Labor, 1990). Unfortunately, the qualifications profile of the majority of persons in this population of "minorities" in New York City does not correspond to the sectorial and occupational needs of the city's economy due to their lack of access to and/or success in the educational and occupational systems.[4] To what extent can these specialized demands and shortfalls in available skills be met with immigrant labor? This can only be determined by the educational and occupational resources brought into New York through future international migratory flows.

The Immigrant Potential

The analysis of the 1980 data strongly suggest that the effect of immigrants on the labor market of New York has been substantial. The state showed to be a powerful attraction not only for manual labor and service workers, but for highly qualified professional and white-collar immigrants, as well as for skilled craftsmen. The immigrant presence in these upper skill levels can only have increased in New York by 1990. While one cannot speculate on the precise volume of future flows, new immigrants are expected to continue coming into New York to help vitalize the city's productivity levels, respond to shortages in professional and technical employment and promote new investments into the state. What changes might one expect to occur in light of the contemporary occupational profile of New York's foreign-born work force and the newly adopted policy linking immigrant admission standards more closely to labor market considerations?

New York is expected to continue to provide an expanded point of entry for a mixed group of immigrants because of the duality that characterizes the labor market structure of its metropolis. Side by side with emerging demands for highly specialized manpower in professional and technical specialties, the major growth sectors in the city are expected to continue expanding the supply of low-wage manual and service jobs, particularly in subsectors of employment related to product services, consumer services, construction and in the renewed industrial activities in the informal economy (Portes and Rumbaut, 1990). The applicants for these jobs will be a mix of occupational immigrants admitted to date under the sixth preference category of workers, permanent residents admitted under the family reunion provisions and refugees. Nationwide data show that among the two latter groups only one adult in ten qualifies as professional (Vernez and McCarthy, 1990).

Shortages forecast in professional and technical specialties in New York will be alleviated not only by the expansions in the number of visas earmarked for professional immigrants under the new bill, but also by the growing pool of would-be qualified and skilled workers from among the foreign community living in the United States who entered the country as nonimmigrants for purposes of temporary work, education and business. By 1988, the nationwide number of temporary nonimmigrant workers totaled 685,000; two-thirds among them equipped with professional and technical skills (Vernez and McCarthy, 1990).

By redefining the basis of admission for a fraction of future immigrants, the 1990 Immigrant Act is expected to effect some changes in the nationality mix of the new flows of professional immigrants coming into New York. These changes will not outweigh the overall compositional mix, since the large majority of persons admitted qualify under the family reunion provisions.

Except for Asian Indians and a selected group from among the English-speaking Caribbean countries, the dominant nationality composition of New York's immigrants do not correspond to the particular groups who have supplied the state's labor market with top-level resources at professional and management levels, as immigrants from Africa, the Middle East and northwest Europe have done. The Korean and Chinese, though numerically important, are more prominent as ethnic enclave economies in produce, retailing and other small businesses (Portes and Rumbaut, 1990), while many non-English-speaking Caribbeans are in manual labor and in the "lesser-skill" service jobs.

Because the quality level of resources among nationality groups tends to decline with lengthening periods of immigration, it is unlikely that the 1980 nationality profile of the professional immigrant in New York will be replicated in later decades. For some time to come, however, we may expect to see an increasing presence of professional immigrants with origins in selected parts of the Middle East and Africa, many more from India and the English-speaking Caribbean islands.[5] This is, of course, in addition to an expected increase in professional representation from northwest Europe, Eastern Europe and the Soviet Union. These nationality groups will be welcomed not only for the professional specialties they can offer to New York, but also because of the explicit intent of the new Immigration Act to achieve a more balanced representation of nationality origin groups in future migratory streams.

Considerations in the Implementation of a Labor Market-Conscious Immigration Policy

In the planning and implementation of the labor market aspect of the 1990 Immigration Act, concerted efforts need to be extended to ensure that New York's priorities be addressed effectively.

First is channeling an adequate supply of qualified professional immigrants into the New York area who fit the sectorial and occupational needs of the local economy. This means that the country and New York State must attract immigrants more selectively than in the past. The task involves more than the mere lessening of bureaucratic hurdles for immigrants to gain entry into the country. Though still remaining a powerful attraction for professionals coming from countries with lower wages and few employment opportunities, there are clear signs from Western Europe, in particular, that the comparative advantage of the U.S. immigration market has been declining (Vernez and McCarthy, 1990; Borjas, 1990). The New York data confirm this trend: among all New York-bound occupational immigrants admitted under the third preference category, the proportion coming from the northwestern European countries declined from 25 percent in 1980 to 19 percent in 1986.

The second effort involves establishing a monitoring system at the state level to be aware of short-term changes in New York's occupational needs and to be responsive to local requirements related to labor demand (Vernez and McCarthy, 1990). At the national level, policy provisions need to be formulated with sufficient flexibility to allow for swift responses to local changes and to accommodate labor requirements that are regional or state-specific.

Finally, a commitment to initiate appropriate action to minimize the long-term effect of immigration policy on American-born workers is necessary. The search among political leaders to accommodate immigration policy and national man-power needs in a manner that incorporates the interest of the American-born workers is imperative. It can be done foremost by placing priority on action programs that will avoid bringing in immigrants to take over jobs that native workers can potentially fill. An action of this kind is by necessity long term. It calls for full-fledged corrective measures to be taken to address the widespread and pervasive skill mismatches in the country that have been directly caused by the inadequate preparation of American-born workers to meet the specialized demands of the national economy (Bach and Meissner, 1980).

Data Gaps and Research Directions

Data Adequacy

Migration data universally present serious problems of validity and reliability which stem from the incomplete condition of demographic information. As Stolnitz (1979) has so aptly stated, migration information "represents rough orders of magnitude which though they may not be good enough to pass close statistical review are sufficient to cover several central questions."

The scope of this study is too limited to give specific recommendations about ways to upgrade existing data collection practices, restructure current data bases to supplement needed information or initiate new and innovative data collection systems — all of which are needed. A mention of some of the central data gaps encountered in the basic task of developing a "profile" of New York's foreign-born/immigrant population is, however, in order.

As a fundamental basis for understanding the significance of the presence of foreign-born persons in the country, measuring the outcomes of immigration and interpreting its impact, it is essential that one integrated body of data identify the foreign-born population as a collective, classifying them by immigrant status category/subcategory and by birthplace.

The question on birthplace is the best available to identify the foreign-born population, but is not free of all problems. It identifies many immigrants, but tends to overestimate their numbers; misses persons who entered the country but left; provides no reliable information on rates of flow over time; and fails to distinguish between those recently arrived and those who intend to remain.

There is a need for reliable data on return migration, (emigration) to arrive at an estimate of the net immigration rate, identify the actual population base of immigrants and assess their impact.

More detailed information is needed regarding the specifics of nonimmigrant visa categories which apply for adjustment to permanent resident status in order to identify some of the routes used to enter the United States and later settle there permanently. The category of temporary workers also needs to be specified for inclusion into labor force analysis.

There is need to ascertain the accuracy of immigrant reporting regarding the actual geographical destination within the United States. At present, information available on "state of intended residence" filed by immigrants on their visa application is assumed de facto residence and utilized as indicator for immigrants geographical distribution across the country.

There continue to be serious problems in identifying, tracing changes and comparing populations according to characteristics of race and ethnicity despite expansions in those categories. This stems from a continuing lack of uniformity in the manner in which race and ethnicity are defined, classified and coded and from the practice of self-reporting on race which has shown to be influenced by country of origin, social class, changing attitudes about race and self, etc. There is also the problem in the reporting system of New York State agencies of collapsing populations by race and ethnicity without reference to birthplace. This makes it impossible to distinguish characteristics related to factors of race/ethnicity between foreign-born and American-born persons.[6]

Research Directions

Immigration research has generally been faulted for failing to be policy-relevant, and it is true that there is a scarcity of substantive research on which to base immigration policy. Research has the potential for making an input into the formulation of immigration-related concerns by providing some indication of possible adverse effects (if any) that segments of the American-born population may have experienced as a result of the immigrant presence; identifying current and anticipated needs of the older and more recent immigrants; and alerting the policy community through its findings about those particular groups in the foreign-born community who confront the greatest difficulty in becoming incorporated into the mainstream. There is a dire need to direct research more systematically into such policy-relevant realms as well as to assess the impact of immigration from the perspective of the receiving society or locality.

Assessing Impact

In 1988, the U.S. General Accounting Office (GAO) was commissioned by the Senate Subcommittee on Immigration and Refugee Affairs to evaluate the availability and adequacy of data needed to fulfill the reporting requirements stipulated in earlier drafts of the 1990 Immigration Act and which were related to the effect of international migration on the United States. The GAO, report (1988) concluded that: 1) no data are available to measure immigration impacts at the national level and 2) the capacity of data available to analyze and detect regional and local variations in impact is weak.

From the policy perspective, assessment of impact implies efforts and consequences — in this case of international migration as a process and of the presence of international migrants in the receiving site. Impact assessment may be interpreted or conceptualized in three ways, each having different implications for data needs (GAO, 1988): 1) analyses of the current status of immigration relative to some previous status; 2) interpretation of trends and changes over time; and 3) cause and effect (causal) analyses requiring longitudinal data sources.

The present study makes no claim to have provided substantive findings on which to base immigration policy. It does, however, fall within the category of middle range research, providing groundwork for the interpretation of the lesser demanding designs for assessment impact where the primary questions are: What is happening now? and, In what directions and to what extent have there been changes (over a defined period of time)? Interpretation of impact in terms of current status and changing trends may be sufficient to inform immigration policy regarding some outcomes only; for others reliable evidence is needed to suitably address cause and effect questions.

There is yet another important way in which a redirection in thinking needs to take place regarding immigration data collection, analysis and reporting. This incorporates the recognition that the foreign-born/immigrant population should no longer be viewed solely as a national responsibility and the business of only the federal data generation system to worry about. Knowledge, generation of data and responsibility for controlling information on immigrants is of equal concern to those individual states who host the largest immigrant populations.

Thus, one may perceive improvement in immigration data collection systems along the following lines. At the federal level there is a need for continuing corrective and comprehensive reform of data-collection practices and of classification and disaggregation procedures to facilitate state-specific research and for promotion and participation in research focused on the immigration experience of individual host states. At the individual state level, more responsibility needs to be assumed to trace migratory flows into state boundaries, document residential concentrations and develop methodologies to assess the impact of the immigrant presence at various levels (this may require some annual registration procedure in states to identify the residence of all foreign-born persons).

The Importance of a State-Specific Focus in Immigration Research

In considering the role of the state in collecting immigration data, analyzing relevant information and undertaking impact studies of the resident immigrant population, there is need to underline the following. New York State fully recognizes the need to obtain information on the assets and demographics of its immigrant population. According to the Inter-Agency Task Force on Immigration Affairs (1990), "information on the assets and demographics of this population, the extent of their human service needs and how critical they may be in our future labor market would assist those responsible to help meet the challenge of these arrivals" (p. vii). Second, the present scarcity of substantive research on which to base national immigration policy is, in large part, due to the absence of a localized context to serve as a reference point for examining larger policy issues. For example, a perennial concern in the past has been whether or not immigrants hurt the economy in periods of domestic unemployment. This question cannot be honestly addressed without examining the significance of immigrant labor in the context of the local employment situation of those individual states with high immigrant concentrations (*e.g.,* New York, California, Texas, Florida), and singling out the distinctive effect that immigrants may have on the labor market of each of these states.

Aggregate figures based on the nationwide total of immigrants understate the potential regional or local effects of immigration due to the uneven geographical distribution. When over 70 percent of all legal immigrants admitted to the United States establish residence in only six of the 50 states comprising this nation and the concentration of the undocumented population is predicted to be in the same geographical location as are legal immigrants, it must be conceded that a national perspective on what are the impacts and consequences of international migration for the United States must be formulated on the basis of the specific experiences of those individual states where immigrants have a presence.

The General Accounting Office, which represents the federal level reporting agency on immigration, recognizes this fact, but is somewhat hesitant to fully endorse the undertaking of data collection particular to the regional and local immigrant experience lest it disallow for generalizations to be drawn. One possible move in this direction would be to explore the feasibility of standardizing state immigration data sources and encouraging states with the largest immigration concentration to "restructure the data bases that they may now maintain on immigrants so that they would be compatible with regard to data definitions and formats" (GAO, 1988:45). However, before any standardization and restructuring of the data base is initiated, more focused research on the individual immigration experience of different states and localities needs to be pursued and fed into the system, lest particular characteristics of local experiences be lost in trying to achieve uniformity and compatibility in the data search.

However efficient the federal level accounting system of the foreign-born/immigrant population may be, it cannot be sensitive at all times to regional and local conditions. The principal host states must actively participate in the process of researching their localities. They will themselves benefit and benefit the federal data system when they generate the necessary data to monitor, examine and document information such as the direction and changes occurring in the flow of international migration into the state; the volume of foreign-born persons residing within the state boundary during intercensus periods; the current immigrant "status" of foreign-born residents; and the effect of the immigrant presence upon the local educational system, the labor market, social service delivery systems, etc.

Federal and state agencies will need to collaborate in devising information generation systems to meet these objectives with the GAO possibly acting as coordinating body.

NOTES

[1] An immediate outcome of this trend is the greying of America with census projections showing the median age in the country rising from 33 to 42 years over the next decade.

[2] This trend could continue with the expected drop in the number of young adults in the ages 25 to 34 from 44 million to 37 million over the next ten years. As once-young workers age and low fertility cohorts become a significant part of the work force, recruitment problems could increase in many employment sectors, causing severe dislocation (Wattenberg and Zinsmeister, 1990).

[3] The United States already depends in large part on a foreign-born work force. This fact has assumed greater visibility over the past 5 years with the growing numbers of "temporary" nonimmigrant workers admitted into the country explicitly to meet nationwide labor market needs. By 1988, their total number had reached 685,000. In 1987 alone, temporary foreign workers admitted as nonimmigrants totaled 65,500, exceeding the 54,000 who entered the country that year as permanent residents under the third and sixth preference categories. Among these temporary nonimmigrant workers two in every three come from Europe and Asia, mostly with occupational backgrounds in the professions and in technically skilled work. They add an estimated 300,000 persons per year to the U.S. labor force (Vernez and McCarthy, 1990).

[4] Based on 1980 census data, there were over 50,000 New York City dropouts aged 16 to 19 who were unemployed and not in the labor force: 80% of these jobless dropouts were minority youngsters. In 1989, over 50% of black male dropouts aged 20 to 24 were without jobs. Also, 42% of the city's black population aged 25 and above and 60% of the Hispanics aged 25 and above did not have a high school education compared to 37% of non-Hispanic whites (U.S. Department of Labor, 1990; News, Bureau of Labor Statistics, June 26).

[5] The occupational contribution of immigrants from the Caribbean region is mixed. There are considerable differences in the socioeconomic background between English-speaking and Spanish-speaking Caribbean immigrants in New York. The former tend to export larger numbers of well-educated professionals (Chaney, 1985), and that particular segment appears to be on the increase. In the overall pool of New York-bound occupational immigrants entering under the third preference (professional) category, the proportion who were of Caribbean origin increased from 2% in 1980 to 20% in 1986.

[6] The tentative findings in this study reported in Chapters 5 and 6 strongly suggest that race and ethnicity characteristics of immigrants need to be identified and treated as stratifying variables in the same manner as is done in studies of the American-born population, to explore whether these attributes have different meanings and consequences depending on whether the individual is native born or foreign born.

APPENDIX A

PREFERENCE SYSTEMS: 1952 AND 1965 IMMIGRATION ACTS

Immigration and Nationality Act, 1952

Exempt from preference requirements and numerical quotas: Spouses and unmarried minor children of U.S. citizens.

1. First preference: Highly skilled immigrants whose services are urgently needed in the United States and the spouses and children of such immigrants — 50%.
2. Second preference: Parents of U.S. citizens over age 21 and unmarried adult children of U.S. citizens — 30%.
3. Third preference: Spouses and unmarried adult children of permanent resident aliens — 20%.
4. Fourth preference: Brothers, sisters and married children of U.S. citizens and accompanying spouses and children — 50% of numbers not required for first three preferences.
5. Nonpreference: Applicants not entitled to one of the above preferences — 50% of numbers not required for first three preferences, plus any not required for fourth preference.

Immigration Act of 1965

Exempt from preference requirements and numerical quotas: Spouses, unmarried minor children and parents, and parents of U.S. citizens.

1. First preference: Unmarried adult children of U.S. citizens — 20%.
2. Second preference: Spouses and unmarried adult children of permanent resident aliens — 20% (26% after 1980).
3. Third preference: Members of the professions and scientists and artists of exceptional ability — 10%. Requires labor certification.
4. Fourth preference: Married children of U.S. citizens — 10%.
5. Fifth preference: Brothers and sisters of U.S. citizens over age 21 — 24%.
6. Sixth preference: Skilled and unskilled workers in occupations for which labor is in short supply in the United States — 10%. Requires labor certification.

7. Seventh preference: Refugees from communist countries or communist-dom-inated countries or the general area of the Middle East — 6%. Removed when 1980 Refugee Act enacted, with 6% going to second preference.

8. Nonpreference: Applicants not entitled to one of the above preferences — any numbers not required for preference applicants. Not currently being used because preference applicants take up all available places.

Note: The spouse and unmarried minor children of a visa recipient generally receive visas in the same preference category.

REFERENCES

Alba, R. and K. Trent
1988 "The People of New York: Population Dynamics of a Changing State." In *New York State in the Year 2000.* Edited by J. Mumpower and W. Ilchman. Albany: State University of New York Press. Pp. 21–155.

Alba, R. and M. Batutis, Jr.
1984 *The Impact of Migration on New York State.* Report completed for the Public Policy Institute and the Job Training Partnership Council. Albany: Center for Social and Demographic Analysis at the State University of New York. Pp. 1–15.

Bach, R. and D. Meissner
1990 *America's Labor Market in the 1990s.* Immigration Policy Project of the Carnegie Endowment for International Peace. Washington, DC.

Bach, R. and D. Papademetriou
1989 "Introduction." In *The Effects of Immigrants on the U.S. Economy and Labor Market.* Immigration Policy and Research Report 1. Washington, DC: Department of Labor, Bureau of International Labor Affairs. Pp. 1–20.

Bach, R. and R. Seguin
1986 "Labor Force Participation, Household Composition and Sponsorship among Southeast Asian Refugees," *International Migration Review,* 20(2):381–404.

Badillo-Veiga A., *et al.*
1979 "Undocumented Immigrant Workers in New York City," *The North American Congress on Latin America,* 13(6):2–46.

Bailey, T.
1986 *Immigrant and Native Workers: Contrasts and Competition.* Boulder, CO: Westview Press.

Bean, F. and R. O. de la Garza
1988 "Illegal Aliens in Census Counts," *Society,* March/April. Pp. 48–53.

Bogen, E.
1987 *Immigration in New York.* New York: Praeger.

Bonacich, E.
1973 "A Theory of Middlemen Minorities," *American Sociological Review,* 38(5):583–594.

Borjas, G. J.
1990 *Friends and Strangers.* New York: Basic Books, Inc.

Bouvier, L. and V. Briggs, Jr.
1988 *The Population and Labor Force of New York: 1990 to 2050.* New York: The Population Reference Bureau.

Bouvier, L. and R. Gardner
1986 "Immigration to the United States: The Unfinished Story," *Population Bulletin,* 41(4):3–46.

Briggs, V. Jr.
1985 "Employment Trends and Contemporary Immigration Policy." In *Clamor at the Gates.* Edited by N. Glazer. San Francisco: Institute for Contemporary Studies. Pp. 135–160.

1984 *Immigration Policy and the American Labor Force.* Baltimore: Johns Hopkins University Press.

Bryce-LaPorte, R. S.
1985   "Caribbean Immigration and Their Implications for the United States." In *Focus Caribbean.*
       Edited by S. Mintz and S. Price. Washington, DC: Woodrow Wilson International Center
       for Scholars, The Smithsonian Institute.

_____, ed.
1979   *Sourcebook on the New Immigration.* New Brunswick: Transaction Publishers.

_____
1977   "Visibility of the New Immigrants," *Society,* 14:18–22.

Cafferty, P., B. Chiswick, A. Greenley and T. Sullivan, eds.
1983   *The Dilemma of American Immigration: Beyond the Golden Door.* New Brunswick, NJ:
       Transaction Publishers.

Chaney, E.
1985   *Migration from the Caribbean Region: Determinants and Effects of Current Movements.*
       Georgetown University, Center for Immigration Policy and Refugee Assistance, Hemispheric
       Migration Project, March.

Chun-shing, C.
1984   *Immigration and Immigrant Settlements: The Chinese in New York City.* Hawaii: University of
       Hawaii.

City of New York, Department of City Planning
1985   *Asians in New York City: A Demographic Summary.* City of New York: Office of Immigrant
       Affairs and Population Analysis Division.

_____
1985   *Caribbean Immigrants in New York City.* City of New York: Office of Immigrant Affairs and
       Population Analysis Division.

Cominolli, R.
1990   *Smokestacks Allegro: The Story of Solvay, A Remarkable Industrial Immigrant Village: 1880–
       1920.* Staten Island, New York: Center for Migration Studies.

Commission on Population Growth and the American Future
1972   *Population and the American Future.* Washington, DC: Summary Report.

Couch, S., R.
1979   "Where Do We Go from Here? The New Immigration and Implications for Research." In
       Sourcebook on the New Immigration. Edited by R. S. Bryce-LaPorte. New Brunswick, NJ:
       Transaction Publishers. Pp. 453–458.

Council of Economic Advisors
1986   "The Council of Economic Advisors on U.S. Immigration," *Population and Development
       Review,* 12(2):361–374.

Davis, C., C. Haub and J. Willette
1983   "U.S. Hispanics: Changing the Face of America," *Population Bulletin.* 38(3)1–27. June.

Denton,N.
1988   "Residential Segregation of Blacks, Hispanics and Asians by Socio-Economic Status and
       Generation," *Social Science Quarterly,* 69(4):797–817. December.

Denton, N., and D. Massey
1989   "Racial Identity among Caribbean Hispanics: The Effect of Double Minority Status on
       Residential Segregation," *American Sociological Review,* 54:790–808. October.

DiMarzio, N. and D. Papademetriou
1988   *Toward New U.S. Statutory Standards for Those Who Flee Crises: Humanitarian and Political Responses.* Washington, DC: Migration and Refugee Services of the United States Catholic Conference.

Edmonston, B.
1989   *International Migration and Population Growth: A Paper Assessing Data for Policy Research."* Washington, DC: The Urban Institute.

Fallows, J.
1983   "Immigration: How It is Affecting Us," *The Atlantic Monthly.* Pp. 45–106. November.

Foner, N.
1987   "The Jamaicans: Race and Ethnicity among Migrants in New York City." In *New Immigrants in New York City.* Edited by N. Foner. New York: Columbia University Press. Pp. 195–217.

_____

1983   *Jamaican Migrants: A Comparative Analysis of the New York and London Experience.* Paper presented at the Conference on "Caribbean Migration and the New York Labor Market." Sponsored by the New York Research Program in Inter American Affairs, New York University, May 6.

Francese, P.
1990   "Aging America Needs Foreign Blood," *The Wall Street Journal.* P. A, 20. March 27.

Gardner, R., B. Robey and P. Smith
1985   "Asian Americans: Growth, Change and Diversity," *Population Bulletin.* 40(4):3–41. October.

Gibney, M.
1989   "United States Immigration Policy and the 'Huddled Masses' Myth," *Georgetown Immigration Law Journal,* 3(3):361–386.

Glazer, N., ed.
1985   *Clamor At the Gates: The New American Immigration.* San Francisco: Institute for Contemporary Studies.

Grant, L.
1988   "How Many Americans?" In *U.S. Immigration in the 1980s: Reappraisal and Reform.* Edited by D. Simcox. Washington, DC: Center for Immigration Studies. Boulder: Westview Press. Pp. 269–282.

Grasmuck, S.
1984   "Immigration, Ethnic Stratification and Native Working Class Discipline: Comparison of Documented and Undocumented Dominicans," *International Migration Review,* 18(3):692–713.

Gurak, D. and M. Kritz
1982   "Dominicans and Colombian Women in New York City: Household Structure and Employment Patterns," *Migration Today,* 20(1):15–21.

Helton, A. C.
1988   "The Alien Legalization Problem in New York: A Review. Symposium: Implementation of IRCA, March 25, 1988," *Georgetown Immigration Law Journal,* 2(3):447–460.

Hirschman, C. and E. Kraly
1988   "Immigrants, Minorities and Earnings in the United States in 1980," *Ethnic and Racial Studies,* 11(3):332–365.

Howe, M.
1990   "Fraud Charges Rise as Aliens Seek to Enter through Rulings," *The New York Times.* P. A, 13. April 16.

1990   "Soviet Immigrants Don Blue Collars," *The New York Times.* P. II, 26. June 17.

Inter Agency Task Force on Immigration Affairs
1990   *Immigration in New York State: Impact and Issues.* Albany: New York State Department of Social Services.

1987   *Report of the Task Force.* Albany: New York State Department of Social Services.

Jensen, L.
1989   *The New Immigration: Implications for Poverty and Public Assistance Utilization.* Studies in Social Welfare Policies and Programs. No. 10. New York: Greenwood Press.

Keely, C. B.
1989   Center for Immigration Policy and Refugee Assistance. Personal Communication, January. Georgetown University, Washington, DC.

nd   "E Pluribus Unum." Unpublished.

Kellogg, J. B.
1988   "Immigration," *Phi Delta Kappan.* Pp. 200–204. November.

Kraly, E. P.
1987a "U.S. Immigration Policy and Immigrant Populations of New York." In *New Immigrants in New York City.* Edited by N. Foner. New York: Columbia University Press. Pp. 35–78.

Kraly, E. P.
1979   "Sources of Data for the Study of U.S. Immigration." In *Quantitative Data and Immigration Research.* Edited by S. R. Couch and R. S. Bryce-LaPorte. RIIES Research Notes No. 2. Washington, DC: Smithsonian Institute. Pp. 34–54.

Kraly, E. P. and K. S. Gnanasekaran
1987b "Efforts to Improve International Migration Statistics: A Historical Perspective," *International Migration Review,* 21(4):967–995.

Levine, D., K. Hill and R. Warren, eds.
1985   *Immigration Statistics: A Story of Neglect.* Washington, DC: National Academy Press.

Levine, R.
1990   "New York Region Faces Slowdown of the Economy," *The New York Times.* P. I, 1. February 25.

1990   "Young Immigrant Wave Lifts New York Economy," *The New York Times.* P. A, 1. July 30.

Lindsay-Lowell, B. with K. Johnson
1989   "Regional and Local Effects of Immigration." In *The Effects of Immigration on the U.S. Economy and Labor Market.* Immigration Policy and Research Report I. Washington, DC: U.S. Department of Labor. Bureau of International Labor Affairs. Pp. 47–95.

Mandel, M. J.
1989   "Roll Out America's Red Carpet for the Skilled," *Business Week.* P. 128. October 30.

Marshall, A.
1987   "New Immigrants in New York's Economy." In *New Immigrants in New York City.* Edited by N. Foner. New York: Columbia University Press. Pp. 79–101.

1983   "Immigration in a Surplus-Worker Labor Market: The Case of New York." New York:

Research Program in Inter-American Affairs, New York University. Occasional Papers No. 39.

Meissner, D. and D. Papademetriou
1988   *The Legalization Countdown: A Third Quarter Assessment.* Washington, DC: Carnegie Endowment for International Peace.

Morrison, B.
1990   Chairman of the Subcommittee on Immigration, Refugees and International Law. Opening Remarks at the *Thirteenth Annual National Legal Conference on Immigration and Refugee Policy.* Organized by Center for Migration Studies. Washington, DC. March 29–30.

New York State Department of Health and Human Services
1990   *Immigration in New York State: Impact and Issues.* Albany: Office of Refugee Resettlement cited in Inter Agency Task Force on Immigration Affairs.

Papademetriou, D.
1989   Director, Immigration Policy Group, U.S. Department of Labor. Personal Communication. January.

Papademetriou, D. with B. Lindsay-Lowell
1989   "Summary and Conclusions." In *The Effects of Immigration on the U.S. Economy and Labor Market.* Immigration Policy and Research Report I. Washington, DC: U.S. Department of Labor, Bureau of International Affairs. Pp. 179–301.

Papademetriou, D. with K. Johnson
1989   "The Labor Market Integration and Progress of Immigrants." In *The Effects of Immigrants on the U.S. Economy and Labor Market.* Immigration Policy and Research Report 1. Washington, DC: Department of Labor, Bureau of International Labor Affairs. Pp. 51–178.

Papademetriou, D. and N. DiMarzio
1986   *Undocumented Aliens in the New York Metropolitan Area.* Staten Island, New York: Center for Migration Studies. Pp. 47–109.

Papademetriou, D. and D. Meissner
1988   *The Canadian Immigrant-Selection System: A Technical Report.* Unpublished draft.

Papademetriou, D. and T. Muller
1987   *Recent Immigration to New York: Labor Market and Social Policy Issues.* Report prepared for the National Commission for Employment Policy. Washington, DC.

Passel, J. S. and K. A. Woodrow
1984   "Geographic Distribution of Undocumented Immigrants: Estimates of Undocumented Aliens Counted in the 1980 Census by State," *International Migration Review,* 18(3):642–671.

Passell, P.
1990   "So Much for Assumptions About Immigrants and Jobs," *The New York Times.* P. IV, 4. April 15.

Perez, G.
1981   "The Legal and Illegal Dominicans in New York City." Paper presented at the Conference on Hispanic Migrants in New York. December.

Pessar, P.
1987   "The Dominicans: Women in the Household and the Garment Industry." In *New Immigrants in New York City.* Edited by N. Foner. New York: Columbia University Press. Pp. 103–129.

Portes, A. and R. Rumbaut
1990   *Immigrant America: A Portrait.* Berkeley: University of California Press.

Richman, L. S.
1990   "The Coming World Labor Shortage," *Fortune,* 121(80):70. April 9.

_____
1990   "Let's Change the Immigration Law—Now," *Fortune,* 121(3):12. January 29.

Sassen-Koob, S.
1979   "Formal and Informal Associations: Dominicans and Colombians in New York," *International Migration Review,* 13(2):314–332.

Shokeid, M.
1988   *Children of Circumstances: Israeli Emigrants in New York.* Ithaca: Cornell University.

Simcox, D., ed.
1988   *U.S. Immigration in the 1980's: Reappraisal and Reform.* Boulder: Westview Press.

Simon, J.
1990   "Bring on the Wretched Refuse," *The Wall Street Journal.* P. A. 14. January 26.

Stolnitz, G. J.
1979   "U.S. Immigration Now and in Prospect: Some Population and Policy Aspects." In *Source-Book on the New Immigration.* Edited by R. S. Bryce-LaPorte. New Brunswick: Transaction Publishers.

Sung, B. Lee
1987   *The Adjustment Experience of Chinese Immigrant Children in New York City.* New York: Center for Migration Studies.

Suro, R.
1989   "1986 Amnesty Law Seen as Failing to Slow Alien Tide," *The New York Times.* P. A, 1. June 18.

Sutton, C. and E. Chaney, eds.
1987   *Caribbean Life in New York City: Socio-Cultural Dimensions.* Staten Island, New York: Center for Migration Studies.

Tienda, M.
1983a "Market Characteristics and Hispanic Earnings: A Comparison of Natives and Immigrants," *Social Problems,* 31(1):59–72.

_____
1983b "Nationality and Income Attainment among Native and Immigrant Hispanic Men in the United States," *Sociological Quarterly,* 24:253–272. Spring.

U.S. Bureau of the Census
1989   *Projections of the Population of the United States by Age, Sex and Race: 1988 to 2080.* Current Population Reports. Series P-25, No. 1018. Washington, DC: U.S. Government Printing Office.

_____
1983a *Statistical Profile of the Foreign-Born Population: 1980.* Washington, DC: U.S. Government Printing Office.

_____
1983b *Census of the Population: 1980.* Volume 1, U.S. Summary. Washington, DC: U.S. Government Printing Office.

_____
1983c *Census of the Population 1980: Public Use Microdata Sample.* Washington, DC: U.S. Bureau of the Census. Tape Documentation.

1952 *Census of the Population: 1950*. Volume 2. Washington, DC: U.S. Government Printing Office.

U.S. Department of Commerce
1988 *Statistical Abstract of the United States*. Washington, DC: U.S. Government Printing Office.

U.S. Department of Health and Human Services
1991 *Report to the Congress*. Office of Refugee Resettlement, Washington, DC: U.S. Government Printing Office.

1990 Office of Refugee Resettlement. Unpublished Data.

U.S. Department of Labor
1990 *News*. Bureau of Labor Statistics, Middle Atlantic Regional Office. June 26.

1989 *The Effects of Immigration on the U.S. Economy and Labor Market*. Immigration Policy and Research Report 1. Bureau of International Labor Affairs, Washington, DC: U.S. Government Printing Office

U.S. Department of State
1990 Bureau of Refugee Programs. Unpublished Data.

U.S. General Accounting Office
1989 *Immigration Reform: Major Changes Likely Under S 358*. Report to the Chairman, Subcommittee on Immigration and Refugee Affairs, Committee on the Judiciary, U.S. Senate. Washington, DC: U.S. Government Printing Office. GAO/PEMD. 90–5. November.

1988 *Immigration: Data Not Sufficient for Proposed Legislation*. Report to the Chairman, Subcommittee on Immigration and Refugee Affairs, Committee on the Judiciary, U.S. Senate. Washington, DC: U.S. Government Printing Office. GAO/PEMD 89–8. December.

U.S. Immigration and Naturalization Service
1990 *1989 Statistical Yearbook of the Immigration and Naturalization Service*. Washington, DC: U.S. Government Printing Office.

1989a *1988 Statistical Yearbook of the Immigration and Naturalization Service*. Washington, DC: U.S. Government Printing Office.

1989b *Provisional Legalization Application Statistics: May 12, 1989*. Statistical Analysis Branch, Office of Plans and Analysis, Washington, DC: U.S. Government Printing Office.

1987a *Immigrants Admitted into the United States as Legal Permanent Residents*. Fiscal Years 1978–1986. Washington, DC: Statistical Analysis Branch. Tape Documentation.

1987b *1986 Statistical Yearbook of the Immigration and Naturalization Service*. Washington, DC: U.S. Government Printing Office.

Annual Report Statistical Yearbook. File: 1965–1987. Washington, DC. Unpublished Data.

Vernez, G. and K. McCarthy
1990   *Meeting the Economy's Labor Needs Through Immigration: Rationale and Challenges.* Santa Monica: The Rand Corporation.

Waldinger, R.
1988   *Through the Eye of the Needle: Immigrants and Enterprise in New York's Garment Industry.* New York: New York University Press.

_____
1986   *The Problems and Prospects of Manufacturing Workers in the New York City Labor Market.* Paper prepared for the Worker Literacy Project of the City University of New York. February.

_____
1985   "Immigration and Industrial Change in the New York City Apparel Industry." In *Hispanics in the U.S. Economy.* Edited by G. Borjas and M. Tienda. Orlando: Academic Press. Pp. 323–349.

_____
1984   "Immigrant Enterprise in the New York Garment Industry," *Social Problems,* 32(1):60–71.

_____
1982   *Immigration and Industrial Change: Case Study of Immigrants in the New York City Garment Industry.* Boston: Harvard University Press.

Wall Street Journal
1990   "Review and Outlook: America the Vital," Editorial, *The Wall Street Journal.* P. A, 14. March 16.

_____
1990   "Review and Outlook: The Simpson Curtain," Editorial, *The Wall Street Journal.* P. A, 8. February 1.

Warren, R.
1989   Chief, Statistical Analysis Branch, Immigration and Naturalization Service. Personal Communication. October.

_____
1976   "Volume and Composition of the United States Immigration and Emigration." In *Sourcebook on the New Immigration.* Edited by R. S. Bryce-LaPorte. New Brunswick: Transaction Publishers. Pp. 1–14.

Warren, R. and E. P. Kraly
1985   *The Elusive Exodus: Emigration from the United States.* Population Trends and Public Policy, No. 8. Washington, DC: Population Reference Bureau. Pp. 1–17.

Warren, R. and J. Passel
1983   *A Count of the Undocumentable: Estimates of Undocumented Aliens Counted in the 1980 United States Census.* Paper presented at the 1983 Annual Meeting of the Population Association of America. Pittsburgh.

Wattenberg, B. and K. Zinsmeisters
1990   "The Case for More Immigration," *Commentary,* 89(4):19–25.

Weisser, M. R.
1989   *A Brotherhood of Memory: Jewish Landmanshaft in the New World.* Ithaca: Cornell University.

Wilson, K. and A. Portes
1980   "Immigrant Enclaves: An Analysis of the Labor Market Experiences of Cubans in Miami," *American Journal of Sociology,* 86(2):295–319.

Winnick, L.
1990   *New People in Old Neighborhoods: The Role of New Immigrants in Rejuvenating New York's Communities.* New York: Russel Sage Foundation.

Woodrow, K., J. Passel and R. Warren
1987   "Preliminary Estimates of Undocumented Immigration to the United States 1980–1986: Analysis of the June, 1986 C.P.S. Survey," *Proceedings of the Meetings of Social Statistics Section of the American Statistical Association, August, 1987. San Francisco.*

INDEX

Afganistan: refugee admissions to the United States from, 34, 36–38

Africa: refugee admissions to the United States from, 33, 35, SAW applicants from, 48

Age Structure, of foreign born: impact on economic dependency, 76, 78, on fertility 76; compared to American born, 76, 77; in relation to poverty, 125, 126

Alba, R., 3, 14, 83, 87, 94n, 96, 97, 105, 132, 133

Amerasians: legal status of, 25

Asia: East, refugee admissions to the United States from, 33; immigration from, 51, 53, 54, 61, 62, 65, 66

Austria: immigration from, 61, 62

Bach, R., 96, 132, 133, 162

Badillo, V. A., 132, 133

Bailey, T., 132

Bangladesh: SAW applicants from, 48

Batutis, M., 96, 97, 105, 132, 133

Bean F., 39

Bogen, E., 3, 81, 87

Bonacich, E., 111

Borjas, G. J., 88, 95, 104–106, 117, 124, 125, 142, 161

Bouvier, L., 78, 83

Briggs, V., 1, 6, 7

Bronx, New York: immigrant composition of, 69, 70

Brooklyn, New York: immigrant composition of 69, 70

Bryce-LaPorte, R. S., 13, 114, 156

Bureau for Refugee Programs: as a source of demographic data, 9

Cafferty, P., 110

California: as a preferred destination of foreign born, 16, 17, 28, 29, 58–60; Asian immigrants in, 65, 66; estimate of undocumented residents in, 41; General Legalization Act applicants in, 44, 46; refugees in, 36; SAW applicants in, 44, 46

Cambodia: immigration from, 56; refugee admissions to the United States from, 31–34, 38, 53

Caribbean: immigration from 61–65; New York State undocumented residents from, 44, 46, 63, 65; refugee admissions to the United States from, 33, 35; SAW applicants from, 48

Chaney, E., 3, 77, 80, 82, 166n

Chicago, Illinois: as a preferred destination of foreign born, 17–19

China: General Legalization Act applicants from, 48; immigration from 5, 56, 61, 62, 65–68, 73, 74; SAW applicants from, 48

Class of admission: preference categories of, 25–28, 151–154, 160

Colombia: General Legalization Act applicants from, 48; immigration from, 57, 61, 62, 74

Couch, S. R., 156

Cuba: immigrants from, 56; refugee admissions to the United States from, 31–33, 35, 36

Davis, C., 40, 50n

de la Garza, R. O., 39

Denton, N., 70

DiMarzio, N., 1, 132, 133

Dominican Republic: General Legalization Act applicants from, 48; immigration from, 5, 56, 61–68, 73

Eastern Europe: refugee admissions to the United States from, 33

Economic trends: affect on immigration, 96; effect of 1965 Immigration Act on, 96; in New York, 97, 98, 131, 132;

Ecuador: General Legalization Act applicants from, 48; immigration from, 61, 62, 74

Edmonston, B., 157, 158

Education, of foreign born: 91–94; change in level of, 88–91; controversy over, 104–106; compared to American born, 89-91, 106, in relation to wages, 120–122; to employment status, 106–109, to occupation, 142; wage profile, 120–122

El Salvador: General Legalization Act applicants from, 48; immigration from, 57, 68;

179

refugee admissions to the United States,
33, 36
Employment, of foreign born: Africans, 139–
143, 146–149, 160, 161, Asians, 100,
139–143, 146–149, 153, 154, Asian Indians, 148, 160, Caribbeans, 100, 139–143,
146–149, 153, 154, 160, 161, Central
Americans 100, 140–142, 146–149, 153,
154, Chinese, 160, Europeans, 139–143,
153, 154, 160, 161, Koreans, 160, Middle
Easterners , 154, 160, 161, South Americans, 100, 139–143, 146–149, Soviets, 100,
139–143, undocumented, 132; compared
to American born, gender, 101, 144–145,
labor force participation rates, 99, 100,
102–104, minorities, 111–113, occupation
133–137, 143–145; entrepreneurship,
110, 111; in relation to class of admissions, 153, 154, to language skills, 109,
110, level of education, 106–109, to occupation, 140–143, 145–149, to race/ethnic-
ity, 145–149, to year of admission to the
United States, 150
Ethiopia: refugee admissions to the United
States, 31–33 , 35, 36, 38

Fertility rates, of foreign born: 85; Asian
women, 83, 85, Dominican women, 85,
European women, 83, 85, Greek women,
85, Italian women, 83, 85, Philippine
women, 85; compared to American-born
women, 83
Florida: as a preferred destination of foreign born, 16, 17, 28, 29; estimate of
undocumented in, 41; General Legalization Act applicants in, 44, 46; SAW
applicants in, 44, 46
Foner, N., 36, 79

GAO, see U.S. General Accounting Office
(GAO)
Gardner, R., 78, 3
General Legalization Act, 44, 46–48
Germany: immigration from 61, 62
Gibney, M., 1
Glazer, N., 50n
Gnanasekaran, K. S., 6
Grasmuck, S., 132, 133
Greece: immigration from, 61, 62

Guatemala: refugee admissions to the
United States, 36
Gurak, D., 132, 133
Guyana: immigration from 3, 5, 56, 58, 62–
68, 73, 74

Haiti: General Legalization Act applicants
from, 48; immigration from 5, 56, 62–68,
73; SAW applicants from, 48
Hart-Cellar Act, see Immigration and Nationality Act, 1965
Helton, A., 47–49
Hirschman, C., 111, 129n
Household composition, of foreign born: affect on median income, 87; compared to
American born, 84, 85, 87, 88; female
household heads, 86, 87
Hungary: immigration from, 61, 62; refugee
admissions to the United States, 34, 36–
38

Illinois: as a preferred destination of foreign born, 16, 17, 28, 29; Asian
immigrants in, 65; estimate of undocumented residents in, 41; General Legal
ization Act applicants in, 44, 46
Immigration: data source reliability, 162,
163; general background of, 3–6, 14–16,
23, 51–54; in relation to labor market
needs, 158, 159, to U.S. population
growth, 156–158; legal admissions, see
Class of admission; policy development,
161–163; U.S. General Accounting Office (GAO) evaluation of data, 163–166
Immigration Act, 1990: 161, 163, 164; affect
on U.S. immigration 2, 28
Immigration and Nationality Act, 1952: 52;
affect on class of admissions 167, 168, on
diversity of foreign born, 5, 6
Immigration and Nationality Act, 1965: 2, affect on class of admissions, 167, 168, on
diversity of immigrants, 51, on number
of admissions, 16, 18, 23, 24, on U.S. immigration policy, 51–53
Immigration Reform and Control Act
(IRCA) 1986: 1, 2, 7, 13; affect on illegal
immigration, 44, 46, on number of admissions, 23
INS, see U.S. Immigration and Naturalization Service (INS)

Income, of foreign born: 118, 119, 120; compared to American born, 114–117, in relation to education, 120, 121, to public assistance, 117, to occupation, 120–122, to gender, 120–122; to wages, 117–120

India: immigration from, 5, 56, 61, 62, 65–68, 73, 74; SAW applicants from, 48,

Inter-Agency Task Force on Immigrant Affairs: as a sourc e of demographic data, 9, 10, 165; estimate of foreign-born population, 14, of undocumented population, 41, 47

International Union for the Scientific Study of Population: as a source of demographic data, 8

IRCA, see Immigration Reform and Control Act (IRCA) 1986

Iran: refugee admissions to the United States from, 31–3 4, 36, 38

Italy: immigration from, 61, 62

Jamaica, General Legalization Act applicants from, 48; immigration from, 5, 56, 57, 61–68, 73

Japan: immigration from, 58

Jensen, L., 1

Keely, C., 41

Korea: immigration from, 5, 56–58, 61, 62, 65, 66, 73, 74; SAW applicants from, 48

Kraly, E. P., 4, 6, 17, 57, 58, 68

Kritz, M., 132, 133

Laos: immigration from, 56, 57; refugee admissions to the United States from, 31–34, 38, 53

Latin America: refugee admissions to the United States from, 33

Levine, D., 6

Levine, R., 159

Lindsay-Lowell, B., 96, 98

Los Angeles, California: as a preferred destination of foreign born, 17–19

Marital status: effect of 1965 Immigration Act on, 80, 81; compared to American born 81, 82; in New York, 80; of Caribbean foreign born, 82

Marshall, A., 96, 97, 132, 133, 135

Massey, D., 70

McCarran-Walter Act, 1952, 4, 23

McCarthy, K., 1, 160, 161, 166n

Meissner, D., 96, 162

Mexico: as nonlegalization supplier to the United States, 56; General Legalization Act applicants from, 48; immigration from, 68

Miami, Florida: as a preferred destination of foreign born, 17–19

Muller, T., 41, 88, 90, 92, 93, 96, 106, 110, 118, 132, 133, 136

National Origins Act, 1924, 52

Near East: refugee admissions to the United States from, 33

New Jersey: as a preferred destination of foreign born, 16, 17, 28, 29; Asian immigrants in, 65

New York: as a preferred destination of foreign born, 16 , 17, 28, 29; characteristics of undocumented immigrants in, 44, 45; city of, distribution of foreign born by borough, 20, 21, 68, 70; estimate of undocumented residents in, 41, 42, 63, 65; General Legalization Act applicants in, 44, 46, 47; immigration, general background of, 3–6, 14–16; immigrant heterogenity in, 57–60, 62–65, 71–74; SAW applicants in, 44, 46–48

Nicaragua: refugee admissions to the United States from, 33, 36

Office of Refugee Resettlement: as a source of demographic data, 9

Pakistan: immigration from, 57, 65, 66, 73, 74; SAW applicants from, 48

Papademetriou, D., 1, 3, 31, 41, 49n, 50n, 88, 90, 92, 93, 96, 106, 110, 114, 118, 132, 133, 136

Passell, J., 40, 41, 49n, 50n

Perez, G., 132, 133

Pessar, P., 77, 79

Philippines: as a nonlegalization supplier to the United States, 56; immigration from, 61, 62, 65, 66, 73, 74; SAW applicants from, 48

Poland: immigration from, 61, 62; refugee admissions to the United States from, 31–34, 36–38

Portes, A., 110, 137, 160, 161
Poverty, of foreign born: 127, 128; compared to American born, 127–129; in relation to age, 125–127, to gender, 125–127, to language skills, 109, 110, to national origin, 127, 128, to race/ethnic group, 127–129

Queens, New York: immigrant composition of, 68–70
Quota systems: class of admission 25–27, 151–154, 160; National Origins Act, 52

Refugee Act, 1980: affect on Southeast Asian immigration, 65; special category of admissions, 29, 31
Refugees: admissions to the United States, 29–36; in New York State, 33, 36–39; legal status of, 29
Rumbaut, R., 137, 160, 161
Romania: refugee admissions to the United States from, 31–43, 36–38

San Francisco, California: as a preferred destination of foreign born, 17–19
Sassen-Koob, S., 142
Sequin, R., 132, 133
Sex ratio, of foreign born, 79, 80
Skokeid, M., 3
Southeast Asian refugees: legal status of, 29, 31
Soviet Union: immigration from, 57, 61, 62, 66–68; refugee admissions to the United States from, 31–34, 36–38
Special Agricultural Worker (SAW) provision: 44; applicants from Central America, 48
Staten Island, New York: immigrant composition of, 69, 70
Stolzitz, G. J., 162
Sung, B. L., 79
Sutton, C. R., 3

Taiwan: as nonlegalization supplier to the United States , 56
Texas: as a preferred destination of foreign born, 16, 17, 28, 29; estimate of undocumented residents in, 41; General Legalization Act applicants in, 44, 46; refugees in, 36; SAW applicants in 44, 46
Trent, K., 3, 14, 83, 87, 94n
Trinidad-Tobago: immigration from, 62–65

Undocumented residents: general characteristics of, 42, 44; employment in New York of, 132; U.S. population estimates of, 39–43
United Nations Statistical Office: as a source of demographic data, 8
U.S. Census Bureau: Census, 1980, facilitation of immigration research by, 8; data standardization and reporting bias of, 70, 71; estimate of U.S. undocumented residents by, 40, 41
U.S. General Accounting Office (GAO): evaluation of immigration data by, 163–166
U.S. Immigration and Naturalization Service (INS): as a source of demographic data, 21–23, 150; monitoring of undocumented residents by, 39–41, 47; *Yearbook of Immigration and Naturalization*, 8, 9
U.S. Immigration Policy: 161–163; controversy over, 1, 2

Vernez, G., 1, 160, 161, 166n
Vietnam: immigration from, 56; refugee admissions to the United States from, 33, 35, 38, 53

Waldinger, R., 3, 96, 105, 132
Warren, R., 22, 41, 47, 49n, 50n, 52
Wattenberg, B., 166n
Weisser, M. R., 3
Wilson, K., 110
Winnick, L., 3
Woodrow, K., 40, 41, 49n, 50n

Yugoslavia: immigration from, 61, 62

Zinsmeisters, K., 166n